SCHOLASTIC

100 ENGLISH LESSONS

Terms and conditions

IMPORTANT – PERMITTED USE AND WARNINGS – READ CAREFULLY BEFORE USING

Recommended system requirements:

- Windows: XP (Service Pack 3), Vista (Service Pack 2), Windows 7 or Windows 8 with 2.33GHz processor
- Mac: OS 10.6 to 10.8 with Intel Core™ Duo processor
- 1GB RAM (recommended)
- 1024 x 768 Screen resolution
- CD-ROM drive (24x speed recommended)
- 16-bit sound card
- Adobe Reader (version 9 recommended for Mac users)
- Broadband internet connections (for installation and updates)

For all technical support queries, please phone Scholastic Customer Services on 0845 6039091.

Book End, Range Road, Witney, Oxfordshire, OX29 0YD
www.scholastic.co.uk

© 2014, Scholastic Ltd

3 4 5 6 7 8 9   6 7 8 9 0 1 2 3

British Library Cataloguing-in-Publication Data
A catalogue record for this book is available from the
British Library.

ISBN 978-1-407-12760-6
Printed by Bell & Bain Ltd, Glasgow

Due to the nature of the web we cannot guarantee the
content or links of any site mentioned. We strongly
recommend that teachers check websites before using
them in the classroom.

Extracts from *The National Curriculum in English, English
Programme of Study* © Crown Copyright. Reproduced
under the terms of the Open Government Licence
(OGL). http://www.nationalarchives.gov.uk/doc/open-
government-licence/open-government-licence.htm

Author
Sarah Snashall, Pam Dowson, Jean Evans

Editorial team
Rachel Morgan, Melissa Somers, Vicky Butt, Tracey
Cowell, Sue Walton, Jane Wood, Sarah Sodhi

Cover Design
Andrea Lewis

Design Team
Sarah Garbett, Shelley Best and Andrea Lewis

CD-ROM development
Hannah Barnett, Phil Crothers, MWA Technologies
Private Ltd

Typesetting
Brian Melville

Illustrations
Gaynor Berry

Acknowledgements
The publishers gratefully acknowledge permission
to reproduce the following copyright material:

David Higham Associates for the use of an extract
from *All Afloat on Noah's Boat* by Tony Mitton. Text
© 2007, Tony Mitton (2007, Hachette Children's
Books).
John Foster for the use of the poem 'Magic Horse'
by John Foster from *Twinkle, Twinkle Chocolate Bar*
by John Foster. Poem © 1991, John Foster (1991,
Oxford University Press).
John Foster for the use of the poem 'I went to the
farm' by John Foster from *Farm Poems* by John
Foster. Poem © 1995, John Foster (1995, Oxford
University Press).
Gareth Lancaster for the use of the poem 'Ole'
Blackeye' by Gareth Lancaster. Poem © 2003,
Gareth Lancaster.
Kenn Nesbitt for the poem 'Meanest Pirate' by
Kenn Nesbitt. Poem © 1998 Kenn Nesbitt. All Rights
Reserved.
Penguin Group (NZ) for the use of an extract from
The Other Ark by Lynley Dodd.

Every effort has been made to trace copyright
holders for the works reproduced in this book,
and the publishers apologise for any inadvertent
omissions.

Contents

Introduction

About the series

The *100 English Lessons* series is designed to meet the requirements of the 2014 Curriculum, English Programmes of Study. There are six books in the series, Years 1–6, and each book contains lesson plans, resources and ideas matched to the new curriculum. It can be a complex task to ensure that a progressive and appropriate curriculum is followed in all year groups; this series has been carefully structured to ensure that a progressive and appropriate curriculum is followed throughout.

About the new curriculum

The curriculum documentation for English provides a single-year programme of study for Year 1 and Year 2, but joint programmes of study for Years 3–4 and Years 5–6.

There is a much greater focus on the technical aspects of language – including grammar, punctuation, spelling, handwriting and phonics. These are the building blocks to help children to read and write. It has been perceived that these aspects have to be taught discretely, however the approach encouraged in this series is to embed these elements into existing learning. For example, using a focus text to identify the use of punctuation and using that as a springboard to practise it.

There is a spoken language Programme of Study which outlines statutory requirements across Years 1–6. Within the English curriculum there are also attainment targets that involve 'discussion', 'talking', 'participating' and 'listening'. The aims of speaking and listening are below:

> *The National Curriculum for English reflects the importance of spoken language in children's development across the whole curriculum – cognitively, socially and linguistically. The quality and variety of language that children hear and speak are vital for developing their vocabulary, grammar and their understanding for reading and writing. Teachers should therefore ensure the continual development of children's confidence and competence in spoken language. Children should develop a capacity to explain their understanding of books and other reading, and to prepare their ideas before they write. They must be assisted in making their thinking clear to themselves as well as to others and teachers should ensure that children build secure foundations by using discussion to probe and remedy their misconceptions. Children should also be taught to understand and use the conventions for discussion and debate.*
>
> *Statutory requirements which underpin all aspects of speaking and listening across the six years of primary education form part of the National Curriculum. These are contextualised within the reading and writing domains which follow.*

Terminology

The curriculum terminology has changed; the main terms used are:

- **Domains:** The area of the subject, for English the domains are 'Reading' and 'Writing'.
- **Sub-domains:** The next level down to the domains. In English, Reading's sub-domains are 'Word reading' and 'Comprehension' and Writing's sub-domains are 'Transcription' and 'Composition'.
- **Curriculum objectives:** These are the statutory programme of study statements or objectives.
- **Appendix:** Any reference to an appendix refers to an appendix of the National Curriculum for English document. There are two appendices – one for spelling (Appendix 1) and one for vocabulary, grammar and punctuation (Appendix 2).

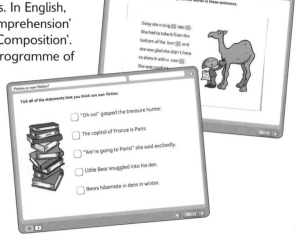

SCHOLASTIC

About the book

This book is divided into six chapters; each chapter contains a half-term's work and is based around a topic or theme. Each chapter follows the same structure:

Chapter introduction

At the start of each chapter there is a summary of what is covered. This includes:

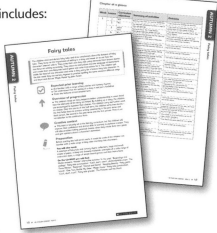

- **Introduction:** A description of what is covered in the chapter.
- **Expected prior learning:** What the children are expected to know before starting the work in the chapter.
- **Overview of progression:** A brief explanation of how the children progress through the chapter.
- **Creative context:** How the chapter could link to other curriculum areas.
- **Preparation:** Any resources required for the teaching of the chapter, including things that need to be sourced or prepared and the content that can be located on the CD-ROM.
- **Chapter at a glance:** This is a table that summarises the content of each lesson, including: the curriculum objectives (using a code system, please see pages 8–10), a summary of the activities and the outcome.
- **Background knowledge:** A section explaining grammatical terms and suchlike to enhance your subject knowledge, where required.

Lessons

Each chapter contains six weeks' of lessons, each week contains five lessons. At the start of each week there is an introduction about what is covered and the expected outcomes. The lesson plans then include the relevant combination of headings from below.

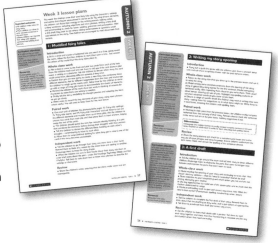

- **Curriculum objectives:** A list of the relevant objectives from the Programme of Study.
- **Resources:** What you require to teach the lesson.
- **Introduction:** A short and engaging activity to begin the lesson.
- **Whole-class work:** Working together as a class.
- **Group/Paired/Independent work:** Children working independently of the teacher in pairs, groups or alone.
- **Differentiation:** Ideas for how to support children who are struggling with a concept or how to extend those children who understand a concept without taking them onto new work.
- **Review:** A chance to review the children's learning and ensure the outcomes of the lesson have been achieved.

Assess and review

At the end of each chapter are activities for assessing and reviewing the children's understanding. These can be conducted during the course of the chapter's work or saved until the end of the chapter or done at a later date. There are four focuses for assess and review activities in each chapter:

- Grammar and punctuation
- Spelling
- Reading
- Writing

Elements of speaking and listening will be included where relevant within these four areas.

All four focuses follow the same format:

- **Curriculum objectives:** These are the areas of focus for the assess and review activity. There may be one focus or more than one depending on the activity.
- **Resources:** What you require to conduct the activities.
- **Revise:** A series of short activities or one longer activity to revise and consolidate the children's learning and ensure they understand the concept(s).
- **Assess:** An assessment activity to provide a chance for the children to demonstrate their understanding and for you to check this.
- **Further practice:** Ideas for further practice on the focus, whether children are insecure in their learning or you want to provide extra practice or challenge.

Photocopiable pages

At the end of each chapter are some photocopiable pages that will have been referred to in the lesson plans. These sheets are for the children to use; there is generally a title, an instruction, an activity and an 'I can' statement at the bottom. These sheets are also provided on the CD-ROM alongside additional pages as referenced in the lessons (see page 7 About the CD-ROM). The children should be encouraged to complete the 'I can' statements by colouring in the traffic lights to say how they think they have done (red – not very well, amber – ok, green – very well).

English starter activities

At the beginning of the book there is a bank of English starter activities (pages 11–14). These are games and activities that will help children familiarise and consolidate their knowledge of grammar, punctuation and spelling. The use of these will be suggested throughout the chapters, but they are also flexible and therefore could be used at any time.

About the CD-ROM

The CD-ROM contains:

- Printable versions of the photocopiable sheets from the book and additional photocopiable sheets as referenced in the lesson plans.
- Interactive activities for children to complete or to use on the whiteboard.
- Media resources to display.
- Printable versions of the lesson plans.
- Digital versions of the lesson plans with the relevant resources linked to them.

Getting started

- Put the CD-ROM into your CD-ROM drive.
  - For Windows users, the install wizard should autorun, if it fails to do so then navigate to your CD-ROM drive. Then follow the installation process.
  - For Mac users, copy the disk image file to your hard drive. After it has finished copying double-click it to mount the disk image. Navigate to the mounted disk image and run the installer. After installation the disk image can be unmounted and the DMG can be deleted from the hard drive.
- To complete the installation of the program you need to open the program and click 'Update' in the pop-up. Please note – this CD-ROM is web-enabled and the content will be downloaded from the internet to your hard-drive to populate the CD-ROM with the relevant resources. This only needs to be done on first use, after this you will be able to use the CD-ROM without an internet connection. If at any point any content is updated you will receive another pop-up upon start up with an internet connection.

Navigating the CD-ROM

There are two options to navigate the CD-ROM either as a Child or as a Teacher.

Child

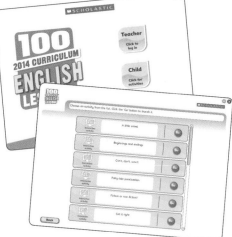

- Click on the 'Child' button on the first menu screen.
- In the second menu click on the relevant class (please note only the books installed on the machine or network will be accessible. You can also rename year groups to match your school's naming conventions via the Teacher > Settings > Rename books area).
- A list of interactive activities will be displayed, children need to locate the correct one and click 'Go' to launch it.
- There is the opportunity to print or save a PDF of the activity at the end.

Teacher

- Click on the Teacher button on the first menu screen and you will be taken to a screen showing which of the *100 English* books you have purchased. From here, you can also access information about getting started and the credits.
- To enter the product click 'Next' in the bottom right.
- You then need to enter a password (the password is: login).
- On first use:

  - Enter as a Guest by clicking on the 'Guest' button.
  - If desired, create a profile for yourself by adding your name to the list of users. Profiles allow you to save favourites and to specify which year group(s) you wish to be able to view.
  - Go to 'Settings' to create a profile for yourself – click 'Add user' and enter your name. Then choose the year groups you wish to have access to (you can return to this screen to change this at any time). Click on 'Login' at the top of the screen to re-enter the disk under your new profile.
- On subsequent uses you can choose your name from the drop-down list. The 'Guest' option will always be available if you, or a colleague, wish to use this.
- You can search the CD-ROM using the tools or save favourites.

For more information about how to use the CD-ROM, please refer to the help file which can be found in the teacher area of the CD-ROM. It is a red button with a question mark on it on the right-hand side of the screen just underneath the 'Settings' tab.

Curriculum grid

This grid shows the full curriculum objectives for Year 2. The codes are referenced in the chapter introductions. Additional information is provided in italics, this includes the statutory information from the appendices.

Domain	Code	Curriculum objective
Reading: Word reading	RWR1	To continue to apply phonic knowledge and skills as the route to decode words until automatic decoding has become embedded and reading is fluent.
	RWR2	To read accurately by blending the sounds in words that contain the graphemes taught so far, especially recognising alternative sounds for graphemes.
	RWR3	To read accurately words of two or more syllables that contain the same graphemes as above.
	RWR4	To read words containing common suffixes.
	RWR5	To read further common exception words, noting unusual correspondences between spelling and sound and where these occur in the word.
	RWR6	To read most words quickly and accurately, without overt sounding and blending, when they have been frequently encountered.
	RWR7	To read aloud books closely matched to their improving phonic knowledge, sounding out unfamiliar words accurately, automatically and without undue hesitation.
	RWR8	To re-read these books to build up their fluency and confidence in word reading.
Reading: Comprehension	RC1	To develop pleasure in reading, motivation to read, vocabulary and understanding by listening to, discussing and expressing views about a wide range of contemporary and classic poetry, stories and non-fiction at a level beyond that at which they can read independently.
	RC2	To develop pleasure in reading, motivation to read, vocabulary and understanding by discussing the sequence of events in books and how items of information are related.
	RC3	To develop pleasure in reading, motivation to read, vocabulary and understanding by becoming increasingly familiar with and retelling a wider range of stories, fairy stories and traditional tales.
	RC4	To develop pleasure in reading, motivation to read, vocabulary and understanding by being introduced to non-fiction books that are structured in different ways.
	RC5	To develop pleasure in reading, motivation to read, vocabulary and understanding by recognising simple recurring literary language in stories and poetry.
	RC6	To develop pleasure in reading, motivation to read, vocabulary and understanding by discussing and clarifying the meanings of words, linking new meanings to known vocabulary.
	RC7	To develop pleasure in reading, motivation to read, vocabulary and understanding by discussing their favourite words and phrases.
	RC8	To develop pleasure in reading, motivation to read, vocabulary and understanding by continuing to build up a repertoire of poems learnt by heart, appreciating these and reciting some, with appropriate intonation to make the meaning clear.
	RC9	To understand books read and listened to by drawing on what they already know or on background information and vocabulary provided by the teacher.

Domain	Code	Curriculum objective
Reading: Comprehension	RC10	To understand books read and listened to by checking that the text makes sense to them as they read and correcting inaccurate reading.
	RC11	To understand books read and listened to by making inferences on the basis of what is being said and done.
	RC12	To understand books read and listened to by answering and asking questions.
	RC13	To understand books read and listened to by predicting what might happen on the basis of what has been read so far.
	RC14	To participate in discussion about books, poems and other works that are read to them and those that they can read for themselves, taking turns and listening to what others say.
	RC15	To explain and discuss their understanding of books, poems and other material, both those that they listen to and those that they read for themselves.
Writing: Transcription	WT1	To spell by segmenting words into phonemes and representing these by graphemes, spelling many correctly.
	WT2	To spell by learning new ways of spelling phonemes for which one or more spellings are already known, and learn some words with each spelling, including a few common homophones.
	WT3	To spell by learning to spell common exception words.
	WT4	To spell by learning to spell more words with contracted forms.
	WT5	To spell by learning the possessive apostrophe (singular).
	WT6	To spell by distinguishing between homophones and near-homophones.
	WT7	To add suffixes to spell longer words, such as '-ment', '-ness', '-ful', '-less' and '-ly'.
	WC8	To apply spelling rules and guidelines, as listed in English Appendix 1 *Including:* ● *Alternative spellings: /j/ sound spelled 'ge' and 'dge'; /s/ sound spelled 'c' before 'e', 'I' and 'y'; /n/ sound spelled 'kn' and 'gn'; /r/ sound spelled 'wr'; /l/ spelled 'le', 'el' and 'al'; /ai/ spelled '-y'; /or/ sound before 'l' and 'll'; /u/spelled 'o'; /o/ spelled 'a' after 'w' and 'qu'; /ur/ sound spelled 'or' after 'w'; /or/ sound spelled 'ar' after 'w'; /zh/ sound spelled 's'* ● *Words ending in '-il'* ● *Adding suffixes to words ending in 'y' and 'e'* ● *Plurals of words ending in 'ey'* ● *Words ending in '-tion'.*
	WT9	To write from memory simple sentences dictated by the teacher that include words using the GPCs, common exception words and punctuation taught so far.
	WT10	To form lower-case letters of the correct size relative to one another.
	WT11	To start using some of the diagonal and horizontal strokes needed to join letters and understand which letters, when adjacent to one another, are best left unjoined.
	WT12	To write capital letters and digits of the correct size, orientation and relationship to one another and to lower case letters.
	WT13	To use spacing between words that reflects the size of the letters.

Domain	Code	Curriculum objective
Writing: Composition	WC1	To develop positive attitudes towards and stamina for writing by writing narratives about personal experiences and those of others (real and fictional).
	WC2	To develop positive attitudes towards and stamina for writing by writing about real events.
	WC3	To develop positive attitudes towards and stamina for writing by writing poetry.
	WC4	To develop positive attitudes towards and stamina for writing by writing for different purposes.
	WC5	To consider what they are going to write before beginning by planning or saying out loud what they are going to write about.
	WC6	To consider what they are going to write before beginning by writing down ideas and/or key words, including new vocabulary.
	WC7	To consider what they are going to write before beginning by encapsulating what they want to say, sentence by sentence.
	WC8	To make simple additions, revisions and corrections to their own writing by evaluating their writing with the teacher and other children.
	WC9	To make simple additions, revisions and corrections to their own writing by re-reading to check that it makes sense and that verbs to indicate time are used correctly and consistently, including verbs in the continuous form.
	WC10	To make simple additions, revisions and corrections to their own writing by proofreading to check for errors in spelling, grammar and punctuation.
	WC11	To read aloud what they have written with appropriate intonation to make the meaning clear.
	WC12	To develop their understanding of the concepts set out in English Appendix 2 by learning how to use both familiar and new punctuation correctly, including full stops, capital letters, exclamation marks, question marks, commas for lists and apostrophes for contracted forms and the possessive (singular).
	WC13	To learn how to use sentences with different forms: statement, question, exclamation, command.
	WC14	To learn how to use expanded noun phrases to describe and specify.
	WC15	To learn how to use the present and past tenses correctly and consistently including the progressive form.
	WC16	To learn how to use subordination (using when, if, that or because) and coordination (using or, and or but).
	WC17	To learn how to use the grammar for Year 2 in English Appendix 2. *Concepts for Year 2 include:* ● *Formation of nouns and adjectives using suffixes.* ● *Suffixes '-er' and '-est' in adjectives and the use of '-ly' in Standard English to turn adjectives into adverbs.*
	WC18	To learn how to use some features of written Standard English.
	WC19	To use and understand the grammatical terminology in English Appendix 2 in discussing their writing. *Terminology for Year 2: noun, noun phrase, statement, question, exclamation, command, compound, adjective, verb, suffix, adverb, tense (past, present), apostrophe, comma.*

English starter ideas

The following activities can be used to support your children's grammar, punctuation and spelling. They can be used as a part of English lessons or at other points over the school day to consolidate and support learning.

Is it a question?

Objectives
● To use punctuation marks correctly.

Begin by reading aloud sentences, some of which are questions and some of which are not. The children should indicate which are sentences, perhaps by holding up an individual whiteboard with a question mark written on it. Extend the activity by having the sentences written on the board for the children to read themselves.

Variations and adaptations
Include sentences that are exclamations, with the children showing either the question mark or an exclamation mark to differentiate between the two types of sentence.

When they are more familiar with both questions and exclamations, give the children short dictated sentences to write on their individual whiteboards, which must include either a question mark, exclamation mark, or full stop, whichever is appropriate to the sentence type.

2 Contractions

Objectives
● To learn to spell more words with contracted forms.

Prepare two sets of A4 cards using a different colour for each set. On one set write the words: *not, will, is, has, have, am, are, would, could, should*. On the other set write the words: *I, we, she, he, they, did, can, who, could, would, should, has, have, who*.

Invite children to select a card from each set, producing phrases such as: *I am*, or *should not*. Ask the class to write on individual whiteboards the correct contracted form of the word pair, such as *I'm, shouldn't*, placing the apostrophe where the missing letters are. They must choose with care, as not all words can be paired to form contractions, for example, *he have* or *did is*.

Variations and adaptations
Smaller versions of the card sets can be produced, so that children can use them individually or in pairs for further practice. They could be challenged to see how many contractions they can make.

3 Why say one word

Objectives
● To use expanded noun phrases to describe and specify.

Create a sentence about an object, or a feeling or an event, for example: *It is a jumper* or *We went to the zoo*. Ask the children to add a word to the sentence for example to: *It is a scruffy jumper*. As the children add adjectives to the sentence, tell them to mentally imagine the commas that would be needed if they wrote them.

Variations and adaptations
You can use this activity to practise connectives, asking the children to choose different ways to continue the sentence, for example: *It is a scruffy jumper but I like it.*

4 Statement changer

Objectives
● To use sentences with different forms.

Sit in a circle with the children and make a statement such as *I have a cat.* Tell the child next to you to turn it into a question (*Do you have a cat?*), the child after that into an exclamation (*You have a cat!*) and the next child into an instruction (*Go and get your cat.*). Continue round the circle with different statement starters.

5 Syllable count

Objectives
● To read accurately words of two or more syllables that contain the same graphemes as above.

Use this activity to help the children become more confident in reading and spelling longer words. Use any new vocabulary, or letter patterns, you are currently working on and break the words into syllables by clapping and counting them as you say them, for example, *yes-ter-day*; *el-e-phant* and so on.

Variations and adaptations

Use simple percussion instruments instead of clapping the syllables.

Give the children a short piece of text for them to find and list words with the same syllable count, listing them under the headings *Two*, *Three* or *Four* syllables. They can swap the lists for others to check and see if they agree.

6 Saying with attitude

Objectives
● To make inferences on the basis of what is being said and done.

This activity gives the children focused practise at changing the way they read different lines and can input into their skills at reading to convey characters' feelings or injecting drama into any presentation. It is also a useful activity to carry out when story writing to help the children think about the way their characters might be speaking.

Ask different children to come to the front and give them a line to say. Link the line to the topic you are studying, the poem you are reading or the genre you are writing. Challenge the children to say the line in different tones and attitudes (sad, gentle, cross, outraged, surprised and so on). Ask the class to suggest the attitude being portrayed.

7 Join together

Objectives
● To understand how nouns can be formed by joining together two words.

Create two sets of word cards that, when paired together, form compound words (*sea* and *shore*, *bed* and *room*). Invite children to sit in two lines facing each other. Give the children in one line a card each from a set. Give the children opposite a card each from the other set. Select a child and ask them to stand facing the two lines before reading their own card and holding it up. The child who can make a word by adding their card to it can then join the first child and both children can hold their cards together to show the compound word. If children are satisfied this is a real word, ring a bell to signal a correct match. If not, hoot a horn to ask them to try again.

Variations and adaptations

Play this game using a timer to see how many words children can make in a given time.

8 Commas for lists

Objectives
● To use commas to separate items in a list.

Practice writing lists with the children and encouraging them to use commas. You could ask them to help you write: a packing list for when you go on holiday; things you need to take on a class trip; the children's favourite footballers, pop stars or TV shows.

Variations and adaptations
Provide word cards that contain, for example shopping list items, ask the children to choose a card and write it down and then choose another one and use a comma between the list.

Play 'When granny went shopping' and ask the children to write down the options with commas between them.

9 This belongs to...

Objectives
● To use the possessive apostrophe for singular nouns.

When reading, ask the children to identify any instances of the apostrophe used for possession (try to stick to singular possession as plural possession is not a requirement in Year 2). Play a game of 'This belongs to' where the children have to say what the possessive apostrophe shows in the format of *The (object) belongs to (name)*. For example, *That is Rachel's bicycle* would be *The bicycle belongs to Rachel*.

This should help to reinforce the purpose of the punctuation.

Variations and adaptations
You can try the activity the other way round so that the children have to add the apostrophe.

This activity can also be used to focus on the conjunctions that join phrases and clauses.

10 Add a suffix

Objectives
● To correctly add suffixes to root words when the ending changes.

Provide sets of word cards with root words on them and sets of suffix cards with suffixes including '-ed', '-ing', '-er', '-est'. Ask the children to play pairs with the cards and try to find root words and suffixes that could go together, tell them to write down the entire word when they find one – the one with the most words is the winner.

Once children understand the concept of adding suffixes to root words, include root words that end in 'y', 'e' or are of one syllable ending in a single consonant letter after a single vowel letter (for example, *pat, hum, sad*). Encourage the children to match the pairs and write the words, correctly dropping the 'y' or 'e' and doubling the consonant as required.

Variations and adaptations
Play the same game with adding '-es' to nouns and verbs ending in 'y'.

Include the suffixes '-ment', '-ness', '-full', '-less' and '-ly'.

11 Homophone snap

Objectives
● To identify homophones.

Create cards with pairs of homophones and near-homophones on them, they could include: *there, their they're; here, hear; quiet, quite; see, sea; bare, bear; one won; sun, son; to, too, two; be, bee; blue, blew; night, knight* and so on. Divide shuffled sets of cards between pairs or groups and encourage them to play snap, calling 'Snap!' when they see a matching homophone pair.

Variations and adaptations
For added challenge, ask the child that calls 'Snap!' to say or write a sentence using each word correctly.

12 's' or 'c'?

Objectives
● To know that the /s/ sound is spelled with a 'c' before 'e', 'i' and 'y'.

Provide the children with letter cards 's' or 'c'. Tell them that you are going to read out a number of words that contain the /s/ sound but that some are spelled 's' and some are spelled 'c'. Explain that they should hold up the card to show which spelling is used.

Include a range of words such as: *race, ice, cell, city, fancy, snake, sausage, sat.* Once the children have voted on which letter is used, invite them to come up and write the word on the board. Once you have a few words, discuss the spellings. Encourage the children to notice that it is often spelled 'c' before 'e', 'i' and 'c'.

13 'wr' quiz

Objectives
● To know when the /r/ sound at the beginning of words is spelled 'wr'.

Arrange a quiz for there all of the answers being with 'wr'. For example:
- *The opposite of correct is... (wrong)*
- *A present is usually... (wrapped)*
- *This joins your arm to you hand... (wrist)*
- *A crashed ship is called a... (wreck)*
- *This is a letter my mother... (wrote)*

Ask the children to write down the words and then review their answers. Discuss how this spelling only occurs at the beginning of words, but not every word beginning with the /wr/ sound has this spelling, for example *run* not *wrun*.

14 'le' or 'el'

Objectives
● To choose the correct spelling of the /l/ sound.

Prepare cards for the children with 'le' or 'el' on them. Read out a series of words that end with the /l/ sound and ask the children to hold up the ending of them. Words could include: *table, apple, bottle, little, middle, camel, tunnel, squirrel, travel, towel, tinsel.*

Discuss the spellings with the children. Explain that 'le' is the most common ending, but that 'el' is often used after 'm', 'n', 'r', 's', 'v', 'w', 's'.

Variations and adaptations

Include the additional endings 'al' and/or 'il' for the children to choose from. Words can include: *metal, pedal, capital, hospital, animal; pencil, fossil, nostril.*

15 Spelling bingo

Objectives
● To recognise unusual spelling representations.

Play spelling bingo with the children. Prepare game boards that contain a range of spelling representations such as 'ey', 'qua', 'wa', 'all', 'war' and provide children with counters. Read out a range of words that contain these spellings such as *donkey, quantity, watch, ball, warm.* Children have to place their counters on the correct spelling representation for the word.

Variations and adaptations

Once the children understand the concept of the game, you could make it more challenging by including words with other spellings.

16 Knowing terminology

Objectives
● To know and understand grammatical terminology.

Prepare cards of grammatical terminology the children should be familiar with and either a range of definitions of technical words. Put the definitions on the board and invite a child to come up and choose a grammatical term from a box and match it to its definition and put it on the board – discuss the outcome.

New vocabulary for Year 2 should include: *noun, noun phrase, statement, question, exclamation, command, compound, adjective, verb, suffix, adverb, tense (past, present), apostrophe, comma.*

Vocabulary that children should be familiar with from Year 1 includes: *letter, capital letter, word, singular, plural, sentence, punctuation, full stop, question mark, exclamation mark.*

17 Common exception words

Objectives
● To recognise and become familiar with common exception words.

Prepare a board with a range of different common exception words on them and also prepare cards with the same words on them. Challenge the children to match the words by placing the word card on top of the board.

Variations and adaptations

To add more challenge, you could time the children doing it and see if they can beat themselves by improving their time.

You could ask the children to create their own game boards using the words, so they practise writing and spelling the words as well.

18 Past or present?

Objectives
● To use the past and present tenses accurately, including the progressive form.

Bring the class together and sit in a large circle. Say: *I am laughing.* Ask the child to your left to put it into the past tense: *I laughed.* Ask them to then give you another present-tense verb phrase, such as *I am juggling.* Tell the next child to put the phrase into the past tense and then say a new phrase *I juggled.* Carry on around the circle. You may wish to have prepared a list of verbs in case any children get stuck.

Variations and adaptations

You could prepare verbs that you want the children to choose beforehand and hand them out as cards.

Food

The introductory theme for the year is that of food. The children will enjoy reading the picture book *Oliver's Vegetables* by Vivian French, build on their understanding of recipes, identify the key features of posters in order to create their own and read two poems about food before writing their own alphabetical list poem. They will find out about and discuss healthy eating, using this knowledge in their writing. They will continue using phonics for decoding and encoding and work on contractions, noun phrases and imperative verbs.

Expected prior learning
- Know what a sentence is.
- Can use decoding, blending and encoding.
- Can understand questions, question marks and exclamation marks.
- Familiar with using ingredients to make something.
- Know what a noun is.
- Familiar with recipes.
- Know what syllables are.

Overview of progression
- Discussion skills will be developed throughout this half term as the children talk about both their reading and their own writing.
- Phonics is used to decode new vocabulary.
- Punctuation knowledge is developed through the use of apostrophes for omission and commas in lists.
- Vocabulary is increased through increased use of noun phrases and further descriptive verbs.
- The way in which characters in a story can change is discussed.

Creative context
- In art, the children can create miniature gardens.
- In science, link to the study of plants and how they grow as well as to the importance of healthy eating.
- Dance and music can be combined by creating sound effects to accompany representations of plants growing from seed.
- The use of recipes lends itself well to mathematics through quantities and measurements.

Preparation
Oliver's Vegetables by Vivian French and Alison Bartlett is the suggested text for this half-term. Also gather together as many child-friendly recipes and recipe books as you can. Find out about any food allergies or eating disorders that children in your class may suffer from, in case these crop up in discussion.

You will also need:
Sticky notes; two large sheets of sugar paper; scissors; A4 paper; lined paper; glue sticks; vegetables from the story; orange; milk; bread; circle-time objects; recipe books, recipes from magazines or supermarkets; flipchart paper; materials to make a cheese omelette (optional); individual whiteboards and pens; small box; healthy food posters; felt-tipped pens; cooked spaghetti; favourite foods; menus; children's books that the children are not familiar with such as *I Do Not Eat the Colour Green* by Lynne Rickards and Margaret Chamberlain, *Dominic Grows Sweetcorn* by Mandy Ross and Alison Bartlett, *Eddie's Garden and How to Make Things Grow* by Sarah Garland.

On the CD-ROM you will find:
Media resources 'Foods from around the world', 'Gardens', 'Healthy foods?'; interactive activities 'Name that food', 'A little snivel', 'Healthy or unhealthy?'; photocopiable pages 'Animal masks' 'Cupcakes recipe', 'Luscious words', 'What happened next?'

Chapter at a glance

An overview of the chapter. For curriculum objective codes, please see pages 8–10.

Week	Lesson	Curriculum objectives	Summary of activities	Outcomes
1	1	RWR: 1, 6 RC: 1, 7, 11, 13	Introduce topic of food and *Oliver's Vegetables*. Use prediction, inference and phonics. Identify favourite words and phrases.	• Can decode new vocabulary, predict events in the story, list foods they like and don't like.
	2	RC: 2 WC: 4, 12	Focus on story sequence. Revise sentence and days of the week – write sequenced sentences.	• Can recap story, re-order and write sentences, including days of the week.
	3	RC: 1, 9, 11	Question Oliver in the hot-seat. Role play characters and feelings.	• Can ask Oliver questions. • Can improvise dialogue. • Can discuss characters' feelings.
	4	RWR: 6 RC: 14 WC: 6	Discuss the setting of the garden and discuss. Discuss what to put in their own garden and note ideas in preparation for display.	• Can discuss types of gardens. • Can identify fruits and vegetables growing. • Can discuss choices of plants.
	5	WT: 1, 10, 12, 13 WC: 4	Create garden displays with captions.	• Can identify real vegetables and describe using senses. • Can design own gardens and write sentences as captions describing them.
2	1	RWR: 7 RC: 1, 3, 5	Introduce 'The Little Red Hen'. Predict, discuss recurring language, join in with repeated phrases. Role play the story.	• Can read 'The Little Red Hen', pausing for predictions. • Can read together in groups. • Can retell story to a partner.
	2	RWR: 8 WT: 4, 8, 9 WC: 19	Introduce writing contractions using the story.	• Can spell words ending in the /l/ sound. • Can identify, understand and write contractions, using apostrophes of omission. • Can write sentences from dictation.
	3	WT: 4 WC: 12, 13, 19	Revise contractions. Sentence types – questions and statements.	• Can identify questions and statements in story. • Can write own questions and statements based on both stories read so far.
	4	RWR: 8 RC: 9, 11, 14	Look at the ending of the story – was Little Red Hen right not to share?	• Can participate in circle-time style discussion. • Can choose preferred ending and explain reasons for choice.
	5	WC: 12, 13	Use last lesson's work and write an alternative ending – thinking about sentence types and punctuation.	• Can participate in hot-seating Little Red Hen. • Can write alternative ending. • Can use questions, statements and contractions.
3	1	RWR: 1 WT1: WC: 14, 19	Introduce *nouns* and *noun phrases*. Introduce the term *adjective*. Write and share noun phrases.	• Can recognise nouns. • Can use adjectives to form noun phrases.
	2	RWR: 1 RC: 4, 9	Introduce recipes and identify key features.	• Can identify and discuss key features of a recipe.
	3	RC: 10 WC: 4, 13, 19	Re-order recipes and look at commands and bossy verbs.	• Can note and list bossy verbs. • Can make own list and re-order recipe instructions.
	4	WT: 1 WC: 4, 12, 19	Commas for lists – shopping lists.	• Can use commas in lists. • Can write shopping lists. • Can read lists aloud, noting comma pauses.
	5	RC: 10 WC: 12, 13	Follow a recipe.	• Can illustrate re-ordered cheese omelette recipe. • Can include bossy verbs and commas.
4	1	WT: 12 WC: 6, 12, 13	Create shared writing of a recipe using commas, command sentences and numbers. Plan recipe ideas.	• Can discuss ideas for new recipes.
	2	WC: 5, 7	Draft own recipe.	• Can use notes to explain recipe orally to partner. • Can write draft recipe using key features.
	3	WT: 10, 12, 13 WC: 4, 8, 10	Review and finalise recipes.	• Can offer feedback on drafts in pairs. • Can create final recipe written in best handwriting.
	4	RC: 15	Introduce and explore food packaging.	• Can explore language use on food packaging. • Can discuss sentence and word types.
	5	RC: 7 WT: 10, 12, 13 WC: 4	Create own packaging.	• Can discuss, plan and create packaging for recipes created earlier, using best handwriting.

Chapter at a glance

Week	Lesson	Curriculum objectives	Summary of activities	Outcome
5	1	RWR: 8 RC: 14 WT: 1 WC: 12	Recap *Oliver's Vegetables* and discuss food categories and healthy vs. not.	• Can discuss healthy eating. • Can design and label a healthy pizza.
	2	RC: 9, 14	Examine posters – what makes them effective?	• Can identify and discuss healthy and unhealthy foods. • Can list key features of effective posters.
	3	WT: 4 WC: 6, 12, 14	Plan poster – recap noun phrases, what text they want, contractions *do/don't*.	• Can revise contractions and noun phrases. • Can gather ideas and language for healthy-eating posters.
	4	WT: 1 WC: 4, 5, 14	Draft poster.	• Can discuss and draft healthy-eating posters.
	5	WT: 10, 13 WC: 8	Finalise poster.	• Can review and create final healthy-eating posters. • Can assess own work.
6	1	RWR: 5 RC: 1, 7, 8, 14	Share poem 'Spaghetti'. Analyse language and punctuation. Rehearse and read poem.	• Can read and discuss poem 'Spaghetti', exploring language and punctuation use. • Can discuss, annotate, practise and read poem aloud.
	2	RWR: 5 RC: 6	Share poem 'Apple pie'. Explore structure and language.	• Can identify 'Apple pie' as alphabetically arranged list poem. • Can decode new vocabulary and mime actions for verbs.
	3	WC: 6, 14	Explore language – ideas for own poem.	• Can gather ideas for writing list poems. • Can select topic and note possible choices.
	4	WT: 1 WC: 3, 5, 8, 12	Draft own poem.	• Can draft alphabetical list poems on chosen food item. • Can share and evaluate drafts.
	5	WT: 10, 13 WC: 3, 8	Finalise own poem.	• Can write up final poems in best handwriting.

Background knowledge

Adjective: A word that modifies a noun. The simplest way to explain it is that it describes a noun.

Contracted forms: The use of an apostrophe to contract two words into one. The apostrophe takes the place of a missing letter or letters.

Noun: The name of something – whether a thing, a person, or an abstract noun such as *happiness*. Common nouns can be preceded by the definite article.

Noun phrases: A cluster of words acting as a noun. For the purposes of this half term, it is when a noun has been modified by descriptive words – for example, *apple* becomes *the ripe apple*.

Week 1 lesson plans

The children begin this half-term's work on food by using Vivian French's picture book *Oliver's Vegetables*. They will be encouraged to use phonic skills to decode and encode new vocabulary as they identify and write about fruits and vegetables. They will choose favourite words and phrases from the story. They will re-order sentences to sequence the story, predict events and, after role playing, they will discuss how characters and their feelings can change. After looking at and talking about different gardens, they will design their own garden, adding captions in complete sentences to describe its features.

1: *Oliver's Vegetables*

Expected outcomes
● All children can use phonic knowledge to decode and encode some new vocabulary. They can retell a story that has been read to them. They can make simple labels.
● Most children can use phonic knowledge to decode and encode most new vocabulary. They can retell a story with some extra detail. They can write captions in correctly punctuated sentences.
● Some children can read most new words with ease. They can retell a story accurately with detail, engaging an audience. They write captions which include additional description.

Curriculum objectives
● To predict what might happen on the basis of what has been read so far.
● To make inferences on the basis of what is being said and done.
● To listen to, discuss and express views about a wide range of contemporary and classic poetry, stories and non-fiction at a level beyond that at which they can read independently.
● To read most words quickly and accurately, without overt sounding and blending, when they have been frequently encountered.
● To continue to apply phonic knowledge and skills as the route to decode words until automatic decoding has become embedded and reading is fluent.
● To discuss their favourite words and phrases.

Resources
Oliver's Vegetables by Vivian French and Alison Bartlett; media resource 'Foods from around the world' on the CD-ROM; sticky notes; two large sheets of sugar paper pinned to the wall

Introduction
● Display the media resource 'Foods from around the world' on the CD-ROM, inviting the children to identify any that they know, and telling them the names of those they are unfamiliar with. Which have they eaten and what did they think of them? Explain that they will be looking at stories and finding out lots of new things about food over the coming weeks.
● Invite the children to tell a partner some of their favourite foods, allowing two or three minutes for them to do this. Ask some children to tell the class the foods their partners chose. Are there any common to many children, or some unusual choices?

Whole-class work
● Read *Oliver's Vegetables* to the class, if possible, using multiple copies so the children can see the written text clearly, and provide the opportunity for them to join in with decoding some of the words. Pause at the end of the third spread, asking the children what they think will happen. Will Oliver find the potatoes straight away? What might happen if he doesn't? Do they think he will eat what else he might find? After the fifth spread, ask if they think he will find the potatoes next. If not, can they suggest what other vegetables he might find? When Grandpa digs up the potatoes, do they think Oliver will still want to eat them after discovering he enjoys the other vegetables? At the end of the book, what difference do they think there could be in Oliver's meals in the future?
● Read through the book a second time, asking the children to listen out for words or phrases they like, pausing after each page or two, for their responses.

Paired work
● Display these words from the story: *finish, wonderful, vegetables, proudly, complaints, bargain, crinkly, spinach, important, rhubarb, beetroot, tangle, delicious*. Working in ability-based pairs, the children should decode the words, using segmentation and blending. Tell them that the words are all from the story they have just heard. Allow a few minutes for them to read the words, then invite pairs to join other pairs to share what they think each word says. Finally, read the words together as a class. Which words did they find easy and which were harder? Can they explain why? Read to the children the sentences from the book in which the words appear.

Review
● Ask the children to think about the foods they like and those they don't like, choosing two or three of each. Give them sticky notes on which to write their choices which they should stick on to the appropriate large sheet of sugar paper, one of which is labelled 'Foods I like' and one 'Foods I don't like'. Encourage the children to use their phonic knowledge for their spelling. Discuss the finished sheets. Which foods are most and least popular?

Curriculum objectives
● To discuss the sequence of events in books and how items of information are related.
● To write for different purposes.
● To learn how to use both familiar and new punctuation correctly (see Appendix 2), including full stops, capital letters, exclamation marks, question marks, commas for lists and apostrophes for contracted forms and the possessive (singular).

Resources
Photocopiable page 40 'Oliver's Vegetables sequence cards'; scissors; A4 paper; lined paper; glue sticks

2: Putting things in order

Introduction
● Use starter activity 1 'Is it a question?'.

Whole-class work
● Through questioning, ask the children to recap the story of Oliver's Vegetables that they heard in the previous lesson.

Paired work
● Give each child photocopiable page 40 'Oliver's Vegetables sequence cards', scissors, glue stick and A4 paper. Explain that they will cut out the sentence boxes and work with a partner to arrange them in the right order to retell the story. Then they will stick the sentence strips onto the sheet of paper.

Whole-class work
● Briefly remind the class about writing in sentences, using capital letters and full stops. Explain that they will use their story sequences to write sentences about what Oliver ate on each day of the week. Remind them to use capital letters for the days of the week, and give them the first sentence as a starter.

Independent work
● Allow the children time to write their sentences.

> **Differentiation**
> ● Give children a list of the days of the week if they are having difficulty.

Review
● Working in pairs, the children will use their work as a guide to retell the story to each other.

Curriculum objectives
● To listen to, discuss and express views about a wide range of contemporary and classic poetry, stories and non-fiction at a level beyond that at which they can read independently.
● To draw on what they already know or on background information and vocabulary provided by the teacher.
● To make inferences on the basis of what is being said and done.

Resources
Multiple copies of Oliver's Vegetables by Vivian French and Alison Bartlett

3: How characters change

Introduction
● Put yourself in the hot-seat, in role as Oliver. Invite the children to ask you questions about what happened to you in the story.

Whole-class work
● Ask the children to name the characters in the story. What can they tell you about each character? Establish that Oliver and Grandpa are the main characters and that they get on well together.

Paired work
● Explain that the children will imagine they are either Oliver or Grandpa, and improvise a conversation in role, based on the events of the week of the story. They should take turns in each role.
● They should repeat the exercise, this time in role as Oliver and his Mum. This time the conversation should be at the end of the week, after Oliver has found and tried all the vegetables.

> **Differentiation**
> ● Some children may find it helpful to have access to the book.

Review
● Talk with the class about how Oliver's feelings about eating different foods changed. Has anything like that ever happened to them? How do they think Mum would feel at the end of the story? What might Grandpa tell Grandma?

Curriculum objectives
- To write down ideas and/or key words, including new vocabulary.
- To participate in discussion about books, poems and other works that are read to them and those that they can read for themselves, taking turns and listening to what others say.
- To read most words quickly and accurately, without overt sounding and blending, when they have been frequently encountered.

Resources
Media resource 'Gardens' on the CD-ROM; interactive activity 'Name that food' on the CD-ROM

4: Into the garden

Introduction
- Display the media resource 'Gardens' on the CD-ROM. Talk about what is in each image and how they differ. Do the children recognise any of the plants?

Whole-class work
- Talk about the setting of Grandpa's garden, establishing that it has vegetable beds. Talk about different gardens the children know. Does anyone grow vegetables, or know someone who does? Show the class the book, so that they may also notice a shed, bench and some trees.
- Conduct the interactive activity 'Name that food' on the CD-ROM. How many can the children identify?

Group work
- Explain to the class that they will be designing their own garden for a display. Working in small groups they will talk about what fruits and vegetables they would choose to grow. They will make notes as they talk, so they can remember their ideas, though they might wish to change them later.

Review
- Look again at the photos of fruit and vegetables. Which of them did children include in their ideas? What other choices have they made? What reasons do they have for their choices? Have they chosen any of the vegetables that Oliver tried?

Curriculum objectives
- To form lower-case letters of the correct size relative to one another.
- To write capital letters and digits of the correct size, orientation and relationship to one another and to lower-case letters.
- To use spacing between words that reflects the size of the letters.
- To segment words into phonemes and represent these by graphemes, spelling many correctly.
- To write for different purposes.

Resources
Children's notes from the previous lesson; real examples of vegetables in the story

5: Designing a garden

Introduction
- Show the children the real vegetables, and see if they are able to identify them. Encourage them to describe the vegetables using all their senses and interesting vocabulary.

Whole-class work
- Remind the class of the work they did in the previous lesson on gardens. Explain that today they will work with a partner to design and label their own garden.
- Their gardens will need explanatory captions, written in sentences. Recap on sentences, starting with capitals, ending with full stops and making sense. Invite suggestions for sentences that might be used in the designs, for example: *A shed for keeping tools. Carrots growing in a row. Flowers for the bees. Potatoes growing underground.*

Paired work
- Allow the children time to design their gardens, adding appropriate captions. While they are working together to share ideas, each child should create their own version of the garden. Encourage them to use phonic knowledge for spelling, and to use good handwriting so others can read their writing, as the gardens will be put on display.

Differentiation
- Extend experienced writers by encouraging them to include more information in their sentences, for example the adjectives they used in the lesson introduction.

Review
- Invite the children to share their designs with others, encouraging them to provide positive feedback. Praise individuals for correct spelling and look at plausible alternative options, discussing differences.

Expected outcomes

● All children can talk about the story and write an alternative ending. They can read and spell most simple contractions and recognise sentences which are questions.

● Most children can give reasons for their opinions about the actions of characters in the story. They can read, spell and form simple contractions. They understand the difference between questions and statements.

● Some children can offer reasons for characters' actions in the story. They can read, spell and form contractions confidently, some of which are more complex in form. They are secure in their knowledge of questions and statements.

Curriculum objectives

● To read aloud books closely matched to their improving phonic knowledge, sounding out unfamiliar words accurately, automatically and without undue hesitation.

● To become increasingly familiar with and retell a wider range of stories, fairy stories and traditional tales.

● To listen to, discuss and express views about a wide range of contemporary and classic poetry, stories and non-fiction at a level beyond that at which they can read independently.

● To recognise simple recurring literary language in stories and poetry.

Resources

Orange; milk; bread; photocopiable pages 41–42 'The Little Red Hen'; photocopiable page 'Animals masks' from the CD-ROM

Week 2 lesson plans

This week the children's attention is focused on the traditional tale, 'The Little Red Hen'. They will read the story, pausing to predict outcomes. They will discuss the characters' actions, giving reasons for their opinions, wear character masks to role play the story and write an alternative ending. They work on reading, forming and spelling simple contractions, and look at the difference between sentences which are questions and those which are statements.

1: 'Little Red Hen'

Introduction

● Begin by asking the children: *Where does food come from?* Listen to some initial thoughts and then focus the discussion on the foods you have collected. Ask, for example: *Where do oranges come from? What journey do they go on to get to our homes? What about milk? What about bread?* Discuss the different starting points and journeys of different food and then ask: *Who works to bring us our food?* Talk about the different people who work to get food to our table. Focus on bread and ask if any of the children have made bread at home. Establish that bread is made from flour, which comes from wheat.

Whole-class work

● Display photocopiable page 41 'The Little Red Hen' and read this first part of the story with the class. What do the children think about the responses of the Dog, Cat and Rat? What do the children think the hen will do with the wheat she harvests?

● Next display and read photocopiable page 42, up to 'I wonder who'll help me eat this bread?' Pause to ask the children to predict what might happen, then read the ending together. Do the children think the hen did the right thing at the end?

● Put the children into four groups – hens, dogs, cats and rats – and encourage them to join in with a second reading of the story, saying their lines in role. Highlight the repeating phrases – and the change at the end.

Group work

● Arrange the class into groups of four, giving each member a role from the story: Hen, Cat, Dog or Rat. Each child will need the appropriate character mask to wear, made from photocopiable page 'Animal masks' from the CD-ROM. (They can be held in front of the face if printed on card.) The children enjoy acting out the story in role.

Paired work

● Working with a partner, encourage the children to retell the story to each other, using appropriate intonation for the characters' spoken voices.

Differentiation

● Ensure the role-play groups are of mixed ability, so that each group has one more confident speaker to take on the role of Little Red Hen, who has most to remember and to say.

Review

● Talk about how the four characters might feel about each other. What words can the children suggest to describe them? What do they think Dog, Cat and Rat might do if Little Red Hen asks them for a favour on another occasion?

Curriculum objectives
- To learn to spell more words with contracted forms.
- To re-read books to build up their fluency and confidence in word reading.
- To apply spelling rules and guidelines, as listed in Appendix 1.
- To write from memory simple sentences dictated by the teacher that include words using the GPCs, common exception words and punctuation taught so far.
- To use and understand the grammatical terminology in Appendix 2 in discussing their writing.

Resources
Interactive activity 'A little snivel' on the CD-ROM; photocopiable pages 41–42 'The Little Red Hen'

2: Contractions

Introduction
- Write 'Little Red Hen' on the board. Discuss the spelling of *little* and talk about the spelling options for words ending in the /l/ sound.
- Carry out interactive activity 'A little snivel' on the CD-ROM or use starter activity 14 'le' or 'el'.

Whole-class work
- Show the children how pairs of words are joined together to form contractions. Explain that we use an apostrophe to show where we have missed out letters. Use simple examples such as: *do not = don't* or *I will = I'll*.
- Use the starter activity 2 'Contractions' with the class.
- Display the text of 'The Little Red Hen' and invite the children to identify the contractions and to expand them into their constituent parts. Note the word *won't* is formed differently, so has to be learned as a tricky word. Explain that when we write contractions it is usually when we write dialogue.

Independent work
- Dictate short sentences for the children to write on their individual whiteboards, which include the contractions covered in the lesson.

> **Differentiation**
> - For any children finding the concept difficult, work individually with them. Write example words to be contracted on a sheet of paper. Give the child a piece of card with an apostrophe written on it. Invite them to cover the missing letters with the card.

Review
- Repeat the starter activity, looking for progress made in the lesson.

Curriculum objectives
- To learn to spell more words with contracted forms.
- To use sentences with different forms: statement, question, exclamation, command.
- To learn how to use both familiar and new punctuation correctly (see Appendix 2), including full stops, capital letters, exclamation marks, question marks, commas for lists and apostrophes for contracted forms and the possessive (singular).
- To use and understand the grammatical terminology in Appendix 2 in discussing their writing.

Resources
Photocopiable pages 41–42 'The Little Red Hen'

3: Who will help me?

Introduction
- Revise the work you did in the previous lesson on contracted forms. Ask the children to turn to their partner and have a pretend argument between two friends, one of whom will not let the other have a turn on the computer. Encourage them to use as many contractions as possible. Write examples on the board for the children to refer to later.

Whole-class work
- To introduce the difference between statements and questions, display and select dialogue from the story of 'The Little Red Hen'. Read the first question, and ask the children what kind of sentence it is, establishing that it is a question. What other questions can they find in the story? How do they know they are questions?
- Next read out the answers from the other characters, explaining that we call them statements. Give the children several more examples of simple statements. Explain that statements tell us (state) things.

Paired work
- Using 'The Little Red Hen' and *Oliver's Vegetables*, ask the children to write questions and statements for each story. Give them a few examples first.

Review
- Scribe some of the children's sentences on the board, asking the class to identify whether they are statements or questions. Omit the question marks, and ask the class which sentences require them.

Curriculum objectives
• To re-read books to build up their fluency and confidence in word reading.
• To draw on what they already know or on background information and vocabulary provided by the teacher.
• To make inferences on the basis of what is being said and done.
• To participate in discussion about books, poems and other works that are read to them and those that they can read for themselves, taking turns and listening to what others say.

Resources
Photocopiable pages 41–42 'The Little Red Hen'; objects to pass round groups in a circle-time activity

Curriculum objectives
• To learn how to use both familiar and new punctuation correctly (see Appendix 2), including full stops, capital letters, exclamation marks, question marks, commas for lists and apostrophes for contracted forms and the possessive (singular).
• To use sentences with different forms: statement, question, exclamation, command.

4: Was the hen right?

Introduction
• With the class, re-read the story 'The Little Red Hen', focusing on the ending. What do the children think about Little Red Hen at the end? Why do they think she didn't share?

Group work
• Encourage groups of children to discuss, in a circle-time way, what they would have done if they were Little Red Hen, and why. Each group should have an object to pass round, the only speaker being the child holding the object, allowing each child to have a turn.

Differentiation
• Ensure the groups are balanced so that less confident speakers are not all in one group.

Review
• Ask the children to stand in one of two places in the room – one for those who would have shared their bread and one for those who wouldn't. Invite individuals to share the reasons for their choice. Explain to the class that in the next lesson they will look at rewriting the ending of the story.

5: A different ending

Introduction
• Put yourself, or a confident child, in the hot seat as Little Red Hen. Invite the children to ask Little Red Hen about the events of the story. They could ask how she felt about the other animals and why she did what she did at the end of the story.

Whole-class work
• Explain to the class that they will write an alternative ending to the story, using ideas they discussed in the previous lesson. For example, if Little Red Hen shared the bread, what difference would that make?

Independent work
The children write their alternative ending. Remind them to think about different sentence types, and to use the correct punctuation. They should also aim to include some familiar contractions.

Differentiation
• Less confident spellers could be given key word lists to help them.
• Encourage more experienced writers to include noun phrases.

Review
• Ask the class for examples of how they altered the ending. Which ending do they prefer – the original or their alternative? Invite the children to choose examples from their writing of questions and statements, and share some of them with the class. Which contractions were they able to include?

Week 3 lesson plans

This week the children build on work they began in Year 1, developing their knowledge and understanding of how recipes are written, by identifying key features and noting the use of 'bossy', or imperative, verbs. They re-order a written recipe, later creating a pictorial version to which they will add descriptive captions. They will learn the terms *noun* and *adjective*, and create noun phrases to describe types of food. Note that they do not need to know the term *noun phrase* at this stage. They will learn how to use commas to separate ideas in simple sentences and use them in creating shopping list sentences.

1: What's in a name?

Introduction

● Write some nouns that the children are likely to be familiar with on the board and ask what the words have in common. Establish that they are all names of things, and that they can be preceded by *the*, *a* or *an*. Introduce the term *noun*. To help the children remember the word, draw attention to the initial letter matching that of *names*. Read out some simple sentences, asking the children to raise their hands when they hear the noun. Ask children to suggest similar sentences, for the others to identify the nouns in the same way.

Whole-class work

● Take a bite of some food in front of the children – real or imaginary. Keep your expression neutral and write on the board: *The teacher ate the cake,* for example. Ask the class to identify the nouns. Take another bite, showing in your face and actions whether you like or dislike the food. Write another sentence on the board, this time adding appropriate adjectives – for example, *The lucky teacher ate the delicious cake.* Ask the children to read both sentences and say which is more interesting and informative for the reader.
● Write the sentence *The boy ate the pie*, on the board. Ask: *What are the nouns in this sentence?* (*Boy* and *pie*). Ask: *How can we make this sentence more interesting? Perhaps we could say what sort of boy and what sort of pie.* Try out different combinations with the children, for example *The hungry boy ate the enormous pie* and ask for their suggestions.
● Draw attention to the words describing the nouns and introduce the term *adjective*. Explain that these words 'add' information about the nouns. Ask for some adjectives to describe objects easily to hand or that can be seen through the window.

Paired work

● Hand out photocopiable page 43 'Tangy tomatoes' to each pair of children. Ask them to use phonics to read the words, then cut out the word cards, muddle them up and place them face down between them.
● Tell the pairs to take turns to turn over a card, then each think of different adjectives to describe the food. Challenge them to use all their senses to find as many as they can for each type of food.

Independent work

● Allow time for the children to write noun phrases about some of the foods, containing one or two adjectives, for example *a juicy pink peach*, and *tasty chocolate ice-cream*. Discourage them from over-using adjectives, and encourage them to use different words for each food.

Review

● Explain that the children have been writing noun phrases and introduce this term to them. Invite the children to share their best phrases, noting unusual examples.

Expected outcomes

● All children can create noun phrases, identify the need for using commas in lists and begin to identify when imperative verbs are being used. They can identify key features of a recipe and add illustrations to a written recipe.
● Most children can re-order a recipe, write sentences with commas to separate items in a list and confidently include their own captions to an illustrated recipe.
● Some children can confidently use imperative verbs in their sentences.

Curriculum objectives

● To continue to apply phonic knowledge and skills as the route to decode words until automatic decoding has become embedded and reading is fluent.
● To use expanded noun phrases to describe and specify.
● To segment words into phonemes and represent these by graphemes, spelling many correctly.
● To use and understand the grammatical terminology in Appendix 2 in discussing their writing.

Resources

Photocopiable page 43 'Tangy tomatoes'

Curriculum objectives
- To be introduced to non-fiction books that are structured in different ways.
- To continue to apply phonic knowledge and skills as the route to decode words until automatic decoding has become embedded and reading is fluent.
- To draw on what they already know or on background information and vocabulary provided by the teacher.

Resources
Photocopiable page 'Cupcakes recipe' from the CD-ROM; a selection of recipe books (some of which the children could bring from home); recipes from magazines or supermarket recipe cards; sticky notes; piece of flipchart paper

2: What's in a recipe?

Introduction
- Carry out starter activity 3 'Why say one word?' using *This is an apple* or *Sam likes curry* as a starter sentence, but don't include the work on commas on this occasion.

Whole-class work
- Display the photocopiable page 'Cupcakes recipe' from the CD-ROM.
- Go through each part of the recipe, highlighting the key features – the title, the list of ingredients with the amounts needed, and the method written as a series of ordered steps.

Paired work
- Give each pair of children a recipe or cookery book to look at. Encourage them to find the key features of recipes that you have identified, labelling them with sticky notes.

> **Differentiation**
> - More experienced readers can be given two different styles of recipe books to look through and make comparisons.

Review
- Ask the children to talk about their investigation. Establish that, even though the books may look different, all of the recipes include the same essential information. Did all the recipes have each point numbered, or did some have bullet points, or simply gaps between each stage? Did the children find different ways in which amounts were given? Write these key features on a piece of flipchart paper so that you can keep it for next week.

Curriculum objectives
- To use sentences with different forms: statement, question, exclamation, command.
- To write for different purposes.
- To check that the text makes sense to them as they read and to correct inaccurate reading.
- To use and understand the grammatical terminology in Appendix 2 in discussing their writing.

Resources
Photocopiable page 44 'Making a cheese omelette'; scissors; glue sticks; A4 paper; materials to make a cheese omelette (optional); individual whiteboards and pens

3: Re-ordering a recipe

Introduction
- Ideally, make a cheese omelette and talk through the process you are using. Alternatively, pretend to make one. Ask the children to watch and to note on individual whiteboards any action words they hear.
- Ask the children to share the action words they noted. Explain that these words that describe actions are known as verbs, and those used in recipes tell us what to do – they could be called *bossy verbs*.

Paired work
- Ask the children to write down all the action words/bossy verbs that describe what can be done when cooking with both eggs and potatoes, for example *crack*, *whisk*, *boil*, *fry*, *poach*, *peel*, *boil*, *mash* and *roast*. Share their results.

Independent work
- Hand out photocopiable page 44 'Making a cheese omelette'. Ask the children to cut up the recipe instructions, re-order them correctly and stick them onto a sheet of paper.

Review
- Go over the correct order for the cheese omelette recipe, allowing the children to check their own work. What bossy verbs are included?

■SCHOLASTIC

Curriculum objectives
• To learn how to use both familiar and new punctuation correctly (see Appendix 2), including full stops, capital letters, exclamation marks, question marks, commas for lists and apostrophes for contracted forms and the possessive (singular).
• To segment words into phonemes and represent these by graphemes, spelling many correctly.
• To write for different purposes.
• To use and understand the grammatical terminology in Appendix 2 in discussing their writing.

Resources
Any text which includes commas to read aloud (perhaps the method from a recipe); photocopiable page 'Cupcakes recipe' from the CD-ROM; recipes from books, magazines or cards

4: Let's go shopping

Introduction
• Read your chosen text aloud to the class, ignoring the commas, exaggerating the difference this makes. Ask for the children's comments. Do they know what is needed to improve the reading? Explain that we use commas to separate parts of longer sentences so that they are easier to both read and understand.
• Display photocopiable page 'Cupcakes recipe' from the CD-ROM, noting where commas are used to separate parts of sentences. Read the sentences together, telling the children to write a comma in the air each time one occurs.

Paired work
• Give each pair a recipe to use, and ask them to write a shopping list for the items they would need in order to make it.

Whole-class work
• Play the game 'When granny went shopping', following that initial sentence with one item. Each new speaker adds an item to the list, pausing between each, where the comma would go.

Independent work
• Model how to write shopping list sentences, using commas to separate the items, for example *Granny went shopping and bought a bucket, a mop, some floor cleaner and a bar of chocolate.*
• The children will write their own shopping list sentences, either serious or silly. You could suggest themes, such as baking, decorating and gardening.

Review
• Invite children to read their lists, pausing for the commas. Can the others guess the theme of the sentence?

Curriculum objectives
• To check that the text makes sense to them as they read and to correct inaccurate reading.
• To learn how to use both familiar and new punctuation correctly (see Appendix 2), including full stops, capital letters, exclamation marks, question marks, commas for lists and apostrophes for contracted forms and the possessive (singular).
• To use sentences with different forms: statement, question, exclamation, command.

Resources
Children's correctly ordered version of photocopiable page 44 'Making a cheese omelette'; plain A4 paper folded into quarters

5: Following a recipe

Introduction
• As you read photocopiable page 44 'Making a cheese omelette', correctly ordered, ask the children to mime the actions. Read it a second time, asking the children to raise a hand when they hear a comma pause.

Whole-class work
• Explain that recipes with illustrations are often easier to understand – remind them of the omelette video they watched in lesson 3, and refer to recipes they have worked with. Tell the class to create a simple close-up picture for each step of their re-ordered recipe. They will need eight pictures (four on each side of a folded piece of A4 paper). Each picture must be numbered and include a short descriptive caption, explaining what to do for each step. They will be using bossy verbs.

Independent work
• The children will spend most of the lesson creating their illustrated recipes.

> **Differentiation**
> • Less experienced writers could use the original sentences as their captions. Encourage more confident writers to expand the originals, creating descriptive sentences.

Review
• Pairs of children should compare their illustrated and captioned recipes. As a class, discuss what bossy verbs were used. Who included commas?

Week 4 lesson plans

Using what they have learned about the structure and language of recipes, this week the children discuss ideas for, plan, draft and write a recipe of their own invention, using identified key features and appropriate language, including imperative verbs and adjectives separated by commas. Having written their recipes, they first investigate food packaging, paying particular attention to the language used, before going on to devise packaging for their own recipe.

1: Creating a new recipe

Introduction

● Tell the children how the French apple pie dish 'Tarte Tatin' was created accidentally over 100 years ago. Stephanie Tatin, working in the kitchen of her family's hotel making an apple pie for the guests, forgot the pan of apples cooking in butter. There was not enough time to make the pie the usual way, so quickly she made some pastry, put it on top of the pan of apples, popped it in the oven and when it was cooked, flipped it upside down to serve. Everyone loved it and now the dish is famous. The story demonstrates how new recipes can be created in often unexpected ways.

Whole-class work

● Explain that the children will be inventing their own recipes, of anything they can imagine. It could be a delicious dogs' dinner, a fairy's favourite feast or a cake fit for a king. What ideas can the children think of?

Group work

● Working in small groups, the children will discuss the suggested ideas, and think of others, noting them on individual whiteboards. From their lists, ask them to choose two or three to develop further, sharing ideas and writing on paper what ingredients they would use for each recipe. Remind them to use commas to separate items in their lists. They should also discuss the method of making their recipes, noting the bossy (imperative) verbs that they might use and numbering each step. They need to think about quantities too – these could be in standard measurements, or non-standard relevant to the type of recipe. For example, fairy food might use thimblefuls or drops, while giant recipes might have barrels or wheelbarrows as measurements. Remind them to use writing that they will be able to read easily when they use their notes later. By the end of the lesson, the children should have two or three ideas from which they will be able to select the one that they will later write up in full recipe form.

> **Differentiation**
> ● You may wish to provide less experienced learners with lists of appropriate verbs from which to choose, and perhaps limit their choice of ideas to enable them to focus more clearly on just one recipe.

Review

● Bring the class together to share ideas. Ask one representative from each group to tell the class what their final recipe choices were, and invite comments and questions. Tell the children that in the next lesson they will be drafting their chosen recipe, using the ideas and notes they made today.
● Use starter activity 8 'Commas for lists' to revise the use of commas.

Expected outcomes

● All children can plan, draft and write a recipe of their own invention. They can design packaging for their recipe.
● Most children can include all key features in their recipes and use appropriate language for their packaging.
● Some children can extend the language in their description of how to make their invented recipe and use highly expressive language for their packaging.

Curriculum objectives

● To learn how to use both familiar and new punctuation correctly (see Appendix 2), including full stops, capital letters, exclamation marks, question marks, commas for lists and apostrophes for contracted forms and the possessive (singular).
● To use sentences with different forms: statement, question, exclamation, command.
● To write capital letters and digits of the correct size, orientation and relationship to one another and to lower-case letters.
● To write down ideas and/ or key words, including new vocabulary.

Resources

Individual whiteboards and pens

SCHOLASTIC

2: Drafting the new recipe

Introduction

● Display a set of your own notes for an invented recipe. Model how to use them to draft a properly written recipe, reminding the children of the key features of a recipe. Commentate on your thinking and actions as you write, for the children to absorb the process of drafting from notes. You do not need to draft the whole recipe.

Paired work

● Using their notes from the previous lesson, ask the children to choose the one recipe that they will be writing in full. With the notes as a prompt, ask them to tell their partner the recipe orally. Encourage the children to listen carefully, asking for clarification if necessary and offering positive comments. The children may adapt their initial ideas following their feedback if they wish. Explain that this sharing of ideas is a valuable part of the writing process.

Independent work

● Let the children work individually to write their recipe drafts.

> **Differentiation**
> ● Pair the children according to ability, so that less experienced learners are not overwhelmed by their more confident peers, but be prepared to support them if necessary.

Review

● Ask the children to review their drafts. Did they remember to include all the key features? Which bossy verbs did they use? Who used commas in their instructions?

Curriculum objectives
● To plan or say out loud what they are going to write about.
● To encapsulate what they want to say, sentence by sentence.

Resources
Children's recipe notes from the previous lesson

3: The final recipes

Introduction

● Display your own draft recipe that you worked on with the class in the previous lesson, perhaps with a little more added. Ensure that there are some obvious errors and places needing improvement, such as missed commas or numbers, or badly chosen verbs, for example. Ask the children to read it to themselves before sharing with a partner their ideas for changes. Invite the children to offer their suggestions, and re-draft your recipe appropriately. Explain that they will be doing the same thing with their own drafted writing.

Paired work

● Set the children to read each others' drafts, giving feedback for revisions and corrections, and making any changes to their work that they feel is appropriate. Remind them to look for clear instructions which are properly sequenced.

Independent work

● The children now use their drafted recipe to re-write using their best handwriting. When they have finished, they should proofread their work, neatly correcting any errors they discover.

Review

● Invite some children to read out a favourite section of their recipe.

Curriculum objectives
● To form lower-case letters of the correct size relative to one another.
● To use spacing between words that reflects the size of the letters.
● To write capital letters and digits of the correct size, orientation and relationship to one another and to lower-case letters.
● To write for different purposes.
● To proofread to check for errors in spelling, grammar and punctuation.
● To evaluate their writing with the teacher and other children.

Resources
Children's draft recipes from the previous lesson

Curriculum objectives
● To explain and discuss their understanding of books, poems and other material, both those that they listen to and those that they read for themselves.

Resources
Ask the children to bring in a range of clean, empty food packets and packaging from home

4: It's on the packet

Introduction
● If possible, visit a local supermarket and look at the different types of packaging on the shelves. Encourage the children to talk about the different ways that foods are packaged and the packaging's various purposes – it has to protect the food, inform us about what is inside, how to prepare and cook some foods and also persuade us to buy that particular product.

Whole-class work
● Sit in a circle and spread out your collection of packaging. Ask the children to choose one and point out what they notice to their neighbour.
● Invite several children to read you something from their packaging.

Paired work
● Hand out two or three examples of packaging to pairs of children. Challenge them to find some of the following: adjectives, bossy verbs, an instruction, a description, a question, a warning, a statement, a list.

> **Differentiation**
> ● Bear in mind children's reading ability when you distribute the packaging. Children can work in mixed-ability pairs so that they can support each other.

Review
● Ask the pairs to feed back some of what they found on the packaging, using the list above as a guide. For example, what adjectives, bossy verbs and questions did they find? Did anyone find something that surprised them? Did they find words that were new to them?

Curriculum objectives
● To write for different purposes.
● To form lower-case letters of the correct size relative to one another.
● To use spacing between words that reflects the size of the letters.
● To write capital letters and digits of the correct size, orientation and relationship to one another and to lower-case letters.
● To discuss their favourite words and phrases.

Resources
Food packaging from the previous lesson; children's own recipes from lesson 3; photocopiable page 45 'My packaging plan'

5: Creating packaging

Introduction
● Give pairs of children different items of packaging from those they used in the previous lesson. Ask them to look at the language and find words and phrases that they particularly like.

Whole-class work
● Explain to the children that they will be writing what might go on the packaging for their own recipes that they created earlier in the week. Recap on what they found on the packaging in the previous lesson, covering sentence types and language use. Remind the children of the jobs that the writing on the packaging has to do.

Independent work
● Hand out photocopiable page 45 'My packaging plan' and go through it so the children understand how to use it. They should think about the target audience for their recipe – is it adults or children, or a specific group such as pet owners, pirates or witches? Explain that the words and phrases they choose should try to match the people who are likely to buy their product. Encourage them to consider all their senses when writing words and phrases to describe their recipe.
● Using their completed plans, the children should then use their ideas to write sentences and lists that would be included on the packaging for their recipes. They should write their recipe/product name as the heading. They must use their best handwriting.

Review
● Invite some children to read out their favourite descriptions.

Week 5 lesson plans

This week links healthy eating with creating a poster. The children will look at and discuss healthy and unhealthy foods, devising noun phrases to describe them. They will identify the key features of effective posters, listing these to use as a guide when creating and evaluating their own and others' healthy-eating posters. They will revise contractions, some of which may also be used in their posters.

1: Healthy eating

Introduction

● Do the children understand what we mean by 'healthy', especially in relation to food? Are they aware of the types of foods that are thought to be unhealthy, especially if taken in excess, such as sugar or fats? Have they heard of 'five a day' and do they know what it means?

● Display the media resource 'Healthy food?' on the CD-ROM. Discuss whether these foods are generally healthy or not. What about the fish if it didn't have the batter on? Would it make any difference if the egg was fried? What if the bread was white, not wholemeal? Is it OK to eat unhealthy foods sometimes? What did Oliver eat in the story of *Oliver's Vegetables*, and why was Grandpa so keen to get him to try the vegetables in his garden?

Whole-class work

● Ask the children to imagine they have been asked to invent a healthy pizza. Ask: *What is a pizza base made from?* Link this back to the story of 'The Little Red Hen'. What was the main ingredient for her bread, and what was that made from?

● Talk about toppings for the pizza. Give them the headings: vegetables, meat, fish, fruit, others. Ask for some initial suggestions for each heading, for example 'others' might include herbs or cheese.

Paired work

● The children work together to make lists of healthy foods for each of the headings, noting their ideas on individual whiteboards. They must think about what flavours would taste good together before finally choosing the ingredients for their own healthy pizza.

Independent work

● The children will now draw and label their pizza. They should add arrowed captions for each ingredient, and list them all under the illustration, separating each with a comma as they did in week 4. Encourage the children to devise a name for their newly created pizza, writing this as a heading.

Review

● Ask the children to place their pizza pictures on their tables. Allow the class to walk around this pizza gallery, looking at each others' work to decide which three pizzas they think are the healthiest and that they would most enjoy eating. Invite them to copy the names of the pizzas of their choice onto three separate small slips of paper, fold them and post them into your 'ballot box'. Explain that you will count the votes later and tell the class the results of the top three healthy pizzas. (Remember to do this as soon as possible, when you have chance.) Ask for comments about a few of the children's choices.

Expected outcomes

● All children can identify key features of effective posters. They can use some noun phrases in creating a healthy-eating poster.
● Most children can discuss and suggest ideas for posters and review their own and others' work against a list of criteria.
● Some children can include all identified key features and a range of noun phrases in their posters which they can evaluate critically.

Curriculum objectives

● To participate in discussion about books, poems and other works that are read to them and those that they can read for themselves, taking turns and listening to what others say.
● To re-read books to build up their fluency and confidence in word reading.
● To learn how to use both familiar and new punctuation correctly (see Appendix 2), including full stops, capital letters, exclamation marks, question marks, commas for lists and apostrophes for contracted forms and the possessive (singular).
● To segment words into phonemes and represent these by graphemes, spelling many correctly.

Resources

Media resource 'Healthy food?' on the CD-ROM; individual whiteboards and pens; small slips of paper; an empty box

---

Curriculum objectives
• To draw on what they already know or on background information and vocabulary provided by the teacher.
• To participate in discussion about books, poems and other works that are read to them and those that they can read for themselves, taking turns and listening to what others say.

Resources
Interactive activity 'Healthy or unhealthy?' on the CD-ROM; a selection of healthy food posters; flipchart paper; felt-tipped pens

2: Healthy/unhealthy

Introduction
• Display the interactive activity 'Healthy or unhealthy?' on the CD-ROM and work through it with the class. Ask the children to justify their answers.

Whole-class work
• Label each piece of flipchart paper with one of the main food groups (fruit and vegetables; breads, cereals and potatoes; milk and dairy; meat, fish and beans; fats and sugars) and put them around the room.
• Give pairs of children a coloured pen and ask them to write as many foods as they can from each group on the appropriate sheet.
• Explain to the children that they will be creating a poster about healthy foods and show them an example, identifying key features, including layout, font size, clarity, illustration, information included.

Group work
• Provide each mixed-ability group with a poster to share. Tell them to look carefully at their poster, listing the key features already discussed as well as any other important things that they notice, for future reference.

> **Differentiation**
> • Choose a confident speaker from each group for the feedback, warning them of their task in advance.

Review
• Ask a representative from each group to feed back their findings to the class. Go through the key features, asking for examples from each poster, and asking how effective the various parts of the posters were. What made them work well, or what could have been improved? Did they get their message across clearly and quickly? What were the most effective words and phrases?

Curriculum objectives
• To use expanded noun phrases to describe and specify.
• To write down ideas and/ or key words, including new vocabulary.
• To learn how to use both familiar and new punctuation correctly (see Appendix 2), including full stops, capital letters, exclamation marks, question marks, commas for lists and apostrophes for contracted forms and the possessive (singular).
• To learn to spell more words with contracted forms.

Resources
Individual whiteboards and pens

3: Planning a poster

Introduction
• Use starter activity 2 'Contractions'. Include the word *don't*, as this may be useful when they create their healthy-eating posters.

Whole-class work
• Explain that the children will be gathering ideas for a poster about healthy eating. Use starter activity 3 'Why say one word', focusing on healthy and unhealthy foods, to get the children thinking about noun phrases for their posters.
• Invite ideas for healthy-eating posters, reminding the class of their previous work on healthy foods. They could focus on positive messages about what to eat, including the five-a-day regime, guarding against dangers by saying what not to eat, or a combination of both.

Paired work
• Ask the children to talk together, sharing ideas for their posters and making notes as they go along. After a few minutes, they should select one idea for their poster. They should note words and phrases including adjectives and contractions, for example 'Don't forget your five-a-day.'

Review
• Invite children to share some of their noun phrases, asking the rest of the class to guess what is being described.

4: Drafting healthy-eating posters

Curriculum objectives
● To plan or say out loud what they are going to write about.
● To use expanded noun phrases to describe and specify.
● To write for different purposes.
● To segment words into phonemes and represent these by graphemes, spelling many correctly.

Resources
Children's poster notes from the previous lesson; key features lists from lesson 2

Introduction
● Refer to the lists of the key features of a poster, from lesson 2. Remind the children that they need to consider these when they create their healthy-eating posters. Which would they say are the top three most important criteria? Discuss their suggestions.

Paired work
● Using their previous notes, allow time for the children to use their ideas to discuss and plan their posters. What will the main wording be? Which of their noun phrases will they use? What illustrations will they include?

Independent work
● The children will now make a rough sketch of what their finished poster will look like. Remind them to think about font size and where they will place each piece of information – the wording must fit the paper comfortably. Any illustrations they include must be simple and clear. They should use phonics to encode spellings of words they are unsure of.

Differentiation
● As they are working, check the children's spellings, using any errors as discussion points leading towards corrections.

Review
● Refer again to the list of key features of a poster, from lesson 2. As you go through each item, ask the children to check that they have included them in their poster, noting any areas that may need changing. Allow a little time for them to do this.

5: The final posters

Curriculum objectives
● To form lower-case letters of the correct size relative to one another.
● To use spacing between words that reflects the size of the letters.
● To evaluate their writing with the teacher and other children.

Resources
Children's poster plans from the previous lesson; key features lists from lesson 2; pencil crayons or felt-tipped pens; rulers (optional); rubbers

Introduction
● Ask the children to swap their plans with their original working partner, offering each other comments on layout, contents and language use. They should use the key features lists from lesson 2 as a guide. They may choose to make amendments following their discussions.

Independent work
● The children will spend the majority of the lesson creating their finished healthy-eating posters. Before they begin, remind them that they must work carefully, using their best handwriting and presentation skills, and ensuring that their spelling is as accurate as possible, so that people can easily read and understand the messages in their posters. You may wish to allow the children to use rulers to draw faint guidelines for their writing.

Differentiation
● If there are any children finding difficulty with handwriting and presentation, you may wish to let them use a larger piece of paper.

Review
● Ask the children to look critically at their completed posters. Taking into account all that they have learned about key features, layout and healthy eating, ask them to make a comment on the back of the poster about their work, including perhaps a mark out of ten for their finished work. Display the posters for the class to share and discuss.

Expected outcomes
● All children can comment on different poems, suggest ideas for and compose a list poem. They can use some noun phrases.
● Most children can comment on their own and others' work and write using a range of noun phrases and well-chosen verbs. They can use legible handwriting.
● Some children can make a variety of comparisons between two poems. They can use a wide range of interesting and appropriate noun phrases and verbs. Their handwriting is clear and easily legible.

Curriculum objectives
● To read further common exception words, noting unusual correspondence between spelling and sound and where these occur in the word.
● To listen to, discuss and express views about a wide range of contemporary and classic poetry, stories and non-fiction at a level beyond that at which they can read independently.
● To participate in discussion about books, poems and other works that are read to them and those that they can read for themselves, taking turns and listening to what others say.
● To discuss their favourite words and phrases.
● To continue to build up a repertoire of poems learned by heart, appreciating these and reciting some, with appropriate intonation to make the meaning clear.

Resources
Photocopiable page 46 'Spaghetti'; a plate of cooked spaghetti (kept hot)

Week 6 lesson plans

In this final week of work on the theme of food, the children investigate two poems, comparing their style and vocabulary. They will suggest ways of reading a poem aloud effectively and read it together as a class. They will gather ideas for their own alphabetically organised list poem which they go on to plan, draft and write as a final neat product. Throughout the planning and drafting process they will collaborate with a partner, helping the writing process and offering and receiving comments in feedback.

1: Spaghetti

Introduction
● Display photocopiable page 46 'Spaghetti', covering up the title and the first four lines. Read the poem and ask the children to suggest what food it's about. What clues do they see? Compare answers and encourage the children to pick out words in the poem that support their claim.
● Agree that the poem's about spaghetti. Reveal the title and opening lines of the poem and re-read the poem together. Sound out and blend any longer words and point out the common exception words that appear. Clap the syllables of the list of words describing the spaghetti.
● Reveal the plate of spaghetti and ask as many children as possible to come up and eat some spaghetti, pretending they're eating worms.

Paired work
● The children now work together, exploring the language of the poem. Hand out the photocopiable sheet. Write the following questions on the board to guide their discussion: *What do you notice about the words? What do you notice about the punctuation? What are your favourite words and phrases?* Allow time for the children to explore and discuss the poem.
● Ask pairs to join together to share their observations and word choices.

Whole-class work
● Invite feedback from each group about favourite words and phrases before opening up the discussion about the language and punctuation of the poem. Keep the discussion about language open-ended to see what the children have noticed. They may have noticed sentence length, the way the poem tells a story, the fact that it doesn't rhyme or that it is funny. They may pick up that the descriptive list is made up of adjectives.
● When discussing punctuation, they could have noticed the unusual use of capitalisation, where some lines begin with them while others don't. They should have observed that the list does not include commas, when they have just been learning that lists require commas. Why do they think they have been deliberately omitted? What difference does this make to the way we read the poem?
● Return to the displayed poem. Tell the children that you will be reading the poem together. Ask for their suggestions about how it should be read – the speed, volume, where to pause and for how long and where there should be emphasis. Annotate the poem according to your collective decisions.

Group work
● Allow a few minutes for the children to practise reading the poem aloud together in mixed-ability groups.

Review
● Enjoy reading the poem together. Ask for comments on how useful the discussion and annotation were in preparation for the reading.

Curriculum objectives
● To read further exception words, noting the unusual correspondences between spelling and sound and where these occur in the word.
● To discuss and clarify the meanings of words, linking new meanings to known vocabulary.

Resources
Photocopiable page 47 'Apple pie'

2: Apple pie

Introduction
● Display the poem on photocopiable page 47 'Apple Pie'. Before reading, ask what the children notice about it, agreeing that it is a list poem using the alphabet for its structure. Read the poem.

Paired work
● Hand out the photocopiable sheet and allow time for the children to read the poem. Encourage them to sound out and blend unfamiliar words, underlining any they don't know the meaning of.

Whole-class work
● Go over the tricky and unknown words, explaining the meaning of those they don't know, then read the poem together. Note the use of commas and compare this with the poem 'Spaghetti'. What else do they notice that is different between the two poems, and what similarities can they spot? They may suggest that both include humour and neither rhyme.

Group work
● Invite the children to mime the actions as one of the group reads the poem aloud. Remind them that the words accompanying their actions are verbs.

> **Differentiation**
> ● The groups should be of mixed ability, each needing at least one confident reader.

Review
● Ask the children for their opinions about the two poems they have read this week. Which did they like best and why? Why do the adjectives in the first poem and the verbs in the second make them enjoyable and effective?

Curriculum objectives
● To write down ideas and/ or key words, including new vocabulary.
● To use expanded noun phrases to describe and specify.

Resources
Large sheets of flipchart or sugar paper

3: Food poem ideas

Introduction
● Remind the children about the list poem 'Apple pie' from the previous lesson. Ask for a few ideas of foods that the children could write a list poem about.

Whole-class work
● Pin up the large sheets of paper around the room, each with different food-related topics as a heading, for example *Fruit, Vegetables, Meals, Parties, Picnics, Take-aways*. Invite the children to write ideas for list poems under the headings.
● When the lists are complete, allow time for the children to read through the ideas, selecting one that they will use for their own list poem.
● Explain that they will be writing alphabetical list poems. They could use the same structure as 'Apple pie', using verbs to describe actions, or they could use adjectives to describe nouns, making noun phrases, or a combination of both, for example *Amazing avocados, make a beautiful breakfast, can be cut into chunks, delivered daily to your door*. Work through examples together.

Paired work
● Ask the children to help each other to come up with ideas for their poems, making notes as they work for later use. Encourage them to list several possibilities for their word choices.

Review
● Ask which children will be using adjectives to describe nouns, which verbs and which a combination for their poems. Invite some to share their ideas.

Curriculum objectives
● To plan or say out loud what they are going to write about.
● To write poetry.
● To learn how to use both familiar and new punctuation correctly (see Appendix 2), including full stops, capital letters, exclamation marks, question marks, commas for lists and apostrophes for contracted forms and the possessive (singular).
● To segment words into phonemes and represent these by graphemes, spelling many correctly.
● To evaluate their writing with the teacher and other children.

Resources
Poem notes from the previous lesson; your own notes for a list poem

4: Drafting list poems

Introduction
● Display your own notes for a list poem, similar to those the children made in the previous lesson. Use the notes to model how to begin writing the poem, talking through your thoughts as you select the words for each line, rejecting some and explaining your choices. Change your mind once or twice to demonstrate to the children that this is an acceptable way of working; that we don't always come up with the best ideas straight away.

Independent work
● Using their notes from the previous lesson, ask the children to draft their own list poems. Remind them to try out different options and to be adventurous in their vocabulary choices, using their phonic knowledge to spell words they are unsure of. As they work, look at their spellings, using errors as opportunities to discuss alternatives and make corrections.

Paired work
● Working in the same pairs as in the previous lesson, ask the children to read out their drafts to each other, giving and receiving comments, and making any changes they decide on.

Differentiation
● Allow any children who are struggling to find words for more difficult-to-find letters such as 'j', 'k', 'q', 'x' and 'z', to omit these if they are holding up their writing.

Review
● Ask the children to share some of the most interesting noun phrases and verbs that they have used. Did anyone manage to deal with the trickier letters? What solutions did they come up with?

Curriculum objectives
● To write poetry.
● To evaluate their writing with the teacher and other children.
● To form lower-case letters of the correct size relative to one another.
● To use spacing between words that reflects the size of the letters.

Resources
Children's draft poems from the previous lesson

5: Final list poems

Introduction
● Explain that the children will be writing final drafts of their poems to be displayed or collated into a class anthology. Ask them what important points they will need to consider in writing their poems for others to read, agreeing that good handwriting and accurate spelling are key points.
● Go over elements of handwriting that will help to ensure a neat product, including correct seating position and pencil grip.

Independent work
● Ask the children to write their list poem. This will take most of the lesson.

Paired work
● The children should read aloud their finished work with their original partner. Each child should offer feedback, making comments on how the final poem has developed from its early planning stages.

Differentiation
● Ensure left-handed writers have their paper tilted 45 degrees to the left so they can see their writing more easily, and help them to avoid using a 'hooked' grip.

Review
● Ask the children to read through their poems silently, and invite some to share what they consider to be their best short sections with the rest of the class. Ask the class what they found easiest and what was more difficult in composing their poems.

Curriculum objectives
• To use expanded noun phrases to describe and specify.

Resources
Favourite foods (or pictures of them); a range of menus with descriptive phrases; photocopiable page 'Luscious words' from the CD-ROM

Grammar and punctuation: Using noun phrases

Revise
• Ask the children to bring in a favourite food – or a picture of it. Get the children to spend time describing the food to their partner. Share the best phrases together.
• Share the menus and tell the children to find and circle any descriptive phrases.
• Hand out photocopiable page 'Luscious words' from the CD-ROM. The children should write a food name on a card and then try out the different adjectives from the photocopiable sheet, choosing the best. Tell them to share their created phrases with their partner.

Assess
• Ask the children to create a menu for a restaurant which serves their favourite food – at least two main meals and two puddings. Tell them to write a sentence to describe each food, using a noun phrase for each one.

Further practice
• Ask the children to write descriptions of meals from the rolling menu of school dinners.
• Use starter activity 16 'Knowing terminology'.

Curriculum objectives
• To learn to spell words with contracted forms.

Resources
Individual whiteboards and pens

Spelling: Contractions

Revise
• Use starter activity 2 'Contractions' with the class.
• Write the following pairs of words on the board: *would not, he has, I will, she had, they have, do not, will not.* Ask the children to write the contracted forms on individual whiteboards and show you their results. Follow this up by asking pairs of children to do the same in reverse, so taking turns, one child writes the contraction and shows it to their partner, who writes the expanded form.

Assess
• Read out contractions for the children to write on paper. Include a mixture of straightforward contracted forms and some expanded forms for the children to work out both the contraction and the spelling.

Further practice
• Make a class collection of as many contractions as possible, either as a working wall display or written in an alphabetically indexed notebook. Encourage their use, particularly when the children are writing dialogue.
• For further practice see page 69.

Curriculum objectives
● To predict what might happen on the basis of what has been read so far.

Resources
A couple of children's books (including multiple copies of one title) that the children are not familiar with (as different as possible), for example *I Do Not Eat the Colour Green* by Lynne Rickards and Margaret Chamberlain, *Dominic Grows Sweetcorn* by Mandy Ross and Alison Bartlett, *Eddie's Garden* and *How to Make Things Grow* by Sarah Garland; photocopiable page 'What happened next?' from the CD-ROM

Reading: Predicting events

Revise

● Write a story starter on the board, for example: *I walked into the school dining room.* Ask: *What is a likely next sentence? What isn't?* Ask: *What else do we need to know?* (Is this a real story, or a pirate story, a silly story and so on.) Discuss the different options, and that if the main character is then kidnapped by pirates, then it's unlikely that there will be a spaceship and vice versa.
● Write down five suggested events which could follow *I walked into the school dining room* on five separate large cards. Ask five children to hold the cards up at the front of the class. Following the class's suggestions, shuffle the five children in their line so they are arranged from more likely to less likely.
● Read the first half of one of the children's books and ask the children to predict what might happen next. Encourage the children to discuss their thinking in as much detail as they can. Ask different children to give their thoughts and then read the end of the story. Was anyone right? Was there a surprise at the end? Discuss how we normally expect the hero to end well and he or she normally does (in children's books, anyway).

Assess

● Hand out photocopiable page 'What happened next?' from the CD-ROM. Ask the children to carry out the activity and then discuss their thought processes in small groups.
● Put the children in small groups and then read the first half of the second children's book out loud.
● Hand out copies of the book to each group. Tell them to re-read the part you've read so far and ask them to tell you what they think might happen next. Ask them to discuss events that might be likely and those that are not likely. Encourage them to make reference to what has happened so far to justify their answers. Check for predictions consistent with the story thus far.
● Read the end of the story and compare the ending to the children's ideas.

Further practice

● Ask the children to create a third and fourth line for the story starters from the photocopiable sheet.

Curriculum objectives
- To write down ideas and/or key words, including new vocabulary.
- To write for different purposes.

Resources
Recipes to browse

Writing: A recipe for healthy eating

Revise
- After spending a little time browsing through recipes, recap with the class the key features of a recipe. What must be included?
- Remind them about the use of bossy verbs and ask for some examples.

Assess
- Explain that the children will be linking together what they know about how recipes are written with the knowledge they have about healthy eating to write a fun healthy recipe.
- Briefly discuss what could be included under two main headings: *Ingredients* and *Method* (or *What to do*).
- Ask for a few examples, such as some food types for the ingredients, and suitable verbs for the method such as *Mix in some fresh apple*, or *Stir in a glass of fruit juice*.
- Allow the children some planning time before they write their recipes independently.

Further practice
- Ask the children to copy favourite recipes from home in their best handwriting. Collate them into a class recipe book and encourage the class to make their own copies to take home and ask a member of their family to try them out. Leave space by each recipe for comments.

Oliver's Vegetables sequence cards

■ Cut out the cards and put them in the right order.

✂ -

Oliver agreed to eat the vegetables he found.
Next Oliver found rhubarb.
Finally he found potatoes.
Oliver went to Grandpa's house.
On Thursday he found cabbage.
Then he found spinach.
First he found carrots.
Oliver had enjoyed all the vegetables.
After that he found beetroot.
Oliver scrubbed the potatoes for Grandma to make chips.
When he was playing football, he found peas.

The Little Red Hen (1)

Once upon a time there was a Little Red Hen who lived in a farmyard with a Dog, a Cat and a Rat. One day, the Little Red Hen found some grains of wheat in the yard. She didn't eat them.

"I'll plant them, and grow some wheat" she said.

The Little Red Hen called to the other animals, "I'm planting some seeds. Who'll help me?"

"Not me," said the Dog.

"Not me," said the Cat.

"Not me," said the Rat.

"Then I'll just have to plant them myself," said the Little Red Hen – and she did.

Time went by and the seeds grew into wheat, until the time came to harvest the wheat.

The Little Red Hen called to the other animals, "I'm harvesting the wheat. Who'll help me?"

"Not me," said the Dog.

"Not me," said the Cat.

"Not me," said the Rat.

"Then I'll just have to harvest it myself" said the Little Red Hen – and she did.

The Little Red Hen (2)

The time came to turn the wheat into bread.

The Little Red Hen called to the other animals, "I'm making some bread. Who'll help me?"

"Not me," said the Dog.

"Not me," said the Cat.

"Not me," said the Rat.

"Then, I'll just have to make it myself," said the Little Red Hen – and she did.

Later, the smell of bread filled the air.

The other animals looked and saw the Little Red Hen with freshly made bread.

The Little Red Hen said to herself, "I wonder who'll help me eat this bread?"

"I will," said the Dog.

"I will," said the Cat.

"I will," said the Rat.

The Little Red Hen took one look at the other lazy animals and said, "Oh no, you won't! I'll just have to eat it myself!" And she did.

Tangy tomatoes

■ Cut out these cards and place them face down between you and your partner. Take turns to turn over a card and think of a describing word for the food.

bread	peach
salt	sugar
chicken	peas
tomato	muesli
margarine	mushroom
pizza	lettuce
fish	ice cream

Making a cheese omelette

■ Cut out the sentences and put them in the right order for making a cheese omelette.

■ When you are sure they are right, stick them onto a sheet of paper.

✂ ------------------------------------

Making a cheese omelette.	Add a pinch of salt.
Pour in the eggs, moving the mixture around with a spatula until it is almost cooked.	When the cheese has almost melted, flip half of the omelette over the other half.
Add a pinch of salt and some pepper.	Beat the eggs in a bowl.
Grate the cheese and keep to one side.	Carefully slide the omelette on to a plate.
Heat a little butter in a frying pan.	Add the cheese and continue cooking.

My packaging plan

■ Write down your ideas for what you will include in the packaging for your recipe.

Name of product _____

Who is it for? _____

Words to describe it _____

_____

_____

Phrases to encourage people to buy it _____

_____

_____

Ingredients, most used first _____

_____

_____

■ Underline the words and phrases you think are best.

I can choose good words and phrases to use in my writing.

How did you do?

Spaghetti

A plate heaped high
with spaghetti
all covered with tomato sauce
is just about my favourite meal.
It looks just like
a gigantic heap of:
Steaming
Tangled
Mixed
Up
Twizzled
Twisted
Wound
Up
Woozled
WORMS!
I like picking them up
one at a time;
Swallowing them slowly
head first,
until the tail flips
across my cheek
before finally wriggling
down my throat.
But best of all,
when I've finished eating
I go and look in a mirror
because the tomato sauce
smeared around my mouth
makes me look like a clown.

by Frank Flynn

PHOTOCOPIABLE

Apple pie

A was an Apple pie

B bit it, C cut it, D dealt it,

E enjoyed it, F fought for it,

G got it, H hoped for it,

I inquired about it,

J jumped on it, K kept it,

L longed for it, M mourned for it,

N nodded at it, O opened it,

P peered in it, Q quartered it,

R ran for it, S sat on it, T took it,

U upset it, V viewed it, W wanted it,

X crossed it, Y yearned for it,

And Z put it in his pocket, and said,

'Well done!'

Anon

Fairy tales

The children read and discuss fairy tales and draw conclusions about the features of fairy tales. They recap on the importance of setting in a story and move on to see how the characters interact with it. They write their own fairy tale using elements from known stories and focus on writing accurately. They return to instructions and the language of instructions and create their own fairy-tale board game and write instructions for it. The children get inside the head of one character and write a diary entry for a known fairy-tale character. In the last week they use nursery rhymes to practise spelling the same sound in different ways and learn and discuss 'Magic Horse' by John Foster.

Expected prior learning
- Familiar with a range of fairy stories and nursery rhymes.
- Can understand that the setting of a story is not just a backdrop.
- Know the features of instructional texts.

Overview of progression
- The children recap on story sequence before understanding in more detail how the elements of the story are linked. By building up a story, the children are encouraged to question their choices.
- The children carry out further work on recipes.
- Over the course of this half term, the children write two stories – the first helps them to practise writing consistently in the past tense and third person, the second in the past tense and the first person.
- There is an introduction to the continuous form.

Creative context
- This topic is securely set in the literacy curriculum, but the children will improve their confidence and drama skills in learning to perform a poem.
- They will also practise making personal choices when they create their own game and give opinions about a character's behaviour.

Preparation
Before starting this half-term's work, it would be useful if the children are familiar with a wide range of fairy tales and fairy-tale characters.

You will also need:
Large pieces of paper; coloured pens; collections of fairy and traditional tales; A4 paper; map template on A1 paper; sticky notes; range of suitable instruction texts; simple traditional games; coloured bricks; word cards; nursery rhyme collections; range of musical instruments

On the CD-ROM you will find:
Media resource 'Woods'; interactive activities 'Beginnings and endings', 'In the past', 'Fairy-tale punctuation', 'Can't, don't, won't'; photocopiable pages 'Rapunzel', 'Hansel and Gretel', 'Sleeping Beauty', 'The Three Wishes', 'Fairy game board', 'One, Two, Buckle My Shoe', 'Magic Horse', 'Fairy-tale punctuation', 'Can't, don't, won't', 'Fairy-tale groups', 'The Princess and the Shark'

Chapter at a glance

An overview of the chapter. For curriculum objective codes, please see pages 8–10.

Week	Lesson	Curriculum objectives	Summary of activities	Outcome
1	1	RWR: 1, 7, 8 RC: 3, 9	Read fairy tales and look for similarities.	• Can create a list of fairy-tale elements.
	2	RWR: 1 RC: 5 WC: 6	Use fairy-tale collections to gather a range of fairy-tale openings.	• Can create own fairy-tale openings and ponder how the story might continue.
	3	RWR: 1, 7, 8 RC: 3, 5, 10, 11, 12 WC: 6	Read and discuss 'The Three Wishes'. Think about beginning, middle and end.	• Can ask and answer questions about 'The Three Wishes'.
	4	RWR: 1, 6 RC: 1, 6	Focus on the characteristics and the roles that characters have in fairy tales. Allocate roles to a wide range of fairy-tale characters.	• Can write an adjective to go with each character, expressing an opinion and agreeing on a choice with group members.
	5	RWR: 3, 6 WC: 6	Verbally create a number of new fairy tales inspired by two fairy-tale elements chosen at random.	• Can write a plan for a new fairy tale, writing key words and ideas.
2	1	RWR: 8 RC: 3, 6, 11, 14	Discuss a range of fairy-tale settings, talking about what happened in each one.	• Can list the settings in fairy tales.
	2	RWR: 8 RC: 3, 11, 14 WC: 6	Use role play to investigate settings and infer how the characters feel about them.	• Can think of adjectives inspired by role play.
	3	RWR: 8 RC: 3, 14 WC: 6, 19	Focus on each setting in a story and make links between setting and plot.	• Can write adjectives and noun phrases to describe setting.
	4	RC: 15 WC: 14, 19	Draw and describe a fairy-tale setting and work with a group to create a fairy-tale world.	• Can describe own setting using noun phrases.
	5	RC: 15 WC: 6, 14	See how own story could take place in some of the settings on the map (using story plan created in week 1).	• Can develop own story plan, adding detail and cause and effect.
3	1	WC: 5, 6	Use character, setting and event cards randomly chosen to create a new fairy tale.	• Can write story plan for own story and record some noun phrases.
	2	WT: 3, 8 WC: 1, 5, 9, 15, 19	Write opening sentences of own story, spending time orally rehearsing and ensuring use of a consistent past tense.	• Can write a few well-written and grammatically correct sentences, attempting to spell them correctly.
	3	WT: 11 WC: 10, 12	Write first draft of own story, checking for handwriting, punctuation, spelling, sense and tense.	• Can write and proofread first draft of own story.
	4	WC: 9, 10, 12, 19	Look for places in own story to create a change in tone, for example adding a question or an exclamation.	• Can write and correctly punctuate questions and exclamations.
	5	WC: 9, 11, 15	Check own story for all the elements worked on this week.	• Can write final version of own story and read it aloud to a partner or the class.
4	1	RC: 4, 14 WC: 19	Look at a range of instruction texts to recap on features of instructions.	• Can find and label the features of instruction text in a range of texts.
	2	RC: 2, 4	Follow a poorly explained set of instructions and set about improving them.	• Can rewrite a set of instructions on how to make a paper aeroplane.
	3	RC: 15 WC: 5, 6	Follow instructions to play games and design own game.	• Can discuss and plan options for own game.
	4	RC: 14 WC: 4, 13	Draft a set of instructions for a game.	• Can write a draft set of instructions.
	5	WT: 10, 11, 12, 13 WC: 9	Assess quality of own game, listening to feedback from classmates before writing final version in best handwriting.	• Can produce a proofread and neatly written set of instructions for a board game.

Chapter at a glance

Week	Lesson	Curriculum objectives	Summary of activities	Outcome
5	1	RC: 11 WC: 1, 9, 15	Tell each other about an event in their life and then write this as a diary entry.	• Can write a personal diary entry.
	2	RC: 11 WC: 1	Hot-seat characters from recently studied fairy tales in order to see the same event from different points of view.	• Can take on the role of a familiar fairy-tale character and answer questions in role.
	3	WC: 1, 7	Recap on hot-seating activity, asking each other further questions. Plan out diary entry.	• Can empathise with a character and make notes about an event in first person.
	4	WT: 8, 12 WC: 1, 7, 9	Turn notes into first draft diary entry.	• Can write a diary entry for a fairy-tale character.
	5	WT: 8, 12 WC: 1, 9	Proofread own work and comment on a partner's before writing final draft.	• Can incorporate comments into a final version of their diary entry.
6	1	RC: 6, 8 WT: 3	Match together common exception words that rhyme. Read and learn 'One, Two, Buckle My Shoe', using this to find other rhyming options and discuss the spelling choices. Create own rhyming phrases for version of this verse.	• Can recite 'One, Two, Buckle My Shoe' and find other rhyming words to use in a new version.
	2	WT: 2	Focus on rhyme to discuss spelling options. Search for rhymes in nursery rhyme collections and re-order key rhymes.	• Can find rhymes and re-order verses.
	3	RWR: 2, 5 RC: 8 WT: 2	Read 'Magic Horse' by John Foster and discuss rhyming words with different spellings. Start to learn 'Magic Horse' by heart.	• Can recite one verse of 'Magic Horse'.
	4	RC: 8 WT: 2	Discuss spelling options using 'Magic Horse'. Write new verse for the poem.	• Can write a new verse for 'Magic Horse'.
	5	RC: 8	Use own voices to impart meaning into dramatic version of 'Magic Horse'.	• Can perform a dramatic recitation of 'Magic Horse'.

Background knowledge

Characters: The people in a story.

Fairy tale: A traditional tale, usually without a specific origin, which tells the magical story of princes, princesses, poor people, witches, fairies and other fabulous folk.

Fairy-tale elements: Elements that are common in many fairy tales, for example plot lines such as the 'rule of three' (something happening three times), good vanquishing evil, hidden things being found, fools triumphing against the odds; characters such as woodmen, princesses, dragons and so on; settings such as medieval castles, forests, cottages and so on.

Sequence: The order of the plot from the beginning, to the middle and then the end.

Settings: The place where a story is set. Note: these are more than just places – they form part of the story as well.

Traditional tales: Old stories from around the world, which were originally told aloud rather than read. They include fairy tales, creation myths, legends and other myths.

Week 1 lesson plans

In this week the children read four different fairy tales: 'Hansel and Gretel', 'Rapunzel', 'Sleeping Beauty' and 'The Three Wishes' and discuss the common elements they find in them, gathering recurring language and ideas so they can begin to understand some of the features of fairy tales. They learn about the roles characters have in stories and practise breaking down the plot of a story into beginning, middle and end. The children start to plan ideas for their own fairy tales, experimenting with fairy-tale language.

1: Talk about tales

Introduction
● As a class, list as many fairy tales or traditional tales as the children can.

Whole-class work
● Display and read the photocopiable pages 'Hansel and Gretel', 'Rapunzel' and 'Sleeping Beauty' from the CD-ROM. Pick out and segment difficult words.
● Write the title of one of the stories in each corner of the board.
● Ask the children to think of something that connects two of the stories – for example, a witch, a prince, a wood, a step-mother and so on. When a connection has been made, draw a line linking the two stories and label it with the common feature.

Group work
● Organise the children into groups of four and provide each group with a large piece of paper and individual the photocopiable sheets. Tell them to work with a partner in the group to re-read each of the four stories.
● Tell the children to write the titles of the four fairy tales in the corner of the paper and carry out the activity again.
● Challenge them to make as many connections as they can and to include at least one connection between each story.

Paired work
● Ask the groups to divide into two pairs and give each pair a new piece of paper and two different-coloured pens.
● Ask the pairs to write the titles of two fairy stories or traditional tales that they both know well at the top of the piece of paper. (Remind them of the fairy tales covered in Year 1, and explain that they can also use any of the four stories read during this lesson, if they're not familiar with other stories).
● Tell them to write a list of all the features that these two stories have in common in one colour, and then write a list of all the differences between the two stories in another colour.

Differentiation
● In the group work, suggest that some children just work with two stories.
● Pair up early finishers and ask them to take turns to tell each other one of the stories covered in this lesson. Tell them to work together to point out any detail that has been missed out. Encourage them to use their own vocabulary in their retelling.

Review
● Ask: *What have we learned about fairy tales?* Agree that they share many of the same features.
● Create a list, headed *Key fairy-tale words*, of all the shared features that the children have found in their discussions. Display this in a space in the classroom where it can be referred to and added to throughout the half term.
● Put a tick by any features that more than one group has found. Challenge the children to think of other stories that they know with these features.

Expected outcomes
● All children can identify fairy-tale language.
● Most children are able to identify key elements in a fairy tale.
● Some children can express views about characters.

Curriculum objectives
● To draw on what they already know or on background information and vocabulary provided by the teacher.
● To become increasingly familiar with and retell a wider range of stories, fairy stories and traditional tales.
● To read aloud books closely matched to their improving phonic knowledge, sounding out unfamiliar words accurately, automatically and without undue hesitation.
● To re-read books to build up their fluency and confidence in word reading.
● To continue to apply phonic knowledge and skills as the route to decode words until automatic decoding has become embedded and reading is fluent.

Resources
Photocopiable pages 'Hansel and Gretel', 'Rapunzel' and 'Sleeping Beauty' from the CD-ROM; large pieces of paper; coloured pens

Curriculum objectives

● To recognise simple recurring literary language in stories.
● To write down ideas and/ or key words, including new vocabulary.
● To continue to apply phonic knowledge and skills as the route to decode words until automatic decoding has become embedded and reading is fluent.

Resources

Several different collections of fairy tales and traditional tales; interactive activity 'Beginnings and endings' on the CD-ROM; photocopiable pages 'Hansel and Gretel', 'Rapunzel' and 'Sleeping Beauty' from the CD-ROM

Curriculum objectives

● To read aloud books closely matched to their improving phonic knowledge, sounding out unfamiliar words accurately, automatically and without undue hesitation.
● To write down ideas and/ or key words, including new vocabulary.
● To continue to apply phonic knowledge and skills as the route to decode words until automatic decoding has become embedded and reading is fluent.
● To become increasingly familiar with and retell a wider range of stories, fairy stories and traditional tales.
● To recognise simple recurring literary language in stories and poetry.
● To re-read books to build up their fluency and confidence in word reading.
● To answer and ask questions.
● To check that the text makes sense to them as they read and correct inaccurate reading.
● To make inferences on the basis of what is being said and done.

Resources

Photocopiable page 'The Three Wishes' from the CD-ROM

2: Once upon a time...

Introduction
● Ask the children: *How do fairy tales start?* Listen to a range of suggestions.
● Complete the interactive activity 'Beginnings and endings' on the CD-ROM.

Group work
● Give the children a range of fairy-tale and traditional-tale collections.
● Tell the groups to look through the books and write down the opening line and last line of as many of the tales as they can.

Whole-class work
● Collect the story openings and write them on the 'Key fairy-tale words' list. Practise reading any tricky or key words that crop up. Note these down, too.
● Return to the openings of the four stories from the previous lesson and ask the children to take turns to read these openings to each other a few times.

Paired work
● Tell the children to take the openings listed on the board and verbally create their own versions by changing the person or object.

Independent work
● Invite the children to choose one of their opening lines and make notes about what might happen in the fairy tale.

Review
● Discuss the children's opening lines and ask individuals to discuss what they think might happen in the story. What final line might these stories have?

3: Beginning, middle and end

Introduction
● Read the 'Key fairy-tale words' list together, increasing the children's familiarity with the words.
● Read photocopiable page 'The Three Wishes' from the CD-ROM to the class and enjoy the story together. Remind the children of the work done in the previous lesson and invite them to find any key fairy-tale words in the story. Practise reading them again as sight vocabulary.
● Point out, blend and segment any unfamiliar vocabulary. Ask the children to note down any words that are new to them.
● Ask different volunteers to help you recap on what happened in the story to check their comprehension. Ask the children about the story, such as: *How did the fairy feel? Can you find words in the story that give us clues about this?*
● Hand out copies and ask the children to read the story aloud to their partner, taking turns so that they become familiar with it. Remind them to listen to what they are saying, correcting themselves if it doesn't make sense.

Group work
● Organise the children into groups of three. Tell them in their groups to remember the story of 'The Three Wishes', recalling the details.
● Tell them to each take on a part of the story – beginning, middle or end – and retell the story in two sentences each.
● Ask the trios now to take on one of the characters from the story and ask each other questions in role, for example: *Do you feel happier or sadder now?*

Review
● Listen to some of the trios' simple versions of 'The Three Wishes'. Clarify any issues of beginning, middle and end. Compare the different fairy-tale openings and closings.

Curriculum objectives
- To listen to, discuss and express views about a wide range of stories.
- To continue to apply phonic knowledge and skills as the route to decode words until automatic decoding has become embedded and reading is fluent.
- To read most words quickly and accurately, without overt sounding and blending, when they have been frequently encountered.
- To discuss and clarify the meanings of words, linking new meanings to known vocabulary.

Resources
A small pile of slips of paper for each child

4: Fairy-tale characters

Introduction
- Ask: *Who is your favourite fairy-tale character?* Encourage as many children as possible to give their opinion and explain why.

Whole-class work
- Write the headings *Hero, Heroine, Helper, Villain* and *Friends and family* on the board, reading and discussing their meaning. Ask: *Who takes on these roles in 'Rapunzel'?* (Point out there is no helper.) Do the same for 'Sleeping Beauty'.
- Encourage the children to voice different opinions on the roles of the characters. Practise reading any new vocabulary and add to the keywords list.

Paired work
- In pairs, ask the children to think of as many characters as they can from fairy stories. Tell them to write the name of each one on a piece of paper.
- Ask the pairs to join with another pair and sort their characters into piles of heroes, heroines, villains, helpers, and friends or family.
- Tell them to jointly agree an adjective for each character, using their phonic knowledge to attempt to spell the word.

Whole-class work
- Share the characters and adjectives and write these under the headings you already have on the board. Discuss the different adjective choices.
- Ask: *What sort of characters do you find in fairy tales?* Agree that most characters in these stories have only one main characteristic.

Review
- Ask the children to read – quickly and accurately – the list of fairy-tale names and adjectives drawn up. Use them to create a character profile for a new fairy-tale villain and a fairy-tale heroine as a piece of shared writing.

Curriculum objectives
- To read most words quickly and accurately, without overt sounding and blending, when they have been frequently encountered.
- To read accurately words of two or more syllables that contain the graphemes taught so far.
- To write down ideas and/or key words, including new vocabulary.

Resources
Photocopiable page 72 'Fairy-tale elements'

5: Fairy-tale elements

Introduction
- Recap on the elements of fairy-tales that you've discovered this week.
- Re-read with increased speed and confidence the 'Key fairy-tale words' list.

Paired work
- Hand out photocopiable page 72 'Fairy-tale elements' and check that the children can read all the words swiftly and accurately, using phonics to read any that are new and adding them to the 'Key fairy-tale words' list.
- Ask pairs to cut out and muddle up the elements. They should place them upside-down on the table and turn over one card each.
- Tell the pairs to spend a few minutes discussing a possible fairy tale that could include the two elements, briefly thinking about characters and a plot.
- Ask them to choose two more cards to create another fairy tale together.

Independent work
- Encourage the children to choose their favourite plot and use it to plan their own fairy tale: writing down main plot ideas and key words.

Differentiation
- Choose four elements for less confident learners to work with.

Review
- Invite the children to share their story plans with their partner. Have they used traditional fairy-tale elements, characters and language?

Week 2 lesson plans

This week focuses on settings and helps children to see that settings aren't just the backdrop of a story, but can also create some of the action. After spending the beginning of the week discussing, describing and pretending to be the settings from the fairy tales they've been reading, the children create a map of a fairy-tale kingdom and discuss a story that could take place in it.

1: The dark, dark woods

Introduction
● Display the two photographs from the media resource 'Woods' on the CD-ROM. Ask: *Which of these two woods would you like to find yourself in?* Take each photograph in turn and ask the children to turn to their partner and discuss what they would smell, hear, feel and see in each of the woods.
● Ask: *Which wood do you think the wood in 'Hansel and Gretel' would be like?*

Whole-class work
● Re-read last week's stories, and recap on what the children learned about plot and characters. Ask: *What settings do we find in these stories?*
● Add any appropriate setting words that the children come up with to the 'Key fairy-tale words' list.
● Share the fairy-tale collections and compare different illustrations of the same settings. Ask: *What do they have in common? How are they different? What mood or feeling do they have?* Help the children to draw out inference from the pictorial clues. Discuss and note any new vocabulary to describe these settings, talking about the spelling choices as you write them on the list.

Paired work
● Give each pair of children the settings from photocopiable page 73 'Fairy-tale settings'. Ask them to discuss each setting in turn and think of a fairy tale that they know that includes this setting. Point out that there will be different options for each setting depending on what fairy tales they know.
● Ask them to think of two adjectives to describe each setting and write them underneath the picture.
● Give each pair one of the stories read from photocopiable sheets in the previous week ('Hansel and Gretel', 'The Three Wishes', 'Sleeping Beauty' and 'Rapunzel'). Ask them to read the story together. Listen to them as they do this, praising any particularly confident or improved reading.
● Give each pair a piece of paper and ask them to make a note of all the settings in their story spread out across the piece of paper. Encourage the children to think about the different parts of each location. Ask the following for discussion:
  ● *What happened at this setting?*
  ● *How did the main character feel?*
  ● *What or who else was found at this setting?*
  ● *Is the setting important to the plot?*
● Ask them to make notes around the setting word on their piece of paper.

> **Differentiation**
> ● Provide less confident children with the setting cards for 'Hansel and Gretel' (poor cottage in the village, woods and the gingerbread house) cut out from photocopiable page 73 'Fairy-tale setting'. Discuss the settings as a group.

Review
● Invite different pairs to talk about the settings in their story. Encourage the other children to say if they agree or disagree with the pair's thoughts.
● Share the setting adjectives and write any new ideas on the 'Key fairy-tale words' list.

Curriculum objectives
- To make inferences on the basis of what is being said and done.
- To re-read books to build up their fluency and confidence in word reading.
- To become increasingly familiar with and retell a wider range of stories, fairy stories and traditional tales.
- To participate in discussion about books, poems and other works that are read to them and those that they can read for themselves, taking turns and listening to what others say.
- To write down ideas and/ or key words, including new vocabulary.

Resources
Photocopiable pages 'Hansel and Gretel', 'Rapunzel', and 'Sleeping Beauty' from the CD-ROM; pairs' settings notes from the previous lesson

2: Setting role play

Introduction
- Ask pairs of children to revisit the notes they made about the settings in their story and share them with another pair, adding further notes to each other's thoughts.

Group work
- Tell these groups to create a short role play of a scene, with one child as the main character and the others as the setting.
- Ask them to think how they could move or stand to make the setting seem dangerous, or lonely, or wondrous. Might there be a sound effect that they can make with their voice, such as the whistling wind?

Whole-class work
- Share the different scenes that the groups have created. Model making notes of some of the most successful ideas, introducing suitable vocabulary for their actions, for example *crouch*, *grab*, *swaying*, *threatening*.

Differentiation
- Ask more confident children to create a setting introduction for their scene, using dramatic vocabulary.

Review
- Share the revised scenes and ask each group to talk about their setting using specific vocabulary to discuss the setting and how they created it.

Curriculum objectives
- To re-read stories to build up their fluency and confidence in word reading.
- To write down ideas and/ or key words, including new vocabulary.
- To become increasingly familiar with and retell a wider range of stories, fairy stories and traditional tales.
- To use and understand the grammatical terminology in Appendix 2 in discussing their writing.
- To participate in discussion about books, poems and other works that are read to them and those that they can read for themselves, taking turns and listening to what others say.

Resources
Photocopiable pages 'The Three Wishes' and 'Hansel and Gretel' from the CD-ROM; strips of paper made by cutting A4 paper in half vertically (four for each child)

3: Describing settings

Introduction
- Remind the children of their setting role plays in the previous lesson. Thinking about the work they've done so far on noun phrases, create some noun phrases for the settings they explored.

Whole-class work
- Read the photocopiable pages 'Hansel and Gretel' from the CD-ROM.
- Divide the board into three and label the sections: *Home*, *Woods* and *Gingerbread house*. Ask the children to help you fill each section with as many adjectives for the three settings as possible. Encourage the children to give reasons for their choices. Model expanding the adjectives into noun phrases.

Independent work
- Give each child two strips of paper and the photocopiable page 'The Three Wishes' from the CD-ROM and ask them to label them: *Cottage* and *Wood*. Ask them to write as many words as they can to describe each setting.
- Challenge them to write at least one noun phrase for each setting.

Paired work
- Tell the children to compare and discuss their strips with a partner.

Differentiation
- Challenge children to discuss which settings are most important to the plot.

Review
- Discuss the impact each setting has on the story. Ask: *What would happen to the story if the setting was different?*

Curriculum objectives
● To use expanded noun phrases to describe and specify.
● To explain and discuss their understanding of books, poems and other material, both those that they listen to and those that they read for themselves.
● To use and understand the grammatical terminology in Appendix 2 in discussing their writing.

Resources
A map template for each group, plus one extra per group (approximately A1 size – use flipchart or brown paper, crumple it up and rip the edges); squares of plain paper

4: Fairy-tale map

Introduction
● Write a list of well-known fairy tales and their related settings on the board.

Whole-class work
● Model drawing a fairy-tale land on one of the map templates. Include a large area of woods, a woodman's cottage and grandmother's house. Add a mountain with a lonely cave, a castle and other settings from your list.
● Organise the children into groups and explain that they are going to make their own maps. Each child needs to choose a setting to add.

Independent work
● Remind the children about their work on expanded noun phrases and the settings that they described in the previous lesson.
● Give each child a square of paper and ask them to draw their setting and write an expanded noun phrase to describe it.

Group work
● Give each group one of the blank maps and encourage them to work together to decide where to stick their settings. Ask them to discuss what each other's phrases mean and how they fit the story.
● Allow time for them to draw in extra trees, rocks and paths.

Review
● Pin up the maps and pick out successful language to share with the class.

Curriculum objectives
● To write down ideas and/ or key words, including new vocabulary.
● To explain and discuss their understanding of books, poems and other material, both those that they listen to and those that they read for themselves.
● To use expanded noun phrases to describe and specify.

Resources
Story plans from Autumn 2, week 1, lesson 5; group maps from previous lesson

5: Fairy-tale journey

Introduction
● Pin up the maps. Choose one (or more) of the maps and walk through it with your fingers pretending to be a fairy-tale character of your choosing. Make up a story as you go along, finding objects and meeting magical people.
● Emphasise the reasons that the story moves from one setting to the other. It is crucial they see this cause-and-effect element of story planning.

Paired work
● Ask the children to share their story plans from the previous week with a partner from their map group.
● Encourage the pairs to discuss each story, talking about how it could fit into the story land and suggesting magical things to enhance it.
● Challenge them to bring into their story why the character moves from one setting to another.

Independent work
● Tell the children to develop their story plan so that their story takes place in three settings, making notes on why the plot moves location. Ask them to write one sentence about each setting, including a noun phrase to describe it.

> **Differentiation**
> ● Ask less confident learners to concentrate on one change of scene.

Review
● Encourage the children to tell you one element from their story plan, explaining what happens to make the story move on, and giving a sentence that includes an expanded noun phrase that they hope to use in their story.

Week 3 lesson plans

This week the children write their own fairy tale using the characters, settings and events that they've encountered in stories so far. By using known elements, the children can focus their energy on the writing process: making notes, writing sentences, including adjectives and noun phrases, writing a first draft and proofreading to check for tense, spelling, grammar and punctuation. After a first draft they look to see where adding exclamations or questions could add interest to the story. The children are encouraged to read aloud their final version.

1: Muddled fairy tales

Introduction

● Sit in a circle and create a traditional tale one word at a time, going round the room. Allow the first four children to start *Once upon a time...* but remind the others of the world that this story takes place in.

Whole-class work

● Ask a child to come to the front and pick two cards from each of the hats. Show the children each card and ask them to tell you if the card shows a plot event, a setting or a character. Ask the children to discuss which story the card could come from, discussing different opinions if they arise.
● Explain that you are now going to create a new fairy tale combining these different elements. Ask for different suggestions from the class and encourage the children to weigh up the merits each. Allow time for the children to come up with a range of crazy plot twists to accommodate the cluster of elements.
● Remind the children of the work done last week in thinking of reasons for characters to move from one setting to another.
● Orally tell the story, modelling the thought process and adapting the ideas as you go along.
● Make notes to record the key elements of your story, using noun phrases where useful. You will need to keep these for the next lesson.

Paired work

● Give each pair of children the photocopiable pages 73 'Fairy-tale settings', 74 'Fairy-tale events' and 75 'Fairy-tale characters' and ask them to cut out the different elements and muddle them up in three piles. Ask the children to choose two cards from each pile and then place them in front of them, tidying away the rest of the cards.
● The children should spend the next few minutes silently thinking of a plot that combines the elements, before sharing their thoughts with their partner.
● Tell the children to discuss the different ideas, building on each other's thoughts – remembering to listen to each other.
● Allow them to swap (without looking for what they get in return) one of the cards if the story becomes unworkable.

Independent work

● Tell the children to go through their story one more time in their head. Remind them to think of a reason for the move from one setting to another. Encourage them to keep the story simple.
● When the children are sure in their heads about their story, ask them to write brief notes about the plot – under the headings *Beginning*, *Middle* and *End* if helpful. Tell them to note down two or three noun phrases to describe the settings or characters.

Review

● Share the children's notes, ensuring that the plans make sense and are manageable.

Expected outcomes
● All children make notes for story ideas.
● Most children use ideas to write accurate sentences in the past tense.
● Some children can improve their story with varying sentences and adding noun phrases.

Curriculum objectives
● To plan or say out loud what they are going to write about.
● To write ideas and/or key words, including new vocabulary.

Resources
Photocopiable pages 73 'Fairy-tale settings', 74 'Fairy-tale events' and 75 'Fairy-tale characters' – each page cut up into cards and placed in a different hat and a further copy for each pair of children

Curriculum objectives

- To apply spelling rules and guidelines, as listed in Appendix 1.
- To plan or say out loud what they are going to write about.
- To write down ideas and/ or key words, including new vocabulary.
- To re-read to check that their writing makes sense and that verbs to indicate time are used correctly and consistently, including verbs in the continuous form.
- To learn to spell common exception words.
- To write narratives about personal experiences and those of others (real and fictional).
- To use the present and past tenses correctly and consistently including the progressive form.
- To use and understand the grammatical terminology in Appendix 2 in discussing their writing.

Resources

Whole-class and individual story plans from previous lesson

2: Writing my story opening

Introduction

- Carry out a quick-fire game with the children: give them a present tense verb and ask them to quickly answer with the past tense in unison.

Whole-class work

- Return to the story plan that you drew up in the previous lesson and use it to retell the story.
- Model writing some complete sentences from the opening of the story – using a typical fairy-story opener for the first sentence. Model composing sentences orally, then repeating them aloud as you write them. Think aloud about tenses, drawing out use of past. Highlight any spelling patterns or common exception words as you come across them.
- Discuss a range of specific words the children may need in writing their own story – asking them for suggestions as to what these might be. Write these as a word bank, involving the children with spelling them.

Paired work

- Working in their pairs from the previous lesson, the children orally compose sentences from the opening of their story. Partners should check the sentences make sense and are in the past tense, making suggestions if not.

Differentiation

- Encourage less confident learners to orally compose complete sentences in the past tense. Organise an adult helper to scribe for them, discussing their spelling choices.

Review

- Share the story openers and check for a consistent past tense and praise any use of noun phrases and story language. Ensure children understand the term *tense*. Check and discuss the spelling of the sentences shared.

Curriculum objectives

- To start using some of the diagonal and horizontal strokes needed to join letters and understand which letters, when adjacent to one another, are best left unjoined.
- To learn how to use both familiar and new punctuation correctly (see Appendix 2), including full stops, capital letters, exclamation marks, question marks, commas for lists and apostrophes for contracted forms and the possessive (singular).
- To proofread to check for errors in spelling, grammar and punctuation.

Resources

Story plans and story openers from previous lesson

3: A first draft

Introduction

- Tell the children to go around the room and tell their story to three different children. Encourage them to elaborate the parts that seem to intrigue their listeners and improve the parts that don't seem to work.

Whole-class work

- Model reading the opening of your story and continuing to write. Ask: *How should I start my sentence – what do I need to remember? And at the end?*
- Draw attention to your handwriting and which letters you are and are not joining, discussing your choices.
- Use any opportunities to model use of the apostrophe, and to check that the children understand its usage.
- Model proofreading work to spot and correct any errors. Ask: *What do I need to look out for?* (Punctuation, spelling, handwriting, sense, tense.)

Independent work

- Tell the children to complete the first draft of their story. Remind them to think about their handwriting as they write, and to join letters as appropriate.
- Tell them to proofread their draft and correct any errors.

Review

- Ask the children to share their drafts with a partner. Tell them to read each story together and check that their handwriting is readable and for any punctuation errors that need correcting.

Curriculum objectives

● To learn how to use both familiar and new punctuation correctly (see Appendix 2), including full stops, capital letters, exclamation marks, question marks, commas for lists and apostrophes for contracted forms and the possessive (singular).
● To proofread to check for errors in spelling, grammar and punctuation.
● To re-read to check that their writing makes sense and that verbs to indicate time are used correctly and consistently, including verbs in the continuous form.
● To use and understand the grammatical terminology in Appendix 2 in discussing their writing.

Resources

The children's first draft stories from previous lessons

4: Varying sentences

Introduction

● Carry out starter activity 4 'Statement changer' with the class sat in a circle.

Whole-class work

● Display your story on the board and look for a place where an exclamation or question could be added. Write these, asking the children to help you read them with proper expression. Ask: *How should these sentences be punctuated?*
● Model adding new exclamations or questions, reading the new sentences in context so they can appreciate the improvement to the story.

Paired work

● Encourage the children to work with a new partner and ask them to explore opportunities to add questions or exclamations to each other's writing. Tell them to work together to write and punctuate these correctly.
● Tell them to look out together for any places where they should have used an apostrophe and help each other to use these correctly.

Independent work

● Ask the children to continue to look for two more places where questions or exclamations can be added. Then recap how to proofread finished work.

Review

● Ask the children to share their new sentences, checking that they are correctly punctuated.

Curriculum objectives

● To re-read to check that their writing makes sense and that verbs to indicate time are used correctly and consistently, including verbs in the continuous form.
● To read aloud what they have written with appropriate intonation to make the meaning clear.
● To use the present and past tenses correctly and consistently including the progressive form.

Resources

The children's draft stories from the previous lesson; interactive activity 'In the past' on the CD-ROM

5: Checking and reading aloud

Introduction

● Ask the children to work in pairs to complete the interactive activity 'In the past' on the CD-ROM. Remind them that some verbs have an irregular spelling in the past tense.
● Recap on the writing process they've used this week. Ask the children to look at their original notes and drafts to see how the story has developed. Ask them to evaluate how useful it was to tell their story orally before writing.

Independent work

● Ask the children to read the first draft of their story. Have they included all their best ideas? Tell them to ask themselves:
  ● *Does the story make sense?*
  ● *Is it written in the past tense?*
  ● *Does one event lead to another?*
  ● *Does something happen to make the character move between settings?*
  ● *Have they included noun phrases and other adjectives to describe the setting?*
  ● *Have they included an exclamation or a question to vary the tone?*
● Tell the children to make revisions to their stories as necessary and then swap stories with a partner.
● Ask the children to review their partner's story with the same criteria, and to feed back sensitively, pointing out parts of the story that they thought were particularly successful.
● Tell the children to write out a final version in their best handwriting.

Review

● Ask as many children as possible to read their story aloud, reading clearly and with expression.
● Encourage the children to discuss how the story built on their notes and how the review process improved the story.

Curriculum objectives
● To participate in discussion about books, poems and other works that are read to them and those that they can read for themselves, taking turns and listening to what others say.
● To be introduced to non-fiction books that are structured in different ways.
● To use and understand the grammatical terminology in Appendix 2 in discussing their writing.

Resources
Sticky notes (one packet per group); a range of instruction texts of a suitable reading age: recipes, game instructions, flat-pack furniture instructions, toy-building instructions, a poster about how to behave in school or at the swimming pool, a letter about a school trip, craft books and so on

Week 4 lesson plans

This week the children build on their previous work on recipes to write a set of instructions for a fairy-tale themed game. First the children use a range of different instruction texts to recap on the features of such text before writing a set of instructions for making a paper aeroplane with support. Finally they design, draft and make a final version of a fairy-tale game.

1: Instructions recap

Introduction
● Hold up a pen and tell the children that it is magical. Ask them to tell you how. (It writes only the truth, it can turn into a rocket, anything it draws becomes real and so on.)
● Place it on the floor and ask the children to take turns to come to the front and say something about the pen. Challenge the first few to say a simple statement (*Someone has left a pen.*), the next few a question (*What's this doing here?*), the next few a command (*Someone pick up this pen.*) and finally an exclamation (*There's my magic pen!*).

Whole-class work
● Write one of each type of sentence that came out of the introduction activity on the board. Focus on the command sentence (*Pick up this pen.*) Ask: *What sort of non-fiction text uses this type of sentence?* Agree that instruction texts use command sentences.
● Remind the children about the work they did in Autumn 1 on instructions and recipes and explain that they are going to be recapping on that work this week – and writing instructions for a fairy-tale game that they create.

Group work
● Give each group a range of different instruction texts, as varied as possible while still being at their reading age. Give each group a packet of sticky notes.
● Ask the children to look through the books and together remember the features of instructions. Ask them to use the sticky notes to label the features they find in the instruction texts. (Title, what you need, what do to, command (bossy) sentences, numbered steps, photographs, diagrams and so on.)
● Encourage them to label two versions of each feature.
● Ask the children to discuss in their groups how the instructions are the same and how they're different. *Does every – or even any – text have an example of every feature? What's missing in each one?*

Differentiation
● Support children by giving them straightforward instruction texts such as recipes, and pre-written sticky note labels.
● Challenge children by giving them a school trip letter to investigate. Can they find some command sentences? (*Arrive by 8.30am. Bring a packed lunch*) Can they find 'what you need' items? (*Welly boots, packed lunch, waterproof* and so on).

Review
● Ask the groups to present their findings. Ask the rest of the class to comment on whether they agree with the group's instruction features. Make a list of the features on the board.
● Ask the groups to talk about how the different texts differed and to talk about which features were sometimes missing.

2: Improving poor instructions

Introduction

Curriculum objectives
● To be introduced to non-fiction books that are structured in different ways.
● To discuss the sequence of events in books and how items of information are related.

Resources
Before the lesson, teach yourself how to make a simple paper aeroplane; photocopiable page 76 'How to make a paper aeroplane'

● Give every child a piece of A4 paper. Read out the instructions from photocopiable page 76 'How to make a paper aeroplane' without showing the children what to do and without telling them what they are making. How many children ended up with a paper aeroplane?
● Ask the children to tell you what they think would have helped them make a better plane or feel less confused about what they were doing? Share their thoughts.
● Repeat the activity with new paper, this time showing them what to do and giving more detailed instructions.

Paired work

● Give each pair the photocopiable sheet.
● Ask them to follow the instructions with a new piece of paper, discussing what they're doing as they go. Ask them to think about their comments to each other and use these to make notes around the instructions as to how they could be improved by adding words.
● Ask the children to cut out the diagrams and use them to create their own improved set of instructions.
● Tell them to add numbers and a 'What you need' section.

Review

● Ask the children to talk about the two experiences of making the plane.
● Share the different ideas that the children had to improve the instructions.

3: Fairy-tale game

Introduction

Curriculum objectives
● To plan or say out loud what they are going to write about.
● To write down ideas and/ or key words, including new vocabulary.
● To explain and discuss their understanding of books, poems and other material, both those that they listen to and those that they read for themselves.

Resources
A range of simple board games such as 'Ludo' and 'Snakes and ladders'; photocopiable page 'Fairy game board' from the CD-ROM

● Give each group a simple board game and allow time for the children to play the game. Tell them to read the rules before they start.

Whole-class work

● Ask the children to describe the different board games they enjoy and to share some of the elements with you. (Dice, taking turns, youngest first, squares that you land on where you get to go ahead or back or miss a turn, landing on another player and sending them back, and so on.) Capture these on the board.

Group work

● Distribute photocopiable page 'Fairy game board' from the CD-ROM.
● Tell the children that they are going to be inventing their own game – set in a fairy-tale context – and then writing a set of instructions for it later in the week.
● Encourage them to fill in the squares on the game board with things that happen on them. (You get stuck in the woods, miss a go.) They should use pencil for this first draft.

> **Differentiation**
> ● Support some children in an adult-led group.
> ● More confident learners can discuss and create different options for the game board, remembering to listen to each other's thoughts.

Review

● Ask the children to talk about their game. Encourage them to explain their choices and praise their use of new words.

Curriculum objectives
- To write for different purposes.
- To participate in discussion about books, poems and other works that are read to them and those that they can read for themselves, taking turns and listening to what others say.
- To write sentences with different forms: statement, question, exclamation, command.

Resources
A pile of coloured bricks; draft game boards from the previous lesson; photocopiable page 'Fairy game board' from the CD-ROM

4: Instruction drafts

Introduction
- Ask different groups to describe their game board from the previous lesson to you and explain briefly how the game is played.
- Take different elements from each one and model turning the ideas into command sentences.

Group work
- Invite the groups to revisit their game board. Provide counters and dice and tell them to have a go at playing their game. Encourage them to discuss what is working and what is not, revising the game if necessary. (Have extra copies of photocopiable page 'Fairy game board' from the CD-ROM available.)
- Tell them to work together to create a draft version of the instructions for their game. Recap on sentence types and ask them to write a statement that describes what the purpose of the game is, for example *To be the first player to reach the treasure.*
- Tell them to then create the set of instructions for the game, re-reading them to check they make sense and include all the information needed.
- Ask them to add advice and warnings: *Watch out for the dragon!*

Differentiation
- Re-form your group of less confident learners from the previous lesson and support the children as they write the game instructions that you have planned out together.

Review
- Ask groups to present their game, explaining how they created it.

Curriculum objectives
- To re-read to check that their writing makes sense and that verbs to indicate time are used correctly and consistently, including verbs in the continuous form.
- To read aloud what they have written with appropriate intonation to make the meaning clear.
- To write capital letters and digits of the correct size, orientation and relationship to one another and to lower-case letters.
- To start using some of the diagonal and horizontal strokes needed to join letters and understand which letters, when adjacent to one another, are best left unjoined.
- To use spacing between words that reflects the size of the letters.
- To form lower-case letters of the correct size relative to one another.

Resources
The draft board games and instructions that the children have created this week; coloured pens

5: Games day

Introduction
- Ask the children to swap game boards and game instructions with another group and attempt to play the game.
- Tell the groups to feed back to each other. Were the instructions easy to understand? Was the game fun to play? Was there something that didn't work or wasn't clear? Do they have any suggestions on how to improve the game?

Group work
- Tell the groups to discuss the advice they've been given and how they will improve the instructions and game.
- They can work together to colour in their board.

Independent work
- Ask the children to write their own final version of the instructions, remembering to use all the instruction features they need and to write a well-presented final version in clear joined-up handwriting.
- Tell them to proofread for spelling, grammar and punctuation.
- Colour copy the game boards so that the children are able to take home their final version of the game.

Differentiation
- Challenge children to create a cover or a box for their game with questions and exclamations to capture interest: *Watch out for the dragon! Do you want to be a hero?* and so on.

Review
- Ask: *Whose game was easy to follow?* Share these successful games.
- Talk with the class about what they now know about writing instructions.

Week 5 lesson plans

After a recap on diary writing, this week the children make the imaginative leap into the fairy-tale characters' heads. The children will be hot-seating familiar characters – good and bad – about the events in their story. The children will focus on one character and empathise with them, make notes about their thoughts and feelings before writing a first then final version of a diary entry for one key day in their story.

1: Dear diary

Introduction

● Use starter activity 18 'Past or present?'. Sit in a large circle. Say: *I am laughing.* Ask the child to your left to put it into the past tense: *I laughed.* Ask him or her to then give you another present tense verb phrase, such as *I am juggling.* Tell the next child to put the phrase into the past tense and then say a new phrase. Carry on around the circle.

Whole-class work

● Ask: *What is a diary?* Remind the children of the diary entries you wrote for Oliver in Autumn 1, week 5, lesson 3. Agree that some people write down what happened to them every day. Diaries can also be a place where people share their private thoughts, feelings and worries.
● Ask a volunteer to come out to the front and tell you what they did at the weekend. Putting the date at the top, scribe the event as a diary entry for the class. Include details of how the child felt when they did each activity – for example, *I went to the cinema on Saturday to see the new superhero film. We had popcorn – yummy! The film made me jump a few times, but I really enjoyed it.*
● Ask: *What tense is the diary written in? Why is that?* (It relates something that happened in the past.) *What person is it written in?* (First person, I.)
● Circle the verbs in the diary entry on the board. Discuss how they are formed (by adding '-ed', or common exceptions).

Paired work

● Tell the pairs of children to share something that happened to them recently, taking turns to listen to each other's recount. Tell the pairs to ask each other questions about the event such as: *How did you feel? What was the best bit?* and so on.
● Explain that they don't need to go into great detail – they should aim for a short but interesting version of the event.
● Tell the pairs to swap with another pair. They now tell their previous partner's experience to their new partner – this will help them to them to start empathising with and expressing another person's feelings.

Independent work

● Tell the children to write their own event as a diary entry.
● Recap on the writing process – making notes, orally rehearsing, writing sentences and proofreading. Remind them that diary entries are often quite short but include the main facts and feelings.

> **Differentiation**
> ● Challenge children to use adventurous verb choices and connectives in their diary entries.

Review

● Encourage the children to read out their diary entries. Discuss the use of past tense verbs. Highlight any exceptions to the '-ed' rule. Check that the children have included feelings as well as events.

Curriculum objectives
● To write narratives about personal experiences and those of others (real and fictional).
● To make inferences on the basis of what is being said and done.

Resources
Photocopiable page 77 'Past and present'

2: Seeing another point of view

Introduction

● Hand out photocopiable page 77 'Past and present' to pairs of learners. Ask the children to first cut out and pair up the verbs and then to use the cards to play a game of pairs.

Whole-class work

● Recap on the diary entries the children wrote in the previous lesson. Explain that today they will be considering what fairy-tale characters think about the events in their story.
● Ask two children to come up to the front and take the hot-seat as Rapunzel and the witch. The rest of the class to question them about the events in the story and for the characters to explain what happened from their point of view.
● Model questioning to help the characters to deepen their thinking: for example: *What did you think/hope/fear would happen?*

Paired work

● Ask the children to work in pairs to repeat the activity but using two new opposing characters, for example: Hansel and the witch, or Sleeping Beauty and the bad fairy. Tell them to ask each other questions.
● Challenge the children playing the 'bad' character to find some way to make them seem less bad. Say: *Tell us something we didn't know about them which explains why they did what they did.*

Review

● Ask different pairs to take on the hot-seat and be questioned by the class. Can they inspire sympathy in the rest of the class?

Curriculum objectives
● To write narratives about personal experiences and those of others (real and fictional).
● To encapsulate what they want to say, sentence by sentence.

Resources
Photocopiable page 78 'Diary questions'

3: Making notes

Introduction

● Tell the children to repeat their hot-seating activity with a new partner (changing character if they wish). Remind them that they can use new details to make their character more interesting/less good/less bad. Hand out photocopiable page 78 'Diary questions' to enhance their questions.

Whole-class work

● Take on the role of the witch from 'Rapunzel'. Tell the class about the day you found out that Rapunzel had met the prince, casting yourself as the victim.
● Model making notes (saw prince arrive and leave, felt betrayed, pleaded with R, R cuts hair and storms out, desperate to find R, I wait for prince, love R like own child).

Independent work

● Tell the children to make notes about the events in preparation for writing a diary entry. Remind them that they're not writing the whole story but only what might have happened on one day.

> **Differentiation**
> ● With a less confident group, take turns to role play the same character then together agree the back story and make notes, ensuring that the children can use the notes to orally retell the character's point of view.

Review

● Share the notes. Have the children written useful notes without writing in sentences? Have they captured feelings, reasons, hopes and fears?

4: Sentence by sentence

Introduction

● Come into the class in role as the witch from 'Rapunzel' and elicit sympathy from the children as you tell them how Rapunzel has abandoned you in your old age and has gone off with a stranger, just as you feared.

Whole-class work

● Say: *It's time to turn my notes into a diary entry. What do I need to remember?* (Date, first person, past tense, details and feelings and reasons, capital letters, full stops, clear handwriting.)
● Model turning your notes into full sentences that describe thoughts, feelings, reasons, hopes and fears about the event that happened, from the character's point of view: *I felt... when....* Orally discuss each sentence as you write so the children can see the careful process of gradually arranging their ideas.

Independent work

● Tell the children to look at their notes and think through what they want to say; orally rehearse (quietly) sentence by sentence; write the date and then each sentence, remembering all the things mentioned above.
● Remind them that you are only asking for the diary for one day, which should be one event, not the whole story turned into first person.

> **Differentiation**
> ● Work with less confident children to help them write three well-constructed sentences. Help them to orally construct these before writing.

Review

● Ask some children to share their first drafts. Ask the other children to sensitively comment on whether the criteria outlined have been met.

5: Building diary memories

Introduction

● Ask one brave child to share their diary entry with the class. Model discussing the diary with the child, praising the work done and talking about how it could be improved. Hot seat the child in role and ask questions to further the child's thinking.

Whole-class work

● Tell the children to turn to their partner and read their diary entry to them, taking turns. Ask the partners to sensitively feed back, discussing whether they've said enough about what they thought and felt, as well as describing what happened; whether they've used the first person, past tense, full stops, capital letters and correct spelling; whether they could read the handwriting; what they liked best about the diary entry.
● Tell the partners to question each other further in role about the event.

Independent work

● Tell the children to make notes of their partner's comments and to mark on their draft how to improve their draft through spelling, grammar and content.
● Tell them to write out a final version of their diary entry.

Review

● Display the diary entries and allow time for them to read each other's work.
● Ask the children to talk about a dairy entry that they particularly liked and say what they like about it.

Curriculum objectives
● To apply spelling rules and guidelines, as listed in Appendix 1.
● To write capital letters and digits of the correct size, orientation and relationship to one another and to lower-case letters.
● To write narratives about personal experiences and those of others (real and fictional).
● To re-read to check that their writing makes sense and that verbs to indicate time are used correctly and consistently, including verbs in the continuous form.
● To encapsulate what they want to say, sentence by sentence.

Resources
Notes from the previous lesson

Curriculum objectives
● To write narratives about personal experiences and those of others (real and fictional).
● To re-read to check that their writing makes sense and that verbs to indicate time are used correctly and consistently, including verbs in the continuous form.
● To apply spelling rules and guidelines, as listed in Appendix 1.
● To write capital letters and digits of the correct size, orientation and relationship to one another and to lower-case letters.

Resources
Diary notes and first draft diary entries from the previous lesson

Week 6 lesson plans

This week begins by looking at nursery rhymes. The children look at some key examples and use these to focus on spelling the same sound in different ways. They also practise spelling some rhyming common exception words and find homophones and rhymes in nursery rhymes. In the second half of the week, we look at 'Magic Horse' by John Foster and the children continue to use rhyme to examine different spellings of the same sound. The children spend time enjoying and learning the poem, imagining where they would go on a magic horse before creating an expressive performance of the poem. Finally, the children write their own version of this poem.

1: One, two, buckle my shoe

Introduction
● Muddle up the cards (see Resources). Give each child one card and ask them to group up into words that rhyme.
● When all the children have found their group, tell the groups to practise spelling all their words.
● Repeat the activity a couple of times.

Whole-class work
● Display a photocopiable page 'One, Two, Buckle My Shoe' from the CD-ROM. Read it to the children and then ask them to join in with the numbers on a second reading.
● Ask the children to help you find the rhyming words. Establish together that some of the rhymes aren't complete rhymes.
● Ask: *What do you think the verse means?* Agree that it doesn't really mean anything; it's just a fun counting rhyme. Explain the meaning of any unknown words (*delve* – dig, *maids a-courting* – young girls looking for a husband, *maids in the kitchen* – servants in the kitchen, *maids in waiting* – women who look after a queen). Use phonics to segment and blend these words to read them.
● Ask the children discuss with their partner whether or not they like the verse.

Paired work
● Give each child the photocopiable sheet and ask them to read the rhyme together, with one child reading the numbers and the other reading the rhyming phrase. Tell them to swap roles and read the poem again. Then ask them to have a go at saying the poem without looking at their copy.
● Ask the pairs to think of more words that rhyme with the numbers.

Whole-class work
● Write the numbers (as words) *two, four, six, eight* and *ten* along the top of the board. Ask the children for the words they came up with and write these as a list under each one (include homophones if they come up). (For example: *to, too, true, blue, blew, grew, stew, new, for, poor, store, claw, picks, Rick's, Nick's, ate, plate, gate, freight, great, pen, again, Ben.*) Add examples of different spellings and homophones if they don't naturally come up.
● Look at the different spelling options under each list.
● Look at the homophones for *four, two, eight, blue* and any others that come up.

Paired work
● Ask the children to return to their pairs and have fun inventing some new rhyming phrases for the poem. Remind them that it doesn't need to make sense.

Review
● Invite the children to share their version of the rhyme. Discuss the spelling of the words chosen each time.

Curriculum objectives
● To learn new ways of spelling phonemes for which one or more spellings are already known, and learn some words with each spelling, including a few common homophones.

Resources
Photocopiable page 79 'Mixed-up nursery rhymes'; a selection of nursery-rhyme collections

2: Nursery rhyming

Introduction
● Sing as many nursery rhymes as you can with the children. Include the ones on photocopiable page 79 'Mixed-up nursery rhymes', plus any others they know.
● Explain that traditional nursery rhymes, like fairy tales, are often very old and have no known author.

Paired work
● Give each pair the photocopiable sheet. Tell them to cut out and arrange the components to recreate the three rhymes.
● They can then circle the rhyming words in each verse.

Whole-class work
● Write the rhyming pairs of words from the photocopiable sheet on the board. Ask the children to tell you which ones are spelled the same (*wall/fall*) and which differently (*sky/high*).
● Together, think of other words that rhyme with these words (*crawl, lie*). Discuss the different spellings of the same sound.
● Clap out the syllables in the rhyming words. *Do they have one or two syllables?*

Paired work
● Provide the children with a large selection of nursery-rhyme collections. Ask them to search through the collections, reading the verses and noting down words that rhyme. Challenge them to find pairs of words with two syllables.

Review
● Share the words the children have found and discuss which are spelled the same and which are not. Discuss the different spellings.

Curriculum objectives
● To learn new ways of spelling phonemes for which one or more spellings are already known, and learn some words with each spelling, including a few common homophones.
● To continue to build up a repertoire of poems learned by heart and recite some of these, with appropriate intonation to make the meaning clear.
● To read further common exception words, noting unusual correspondence between spelling and sound and where these occur in the word.
● To read accurately by blending the sounds in words that contain the graphemes taught so far, especially recognising alternative sounds for graphemes.

Resources
Photocopiable page 'Magic Horse' from the CD-ROM

3: Magic horse

Introduction
● Ask: *If you could go anywhere – real or imaginary – where would you go?* Tell the children to turn to their partner and have a short flight of fantasy.
● Display photocopiable page 'Magic Horse' from the CD-ROM and read the poem to the children. On a second reading, encourage the children to join in with the predictable rhyming words. Point out the repeated verse openings.
● Discuss the spelling of *where* and *river*. Look at *snows* and *blows* and compare this to how we pronounce *growl* and *town*. Point out the repeated 'bl' and 'pl' blends.
● Ask different children to tell you which is their favourite line and why.

Group work
● Organise the class into four groups, each learning one verse by heart.
● Tell the children to circle the rhyming words in the poem and find the rhyme where the words are not spelled the same.

Differentiation
● With less confident learners share the poem as a group. Ask these children to learn the first three lines of each verse, finishing off the rest yourself.

Review
● Agree which is the pair of rhyming words that is spelled differently. Ask: *What other way is there of spelling the /ee/ sound?* ('y')
● Recite the poem together, with each group reciting their verse with meaning.

Curriculum objectives
● To continue to build up a repertoire of poems learned by heart, appreciating these and reciting some, with appropriate intonation to make the meaning clear.
● To learn new ways of spelling phonemes for which one or more spellings are already known, and learn some words with each spelling, including a few common homophones.

Resources
Photocopiable page 'Magic Horse' from the CD-ROM

4: Where will you go?

Introduction
● Read 'Magic Horse' by John Foster, asking the children to join in where they can. The groups from the previous lesson should join in with their particular verse.
● Display the poem. Ask the children to circle the rhymes. Ask: *How else can the /ay/ sound be spelled?* ('a_e' in *haze*, 'ey' in *they*).
● Circle the places the horse goes to in each verse. Write these on the board and then remove the poem. Read the poem again a few times, asking the children to join in where they can.
● Ask: *What other words sound the same as* **where**, **I** *and* **seas**? (*wear, eye* and *sees*). Discuss the different spelling patterns.
● Discuss the different places that the children told their partner they wanted to go to (in the previous lesson).

Independent work
● Hand out the photocopiable page 'Magic Horse' from the CD-ROM. Tell the children you would like them to write two extra verses, saying where they would like the horse to take them.
● Tell the children not to worry too much about getting the verses to rhyme – capturing an interesting place is more important. Suggest that they open with *Black horse/Magic horse/Carry me away...*

Review
● Ask different children to read out their poems, trying to capture their excitement at being taken away. Scribe some on the board. Discuss any rhymes and how the words are spelled.

Curriculum objectives
● To continue to build up a repertoire of poems learned by heart, appreciating these and reciting some, with appropriate intonation to make the meaning clear.

Resources
Photocopiable page 'Magic Horse' from the CD-ROM; a range of musical instruments

5: Performing magic

Introduction
● Make the instruments available to the class and allow them time to experiment with the different sounds each one can make.
● Ask them to try to think what each one could sound like: like a horse trotting, like the wind, like a sandstorm, like a twinkling star and so on.
● Ask: *What sounds can we make with our voices? Can we make the sound of water, the sea...?*

Group work
● Ask the children to get into groups of four and ask them to prepare a dramatic reading of 'Magic Horse' by John Foster. Tell them to discuss:
  ● the meaning of the poem – check that they understand each line. Can they make the poem exciting just by using the words first: *clear, slow and full of wonder?*
  ● adding sounds – are there places where instruments would add meaning or atmosphere? Allow them to try out different options. Can additional sounds be made with their voices?
  ● would the reading be enhanced by adding movement – hand or whole body?
● Encourage the groups to discuss lots of different options, listening carefully to everyone's suggestions.
● Tell them to make their choices and practise a dramatic reading or recitation of the poem.

Review
● Ask the groups to perform their poems to the class. Discuss particularly successful uses of voice, instruments and movement.

Curriculum objectives

- To use sentences with different forms: statement, question, exclamation, command.
- To learn how to use both familiar and new punctuation correctly (see Appendix 2), including full stops, capital letters, exclamation marks, question marks, commas for lists and apostrophes for contracted forms and the possessive (singular).
- To use and understand the grammatical terminology in Appendix 2 in discussing their writing.

Resources

Photocopiable page 'Fairy-tale punctuation' from the CD-ROM; interactive activity 'Fairy-tale punctuation' on the CD-ROM

Grammar and punctuation: Punctuating different sentence types

Revise

- Hand out photocopiable page 'Fairy-tale punctuation' from the CD-ROM (or use the interactive version on the CD-ROM) and ask the children to add appropriate punctuation to each sentence.
- After they have finished, ask them to tell you how they knew what to include.
- Ask the children to decide with a partner whether each sentence on the photocopiable sheet is a statement, question, exclamation or command.

Assessment

- Remind the children of the story of 'Sleeping Beauty'. Ask the children to write, and correctly punctuate, a question, a statement, an exclamation and a command (or warning) about the story.

Further practice

- Continue to ask the children to create the four types of sentences in a variety of contexts (for example, during a game in PE, discussing a history topic), each time ensuring that they can tell you what punctuation ends each type of sentence.

Curriculum objectives

- To spell more words with contracted forms.

Resources

Photocopiable page 'Can't, don't, won't' from the CD-ROM; interactive activity 'Can't, don't, won't' on the CD-ROM

Spelling: Consolidating contractions

Revise

- Display the photocopiable page 'Can't, don't, won't' from the CD-ROM (or use the interactive version on the CD-ROM). Together match up the full and contracted versions of the words, asking volunteers to write the contracted version next to the long version.
- Hand out the photocopiable sheet. Ask the children to cut out the cards from the bottom of the page. Working with a partner, tell them to role play a conversation between two characters from one of the fairy tales that they know well (such as 'Hansel and Gretel', 'The Three Wishes', 'The Little Red Hen' or a story from Year 1 such as 'Jack and the Beanstalk'). Challenge them to use all the contracted words in their role play, taking the word card when they use it.
- Ask the children to rework their role play, remembering and rehearsing what they say.

Assessment

- Ask the children to write down their conversation between their two characters, trying to correctly spell the contracted versions.

Further practice

- Challenge children to use what they know about contracted forms to write contracted versions of *they will, shall not, there will.*
- For support, see page 37.

Curriculum objectives
● To listen to, discuss and express views about a wide range of stories.
● To become increasingly familiar with and retell a wider range of stories, fairy stories and traditional tales.
● To recognise recurring literary language in stories and poetry.

Resources
Photocopiable pages 'Fairy-tale groups' and 'Rapunzel' from the CD-ROM; copies of a fairy tale that the children are not familiar with

Reading: Understanding fairy-tale features

Revise
● Make a list of the traditional tales that the children know – from Year 2 work, Year 1 work and from their general reading.
● Write the story titles on the board, leaving room around each title.
● Ask the children to give you the names of the characters and major objects from the story (Sleeping Beauty, spinning wheel, needle and so on).
● Hand out photocopiable page 'Fairy-tale groups' from the CD-ROM to pairs of children and ask them to find:
  ● Four cards showing important objects
  ● Three cards showing wicked characters
  ● Five cards showing magical characters (good or bad)
  ● Ten cards showing good characters
● Ask the children to sort the cards out into sets of four cards from the same story. Ask the children to remember the story together, using the cards as props.
● Ask the children to create four more sets of cards (for example for 'Little Red Riding Hood', 'The Little Red Hen', 'Hansel and Gretel' and 'Jack and the Beanstalk') and use the cards to play a game of 'Happy families'.

Assess
● Give each child the photocopiable pages 'Rapunzel' from the CD-ROM and ask them to circle all the fairy-tale features they find in it.

Further practice
● Ask the children to write two lists, one labelled *What we might find in a fairy tale* and the other *What we will not find in a fairy tale* (such as space ships, shopping centres, school settings and so on).
● Ask the children to tell you one of the fairy tales that they practised with their partner.
● Give the children copies of a fairy tale that you know they are not familiar with and ask them to find all the fairy-tale characters, features and language that they can.

Curriculum objectives
● To write down ideas and/ or key words, including new vocabulary.

Resources
Photocopiable page 'The Princess and the Shark' from the CD-ROM

Writing: A new fairy tale

Revise

● Challenge the children to create a list of all the elements they've found in a fairy tale – encourage them to think of characters, objects, events and language.

● Ask four different children to give you a number and count down the list to that number and write the four elements that have been selected. Use these elements to start to plan a new fairy tale. Assess what you have so far and ask: *Will these work? Do we need anything else?* Shape the elements to end up with a hero or heroine, a magic object and a villain.

● Ask the children to help you devise a story, discussing different options.

● Draw four large boxes on the board connected by arrows and ask: *What's going to happen first?* Model writing notes for setting the scene and starting the story off.

● Discuss the events for the second box – remind the children that it needs to follow on logically from the first box. Carry on and make notes for the story in the final two boxes.

● Ask different children to tell different parts of the story.

● Together assess what you have written and ask for suggestions for how it can be improved.

Assess

● Ask the children to plan out a new fairy tale.

● Hand out photocopiable page 'The Princess and the Shark' from the CD-ROM and ask the children to choose elements that they could use in their story. Which elements will they definitely not use and why?

● Ask the children to make notes for their story in four boxes connected by arrows. Ask them to use their plans to tell you their story.

● Ask them to comment on whether they feel that their story is a fairy tale. Ask them to assess whether it makes sense as a story and whether the events build logically on from each other.

Further practice

● Ask the children to rework their story following your comments and then write their story, incorporating fairy-tale language.

Fairy-tale elements

■ Cut out these fairy-tale element cards and place them face down on the table. Choose two cards and make up a fairy story that includes both elements.

talking frog	magic apple	magic beanstalk
big bad wolf	glass slipper	witch's house
midnight	magic mirror	magic lamp
trail of crumbs	troll	giant

Fairy-tale settings

■ Think of a fairy tale for each of these settings. Write two words to describe each setting.

_____   _____

_____   _____

_____   _____

_____   _____

_____   _____

_____   _____

I can describe a setting.

How did you do?

Fairy-tale events

■ Cut out these fairy-tale events and muddle them up. Place them upside down on the table and choose three cards at random. Make up a story including the three events.

Lost in woods
Find gingerbread house
Kill witch
Locked in tower
Throws down hair
Meets prince
Meets fairy in a wood
Given three wishes
Wishes for a sausage
Cursed by a bad fairy
Pricks her finger on a spinning wheel
Sleeps for 100 years
Is woken by a kiss

PHOTOCOPIABLE   **SCHOLASTIC**
www.scholastic.co.uk

Fairy-tale characters

■ Cut out these cards and choose two characters at random to use in your story.

How to make a paper aeroplane

■ Use these elements to write your own set of instructions for making a paper aeroplane. Cut out and use the diagrams, but write your own better versions of the instructions. Don't forget to add a title and a 'What you need' section.

1. Fold your piece of paper in half. Open it out again.

2. Fold two corners into the centre.

3. Fold these in again so that the folded edges come to the centre.

4. Fold the paper in half again.

5. Fold down the paper so that the folded edges meet the outside of the fold this time.

6. Open out this last fold half way.

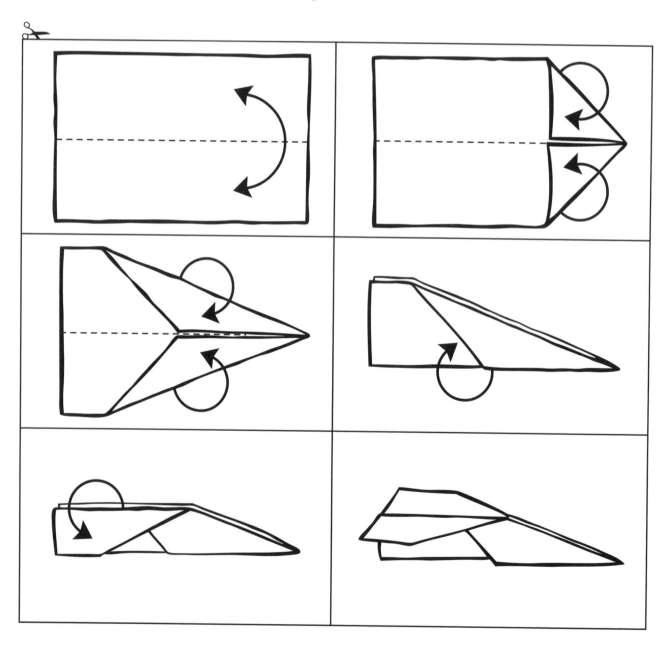

Past and present

- Cut out these verbs and match up the past and present.
- Use the cards to play a game of pairs. Take turns with your partner to turn over two cards. Keep any past and present pairs that you turn over. See who has the most pairs at the end.

talked	see	saw
ask	write	stop
stopped	run	ran
push	walked	wrote
wrap	knock	pushed
help	walk	knocked
learn	learned	wrapped
carry	carried	make
made	start	started
talk	helped	asked

Diary questions

■ Ask your partner these questions during the hot-seating lesson.

Who was there?

What happened?

How did you feel?

Can you remember what someone said?

What was the weather like?

What could you see?

What was the best or worst thing that happened?

What did other people do?

I can ask and answer questions.

How did you do?

Name: _____ Date: _____

Mixed-up nursery rhymes

■ Cut out the mixed-up cards and arrange them in the correct order to recreate three nursery rhymes.

Hey diddle diddle, The Cat and the fiddle, The Cow jumped over the moon,	Baa, baa, black sheep,
The little Dog laughed to see such sport, And the Dish ran away with the Spoon.	One for the master, One for the dame, And one for the little boy Who lives down the lane.
Up above the world so high,	Twinkle, twinkle, little star, How I wonder what you are.
Humpty Dumpty had a great fall. All the king's horses and all the king's men	Yes sir, yes sir, Three bags full.
Like a diamond in the sky. Twinkle, twinkle, little star, How I wonder what you are!	Humpty Dumpty sat on a wall,
Couldn't put Humpty together again	Have you any wool?

Zoo

This half term's zoo theme begins with children discussing their own zoo experiences, stimulated by initial reading of the book *Zoo* by Anthony Browne. They explore this book in detail, discussing the feelings of characters. A zoo visit (real or imaginary) is undertaken and children write a recount of this using subordination and coordination to join their sentences. They focus on their favourite animal and write a factfile about it. They draw and annotate a map of their zoo and then create information to display in a role-play version of this zoo, with individuals conducting guided tours. They read, learn, recite and enjoy poems about zoo animals, and put on a whole-class performance of group poems that they have written.

Expected prior learning
- Know how to combine sentences with *and*.
- Understand the features of a personal recount.
- Have some prior knowledge of conjunctions, suffixes, different sentence types, expanded noun phrases, homophones and spelling rules.
- Have some experience of zoos.
- Are able to use notes to plan writing.
- Know what a map is.
- Know the difference between fiction and non-fiction.

Overview of progression
- During this half term, children learn to read a story at different levels and discuss fiction and non-fiction books.
- They begin to discover conjunctions and use them in their own writing, and learn how to combine sentences using subordination and coordination.
- They are encouraged to see things from different viewpoints, and to ask questions about a text and use questions to improve their writing.
- They write and edit recounts.
- During poetry explorations they offer opinions, recite poems with confidence and use a range of homophones.

Creative context
- Express ideas creatively using paint and collage, drama, music and role-play
- Enhance their knowledge of the countries that zoo animals originate from.
- Understand some different animal habitats, simple animal classification and different animal features.
- Follow timelines and event sequences.

Preparation
Before the half term begins, ask the children to make internet searches for zoo information and help you to write or email two large zoos asking for leaflets to be sent to the school. If possible, arrange to take the children for a zoo visit. The book focused on this half-term is *Zoo* by Anthony Browne.

You will also need:
Individual whiteboards and pens; selection of books from different genres; coloured pens and pencils; small-world models of animals and people; large sheets of paper; card; string; paint; PVA glue; collage materials; large floor mats; camera; posters and leaflets of zoos; selection of different maps; fiction and non-fiction books or resources about zoos; images of animals; outdoor equipment; books and CDs of animal poems; internet access; percussion instruments; green and brown fabric, green curled tissue, brown wool; Blue-Tack®; selection of fiction books the children enjoy; scissors.

On the CD-ROM you will find:
Interactive activity 'Sorting and punctuating sentences'; photocopiable pages 'Zoo animals', 'Zoo enclosures', 'Zoo signs', 'Animal poems', 'I Went to the Farm'

■SCHOLASTIC

Chapter at a glance

An overview of the chapter. For curriculum objective codes, please see pages 8–10.

Week	Lesson	Curriculum objectives	Summary of activities	Outcome
1	1	RC: 9, 12, 14 WC: 15, 19	Discuss zoos and establish knowledge. Identify questions to be answered. Write key questions. Introduce *Zoo* and briefly discuss.	• Can ask appropriate questions. • Can write questions, punctuating accurately. • Can identify fiction and non-fiction books.
	2	RC: 7, 13, 14	Read *Zoo*. Discuss relationship between characters and animals. Predict what might happen and role play these predictions as scenarios using favourite words/phrases.	• Can discuss *Zoo*, and make predictions, becoming increasingly familiar with the story. • Can identify favourite words andphrases.
	3	RC: 1, 15	Explore illustrations in range of book genres. Explore illustrations in *Zoo* and consider how they enhance overall content of book.	• Can discuss views on book illustration across genres and explain their understanding of role of illustration in enhancing book content.
	4	WC: 16	Word game to revise use of *and*. Explore coordinating conjunctions. Make up clauses to extend sentences, joined by conjunctions.	• Can use *and* correctly in sentences. • Can identify coordinating conjunctions in text.
	5	RWR: 2 RC: 11, 12	Answer questions about *Zoo*. Explore and read alternative graphemes. Hot-seat to understand feelings through question and answer techniques.	• Can understand *Zoo* further by answering and asking questions, making inferences based on what is said and done. • Can read alternative graphemes.
2	1	RC: 2, 14	Discuss importance of sequence when remembering story. Sequence animals and events as they occur, by making masks and maps. Re-tell story using aids created.	• Can discuss *Zoo*, taking turns to speak and listen. • Can sequence events and retell through this. • Can establish how information is related.
	2	RC: 11	Explore *Zoo* illustrations. Depict how animals feel. Complete writing exercise involving choosing descriptive words.	• Can make inferences based on *Zoo* illustrations and comments by peers.
	3	RWR: 2 WT: 5, 7	Annotate animal pictures, spelling names of animals in *Zoo* correctly, recalling rules and guidelines, including possessive apostrophe.	• Can read and spell accurately taught graphemes and alternative graphemes. • Can use possessive apostrophe correctly.
	4	WC: 1, 5	Use thought-tracking to establish feelings of animals in *Zoo*. Use information gathered for story plans. Structure plan into separate sections.	• Can plan narrative story with clear structure based on experiences and story read. • Can consider different viewpoints of characters through group work.
	5	WC: 1, 7	Use plan from lesson 4 to rewrite story from animal's viewpoint. Understand need for complete sentences and strong story structure.	• Can rewrite a fictional story from different viewpoint after discussion with others. • Can encapsulate what they want to say in separate sentences.
3	1	WC: 5, 15, 17	Enjoy real or imaginary zoo visit. Make zigzag book recounting visit. Emphasis on interesting choice of words and use of past-tense endings.	• Can plan and say aloud what they will write about. • Can recount and event using the past tense.
	2	RWR: 4 WT: 7 WC: 5, 17, 19	Revise use of suffixes. Learn about noun suffixes. Use subordination and coordination to join sentences.	• Can discuss ideas for sentences. • Can read and write common suffixes. • Can use subordination and coordination to join sentences.
	3	RC: 9 WC: 2	Plan recount of zoo visit using template and own knowledge and photographs.	• Can develop understanding of books read using own experiences and given information. • Can plan recount of event.
	4	WC: 9, 10	Use plans and zigzag books to write first draft of recount. Write final draft and re-read to check sense. Proofread for errors.	• Can write final draft of recount. • Can re-read and proofread to check for sense and for verbs used consistently and correctly.
	5	RC: 9 WC: 16	Study zoo map and answer questions using subordination and coordination.	• Can use subordination and coordination in written responses to questions.
4	1	RC: 1, 12, 14	Find out facts about favourite zoo animals from range of sources. Discuss information and write fact cards based on this.	• Can take part in discussion. • Can read non-fiction to find information and answer questions to use in writing.
	2	RC: 1, 4, 14	Research favourite zoo animal. Discuss fiction and non-fiction as information sources. Create annotated pictures using facts gathered.	• Can explore range of information sources, especially different non-fiction books.
	3	RWR: 6 WC: 13, 16, 19	Join sentence captions from pictures using subordination and coordination. Identify different forms of sentence and add punctuation. Read familiar words quickly.	• Can use subordination and coordination. • Can use different forms of sentences and punctuation. • Can read familiar words quickly and accurately.
	4	WC: 4, 13, 16	Plan individual factfiles on chosen animals. Consider sentence forms and conjunctions.	• Plan a factfile. • Can use sentence forms for specific purposes.
	5	WC: 4, 13, 16	Write factfiles on chosen animals. Consider sentence forms and use of conjunctions.	• Can discuss role of subordination and coordination in creating more effective writing.

Chapter at a glance

Week	Lesson	Curriculum objectives	Summary of activities	Outcome
5	1	WC: 5, 16	Plan an imaginary zoo. Revise subordination and coordination through written exercise.	• Can consider what they write and plan writing. • Can use subordination and coordination.
	2	WC: 5, 18	Create zoo map with annotations using features of Standard English. Plan orally and write annotations for zoo map.	• Can use features of written Standard English. • Can consider, plan and say aloud what they are going to write.
	3	WT: 7 WC: 2, 14, 17	Plan written information for class zoo based on exploration of zoo literature. Use expanded noun phrases and suffixes to enhance written work.	• Can write based on recall of a real event. • Can use expanded noun phrases and suffixes in written work.
	4	WT: 11 WC: 18	Write zoo information documents. Revise letter formation and start to join letters.	• Can use correct letter formation. • Can join letters.
	5	WT: 11 WC: 8	Set up role-play zoo. Use written information on 'tours'. Write building and enclosure labels, attempting joining strokes. Evaluate writing.	• Can join letters. • Can evaluate writing with teacher and peers.
6	1	RC: 1, 7, 8	Listen, explore and recite poems and fictional rhymes. Appreciate rhythm and word choices. Discuss and identify favourite words or phrases.	• Can listen to and discuss poems. • Can recite some poetry by heart. • Can discuss favourite words and phrases.
	2	WT: 2, 6	Revisit poems introduced in lesson 1. Find homophones and homographs. Use in sentences. Learn new spellings. Discuss near homophones.	• Can use new ways of spelling phonemes. • Can use spelling and words in sentences, including common homophones.
	3	WC: 5, 6, 7	Plan a group poem about a favourite zoo animal. Discuss structure and content aloud. Refer to explored poems for structure ideas.	• Can write a plan using ideas and new vocabulary. • Can encapsulate within verses.
	4	WC: 3, 14	Write poem using plans and considering vocabulary and style. Emphasis on applying recent learning, for example, expanded noun phrases.	• Develop positive attitudes towards writing, using poetry as stimulus. • Can use expanded noun phrases.
	5	RC: 14 WC: 11	Put on class or school performance of group poems. Speak confidently with clear intonation. Discuss recitations constructively, taking turns and listening.	• Can read written work aloud, clearly and with appropriate intonation. • Can discuss poems read, waiting for turn to speak and listen.

Background knowledge

Coordinating conjunctions: Links two words or phrases together as an equal pair (*and, but*).

Homonym: Two different words that look exactly the same when written, and sound exactly the same when pronounced.

Homograph: Two different words that look exactly the same when written.

Homophone: Two different words that are pronounced the same.

Inference: Picking up information in a story that is not explicitly told but suggested through text and illustrations.

Standard English: The variety of the English language that is generally used for formal purposes in speech and writing. It is not the English of any particular region and it can be spoken with any accent.

Subordinating conjunctions: Introduces a subordinate clause (*when, because*).

Verbs in continuous form: Verbs which describe an action that continues, or was continuing at the time that is being spoken about – for example, *he is walking, he was walking*.

Week 1 lesson plans

This week children are introduced to the zoo theme. They discuss what they already know and extend their zoo knowledge. Anthony Browne's book *Zoo* is explored throughout the week. Children discuss characters and events, predict what might happen and identify favourite words and phrases. The word *and* is revised through a game, and exploring text helps the children to identify coordinating conjunctions and write sentences using them. Finally, understanding is assessed by asking and answering questions involving reading and discussing alternative graphemes, and by using hot-seat techniques.

Expected outcomes
● All children can talk about *Zoo* by Anthony Browne.
● Most children can understand how to combine sentences.
● Some children can read the story at different levels.

Curriculum objectives
● To answer and ask questions.
● To draw on what they already know or on background information and vocabulary provided by the teacher.
● To participate in discussion about books, poems and other works that are read to them and those that they can read for themselves, taking turns and listening to what others say.
● To use present and past tenses correctly and consistently including the progressive form.
● To use and understand the grammatical terminology in Appendix 2 in discussing their writing.

Resources
Zoo by Anthony Browne; individual whiteboards and pens

1: Discovering zoos

Introduction
● Write the word *zoo* on the board. Ask children to volunteer information about their experiences of visiting or reading about zoos.
● Model how to ask appropriate questions to extend information – for example, *How did the zookeepers make sure that the animal enclosures were similar to their homes in the wild?* Encourage children to answer if they can.
● Ensure whole-class engagement by asking children to clarify vocabulary, such as *enclosures*, with suitable alternative words.
● Encourage children to start asking and answering their own questions.

Whole-class work
● Decide on the key facts established and write these under the word *Zoos*.
● Beneath this, write *Things we would like to find out*, and add interesting facts the children would like to discover.

Paired work
● Provide pairs of children with a whiteboard and ask them to clearly write three more questions attempting to spell any unknown words.

Group work
● Ask pairs to form groups of six to share questions, discuss features chosen and make comments on questions asked.
● Encourage discussion about tenses used for the sentences, and whether correct suffixes have been added, for example, *living, lived*.

Independent work
● Provide individual whiteboards and ask each child to write down the question they would most like to be answered.
● Revise key sentence punctuation briefly before children begin, emphasising the inclusion of a question mark.
● Encourage individuals to consider if they will be writing their sentence in the present or past tense and the significance of suffixes.

Whole-class work
● Bring the class again together to introduce the book *Zoo*.
● Read the story and briefly talk about the experiences of the story family during their day at the zoo.
● Discuss the content and identify whether the book should be categorised as fiction or non-fiction, with reasons for choices.
● Invite children to say whether any of their questions have been answered by the book, and encourage them to ask relevant questions arising from it.

Review
● Ask individuals to read questions from their whiteboards and invite answers wherever possible.
● Focus on how and where answers to unanswered questions might be found.

Curriculum objectives
● To participate in discussion about books, poems and other works that are read to them and those that they can read for themselves, taking turns and listening to what others say.
● To predict what might happen on the basis of what has been read so far.
● To discuss their favourite words and phrases.

Resources
Zoo by Anthony Browne

2: Introducing *Zoo*

Introduction

● Recall lesson 1 discussions about the facts the children already knew about zoos and those they would like to discover.

Whole-class work

● Display the front cover of *Zoo* and read the title together. Explore the illustration of the four characters and ask questions to encourage children to recall things about them.
● Read the first paragraph on the back cover and discuss the notion that it might actually be the animals looking at the people rather than the other way round. Talk about what the animals might think of us as we wave, jump, clap and pull faces at them.
● Read the story, focusing on human and animal reactions and identifying favourite words and phrases, such as *Daylight robbery*.
● Draw five columns on the board headed *Mum, Dad, My brother, Me, Animals*. Invite children to write adjectives the author uses to describe characters and animals in the appropriate columns, for example, *angry, embarrassing, quiet*.

Group work

● Suggest that children role play interactions between the characters and animals, using adjectives and favourite words.

> **Differentiation**
> ● Support less confident children by joining them in character as they role play.

Review

● Bring the class together to re-enact their interactions and discuss how they think the story portrayed a new aspect of life in a zoo.

Curriculum objectives
● To listen to, discuss and express views about a wide range of contemporary and classic poetry, stories and non-fiction at a level beyond that at which they can read independently.
● To explain and discuss their understanding of books, poems and other material, both those that they listen to and those that they read for themselves.

Resources
Zoo by Anthony Browne; a selection of books from different genres such as comics, graphic novels and fairy tales; coloured pens and pencils

3: Effective illustrations

Introduction

● Invite children to bring in their own illustrated books from different genres (see Resources) and supplement these with examples from your class library.
● Ask children to show their books, commenting on the illustrations.
● Encourage discussion about variations in illustrations – for example, comic strip cartoons, line drawings, and black and white or coloured images.

Whole-class work

● Read *Zoo* and ask children for their initial impressions about the illustrations.
● Display the illustration of the traffic jam and discuss what can be learned from the illustration alone. Ask questions to encourage close observation.

Group work

● Ask groups to explore the illustration of the crowd watching the orang-utan.
● Create a freeze frame of the scene, with each child taking on a different role. Encourage close observation of facial expression and posture.

Independent work

● Provide materials for the children to create their own illustrations of a scene they have explored, focusing on facial expression and body language.

Review

● Invite groups to adopt their freeze frames for constructive comment by the class. Ask individuals to show and explain their illustrations. Discuss how the activity has helped raise awareness of how illustration enhances book content.

Curriculum objectives
● To use subordination (using *when*, *if*, *that* or *because*) and coordination (using *or*, *and* or *but*).

Resources
Zoo by Anthony Browne; individual whiteboards and pens

4: Coordinated conjunctions

Introduction
● Revise the use of *and* through a word game.
● Invite children to take turns to add an animal to a list in alphabetical order, for example, *I went to the zoo and saw an antelope.* The next child follows with, *I went to the zoo and saw an antelope and a baboon* and so on.

Whole-class work
● Display the first page of *Zoo* and ask the class to read the two sentences.
● Invite them to link these together with a joining word to make one sentence and write this on their individual whiteboards. Choose children to read out their sentences.
● As most children will use *and* as the joining word, try using other coordinating conjunctions, such as *or* and *but,* and decide whether they 'work'.
● Display the page beginning *We hadn't got a map of the zoo so we just wandered around.* Ask the children to read this sentence and identify the word that joins the two separate facts. Highlight the word (*so*). Do the same with the next sentence, highlighting *but.*

Group work
● Write five short sentences from the book on the board. Ask groups to compose another sentence to join to each one using a 'joining' word, and write this on their boards.

Review
● Gather the groups to share their extended sentences and discuss joining words.

Curriculum objectives
● To answer and ask questions.
● To make inferences on the basis of what is being said and done.
● To read accurately by blending the sounds in words that contain the graphemes taught so far, especially recognising alternative sounds for graphemes.

Resources
Zoo by Anthony Browne; individual whiteboards and pens

5: Question time

Introduction
● Ascertain the children's initial impressions when exploring the cover of *Zoo*, and how these have subsequently changed. For example, ask: *When you first read the book title, what did you think it might be about? How have your thoughts changed since exploring the book in more detail?*

Whole-class work
● Engage children's interest asking them to explain some of Dad's 'bad' jokes, for example the traffic jam and hot dog jokes, and to share some of their own.
● Extend this by encouraging them to use their existing knowledge of graphemes to read words before discussing meaning – for example, reading *you-know-who* and establishing who this refers to.
● Focus on finer detail by displaying and highlighting examples of alternative graphemes used, for example, the sentence *The ele**ph**ant just stood in a corner stu**ff**ing its **f**ace.*

Group work
● Encourage further understanding of the story and insight into characters by asking individuals to take turns to sit in the hot seat while the others question them about how they feel – for example, asking the boy to interpret the dream referred to on the last page or asking Mum why she always looks so sad.

Review
● Bring the class together to discuss the lesson's activities and how they have enhanced their reading skills and understanding of the story.

Curriculum objectives
- To participate in discussion about books, poems and other works that are read to them and those that they can read for themselves, taking turns and listening to what others say.
- To discuss the sequence of events in books and how items of information are related.

Resources
Zoo by Anthony Browne; small models of animals and people featured in *Zoo* by Anthony Browne; large sheets of paper; card; coloured pens; string; individual whiteboards and pens

Week 2 lesson plans

This week, children re-write *Zoo* from an animal viewpoint. They re-tell the story, using the appearance of animals to define the event sequence and creating masks and maps for role-play re-enactments. Discovering animal feelings is enhanced by exploring illustrations of animal actions and appearances, and children collect descriptive words to support ideas. Creating animal pictures, with labels and captions, involves spelling animal names correctly, recalling rules and guidelines, and including the possessive apostrophe. Thought-tracking helps to consider animal feelings in more depth and information gleaned is used for story plans. Children plan different versions of the story, told through the eyes of the animals. Finally stories are written, illustrated and shared with the class.

I: All in order

Introduction
- Ask children to take turns to write the name of an animal that might be found in a zoo on the board.
- Read *Zoo* and then ask the children to circle animals written on the board that also feature in this book.

Whole-class work
- Talk about how sequencing events helps us to remember a story. Recall fairy stories with definite sequences, such as 'Rumplestiltskin'.
- Invite suggestions about possible ways to help remember the sequence of *Zoo*, for example by listing the family's actions in order, such as getting stuck in a jam, buying tickets, eating and watching animals, or by remembering the order in which the animals appear.
- Consider the first suggestion and creating a pictorial map of the zoo depicting the animal enclosures and path taken by the family between them.
- Now consider the second idea. Sit around a pile of model animals and invite individuals to put them in a line to represent the order in which they appear in the book, starting with the elephant. Once everyone agrees the order, talk about each animal in turn, recalling facts given in the book, for example the orang-utan moping in the corner and the tiger pacing up and down.
- Ask children to choose between working in a group of nine to make individual masks or name bands representing the animals in the story, or in fours to create a large pictorial map.

Group work
- Provide those making masks and bands with suitable materials and support with techniques, such as forming a strip to fit around the head with the animal name on the front.
- Ask the children to each compose two sentences about the animal they represent and write these on their whiteboard, for example, *I am a baboon. I sometimes fight with other baboons.*
- Suggest that they now arrange themselves in order, wearing their identity masks and bands, and practise saying their sentences in order.
- Provide those making maps with large sheets of paper, a range of creative materials and model people and animals.
- Invite them to annotate their maps, for example by numbering the points where the family stopped and writing a short caption.
- Encourage them to move the model characters across the map and make up dialogue as they go along.

Review
- Invite groups to wear masks and perform their animal sentences to the class, or to tell the story using their maps as a story aid.

2: Actions and moods

Curriculum objectives
● To make inferences on the basis of what is being said and done.

Resources
Zoo by Anthony Browne; photocopiable page 104 'Actions and moods'

Introduction
● Recall the previous lesson when children explored the sequence of animals appearing in Zoo. Explain that this lesson is about discovering what the illustrations tell us about how the animals might feel.

Whole-class work
● Re-read Zoo, pausing to display animal illustrations as they appear.
● Draw four columns on the board: Appearances, Actions, Moods, Enclosures.
● Take each column in turn, asking children to suggest and write appropriate words in it – for example, tall elegant (giraffes), endless pacing (tigers), serious (gorilla), angry (baboons) and bare boring (the orang-utan enclosure).
● Discuss how illustrations can reflect how animals are feeling, for example the sad orang-utan sitting miserably in a bare enclosure.
● Display photocopiable page 104 'Actions and moods' and work through the first row together, writing in children's suggested words.

Paired work
● Provide pairs of children with the photocopiable sheet to complete.
● Encourage them to discuss their ideas orally before writing them down.

> **Differentiation**
> ● Provide less confident learners with simple 'mood' words on cards, such as happy, sad, lonely, angry. Ask them to match them to the book's animal illustrations.

Review
● Invite pairs to share some of their words with the class. Discuss how listening to the ideas of others extends their own word choices.

3: Follow the rules

Curriculum objectives
● To apply spelling rules and guidelines, as listed in Appendix 1.
● To read accurately by blending the sounds in words that contain the graphemes taught so far, especially recognising alternative sounds for graphemes.
● To learn the possessive apostrophe (singular).

Resources
Zoo by Anthony Browne; coloured paper; paint; PVA glue; collage items such as textured and animal print fabric scraps; thick card

Introduction
● Read Zoo and recall the featured animals. Discuss their appearances, actions and moods.

Whole-class work
● Ask children to call out the names of the animals. Write them on the board.
● Compare the spelling of the phoneme /f/ in elephant and giraffe. Consider the spelling of other animal names using alternative graphemes for this phoneme, such as laughing hyena and fox.
● Discuss the difference in sound made by the letter 'g' in the words giraffe, penguin and orang-utan. Recall the rule for the changing of sound from /g/ to /j/ when followed by 'i', 'e' or 'y'.
● Ask children to identify key features from the illustrations, such as the baboon's teeth and tiger's stripes. Invite them to write these on the board, using the possessive apostrophe.

Paired work
● Suggest that pairs create a picture of an animal. Provide materials to enable the creation of interesting textures.
● Ask them to write sentences about their animal, for example, Look at the baboon's teeth. Emphasise correct spelling and use of possessive apostrophes.
● Glue the sentences around the picture.

Review
● Bring the class together to show the pictures. Comment on correct spelling and apostrophe use.

Curriculum objectives
● To write narratives about personal experiences and those of others (real and fictional).
● To plan or say out loud what they are going to write about.

Resources
Zoo by Anthony Browne; large floor mats

4: Story planning

Introduction

● Identify whose viewpoint Zoo is told from. Consider how the story would change if told from the viewpoints of the animals.

Whole-class work

● Gather in the hall and explain that this lesson involves planning a new version of the story, as told by the animals.
● Introduce mats representing animal enclosures. Identify the zoo entrance and label each mat to represent an animal enclosure in story order.

Group work

● Choose four children to represent the family and divide the rest of the class into eight groups, allocating an 'animal enclosure' to each one.
● Ask groups to think about how their animals might be feeling. Use thought-tracking to identify ideas, with an individual in role as an animal while others touch their shoulder and ask how they feel. Discuss the different thoughts.
● Ask the family to walk around listening to the animals' thoughts.

Paired work

● Back in the classroom, ask pairs to start planning the new version of the story based on the group work in the hall.
● Encourage them to discuss sentence structure, dialogue and illustrations.

Review

● Ask children to share their plans and some of the vocabulary used. Discuss how thought-tracking improved understanding of the views of animals.

Curriculum objectives
● To write narratives about personal experiences and those of others (real and fictional).
● To encapsulate what they want to say, sentence by sentence.

Resources
Zoo by Anthony Browne; children's plans from the previous lesson; paper of different sizes; coloured pens and pencils; card

5: This is our zoo

Introduction

● Write Beginning, Middle and End as headings on the board. Consider the role of each heading in shaping a story.

Whole-class work

● Read the opening sentence of Zoo. Talk about how this might change if written from an animal viewpoint. Write suggestions under Beginning.
● Read a sentence from the middle and end of the book, changing each to reflect an animal viewpoint and writing it down.

Paired work

● In the same pairs as the previous lesson, ask individuals to write their stories under the three headings on the board. Provide them with their plans, and emphasise the need to write in sentences. Briefly revise spelling rules.
● Suggest that they read and discuss each section with their partner, before deciding to make any alterations.

Independent work

● If time allows, suggest that children illustrate their stories, before sticking their writing and pictures to larger pages.

> **Differentiation**
> ● Support children to draw three pictures in order and write a sentence about each one.

Review

● Ask individuals to read their stories and show their illustrations. Invite constructive comments from the class.

Week 3 lesson plans

This week the children enjoy a real or imaginary zoo visit and make a zigzag book. They revise suffixes and learn about noun suffixes, writing them in sentences. Subordination is introduced, and coordination recalled, and used to join sentences. Children plan a zoo visit recount using a template, their own knowledge and photographs. Plans are used to write the first draft of the recount before the final draft is completed, followed by re-reading to check sense and proofreading for errors. Finally children explore maps and study a zoo map. They use information provided to answer related questions, focusing on using subordination and coordination and the grammar of word structure.

Expected outcomes
● All children can write and edit a recount.
● Most children can write and edit a recount, drawing on grammar of word structure.
● Some children can write and edit a recount, drawing on grammar of word structure and using feedback to improve their work.

Curriculum objectives
● To plan or say out loud what they are going to write about.
● To use the grammar for Year 2 in Appendix 2.
● To use the present and past tenses correctly and consistently including the progressive form.

Resources
If you are unable to visit a zoo, create a zoo in the classroom using the photocopiable pages 'Zoo animals', 'Zoo enclosures' and 'Zoo signs' from the CD-ROM; a zigzag book for each child (created by folding strips of landscape A3 paper into four sections); black and coloured pens; cameras; posters and leaflets of zoos; a name for your zoo written on the board; a picnic

1: Visiting the zoo

Introduction
● Go on a trip to the zoo, or create a zoo in the classroom using the resources on the CD-ROM. Further research could be carried out using zoo websites, who occasionally have live webcams of their enclosures. Encourage children to observe animal appearances and actions carefully and take photographs (even in the classroom zoo).
● On return, share experiences of the trip. Recall real or imagined events in order, writing these as sentences on the board.

Whole-class work
● Revise the meaning of *verb*. Invite individuals to circle a verb on the board until all verbs have been identified. Talk about how the trip happened in the past so that these verbs are in the past tense. Point to their '-ed' endings.
● Invite children to suggest other verbs to describe what they did, and include examples of your own.
● Consider all the different noises the children made at the zoo: *whispered, gasped, giggled, screamed, cried* and so on. Discuss how some of these verbs conjure up a more lasting impression of the day.
● Review the verb choices in the sentences on the board and decide whether they could be improved.
● Consider some unusual verbs chosen by the author of *Zoo*, for example *snarled, snorted, whined*, and talk about the 'mind's eye' picture they create.
● Show children a zigzag book and explain that it is for planning a recount of your zoo trip. Choose four key verbs, for example *watched, ate, smelled, laughed*, and model writing one verb in each section.

Group work
● Organise children into groups and ask questions to recall the events in *Zoo*.
● Now invite children to decide on the six most interesting or fun things that they did at the zoo, asking questions to motivate discussion, for example: *Which animal made you go 'Wow'? Which animal was the tiniest?*
● Tell them to put these six events in chronological order, noting an interesting verb for each one and trying to improve the verbs as they go along.

Independent work
● Give each child a zigzag book and ask them to choose four verbs from their group discussion and write one in each section.

Differentiation
● Support children to identify which word is the verb by asking: *What did you do when that happened?*

Review
● Bring the class together to share their zigzag books. Encourage constructive comments about planning and sentence structure.

Curriculum objectives
● To plan or say out loud what they are going to write about.
● To add suffixes to spell longer words.
● To read words containing common suffixes.
● To use subordination (using *when, if, that,* or *because*) and coordination (using *or, and,* or *but*).
● To use the grammar for Year 2 in Appendix 2.
● To use and understand the grammatical terminology in Appendix 2 in discussing their writing.

Resources
Zoo by Anthony Browne; photocopiable page 105 'Adding suffixes'

2: Adding suffixes

Introduction

● Talk about how suffixes can change the tense of verbs or create adjectives that compare, for example size and height.
● Find examples of verb suffixes in *Zoo* and note how they denote past tense.
● Ask children to think of sentences using comparative adjectives, for example: *This giraffe is the tallest.*
● Introduce the concept of forming nouns using suffixes, giving examples, such as *happiness* and *embarrassment*. Model theses in sentences from the story.

Whole-class work

● Revise coordination by writing short sentences on the board and joining them with *or, and* or *but.*
● Introduce subordination by writing this sentence on the board: *We are going to the zoo.* Add the word *when* and ask the children to suggest ways of completing the sentence.
● Repeat with the same sentence and the words *if, because* and *that.*

Independent work

● Provide each child with photocopiable page 105 'Adding suffixes' to complete. Work through the first sentence together so that children understand what to do.

Differentiation
● Help those less confident learners by providing a simplified version of the sheet using only familiar taught suffixes.

Review

● Work through the photocopiable sheet with the class for self-correction. Invite comments on whether this lesson developed their understanding of suffixes and 'joining words'.

Curriculum objectives
● To draw on what they already know or on background information and vocabulary provided by the teacher.
● To write about real events.

Resources
Zoo by Anthony Browne; children's zigzag books from lesson 1; photographs taken on real or imaginary zoo visit (or suitable internet images); photocopiable page 106 'Planning a recount'

3: Planning a recount

Introduction

● Suggest that children plan a zoo visit recount. Recap key recount features, for example discussion, planning, past tense, fact not fiction.

Whole-class work

● Explore your zoo visit photographs (or suitable website images).
● Invite children to arrange them in a timeline along the floor.
● Ask questions to establish a time sequence.
● Display photocopiable page 106 'Planning a recount' and work through the questions, asking children to write appropriate words in the boxes, for example: *When? – last Wednesday, Who? – the whole class.*
● Revise aspects of sentence structure, for example coordination and subordination. Emphasise that this should not result in long lists such as: *We had an ice-cream and saw an elephant and went to the giraffe house and...*
● Write examples of endings that change words from present to past, for example: *The giraffe was stretch**ing**.* Consider comparative suffixes, such as: *One baboon was funny, another was funnier, but the baby was the funniest.*

Independent work

● Provide each child with the photocopiable sheet to complete.

Review

● Invite the class to share their plans.

4: Writing a recount

Introduction
- Explain to the children that they will be writing recounts using their planning sheets and zigzag books to help.
- Recap on previous discussions about the need for past tense and appropriate suffixes in recounts.
- Discuss how expanded noun phrases can add interest and detail to a recount. Work through appropriate examples, such as changing *The boys enjoyed watching the baboons* to *The oldest boys in our group enjoyed watching the angry fighting monkeys.*

Whole-class work
- Display photocopiable page 106 'Planning a recount' and fill it in using children's ideas and your own examples. Leave this on display.
- Recall that the zigzag books identified the sequence of key events.

Paired work
- Provide pairs with their completed planning sheets and zigzag books. Suggest they use these as support as they discuss writing their recounts.
- Ask them to write a first draft and ask their partner for comments.

Independent work
- Allow time for individuals to re-read and proofread their work, checking spelling and considering ways to improve content, for example with expanded noun phrases, before writing a final draft.

Review
- Ask individuals to read their recounts to the class. Praise effective use of verbs indicating time and expanded noun phrases.

Curriculum objectives
- To re-read to check that their writing makes sense and that verbs to indicate time are used correctly and consistently, including verbs in the continuous form.
- To proofread to check for errors in spelling, grammar and punctuation.

Resources
Photocopiable page 106 'Planning a recount'; children's zigzag books from lesson 1 and completed versions of photocopiable sheet; card

5: Map it out

Introduction
- Ask children to recall experiences of themselves or others using maps.
- Show the maps and invite children to decide which to use for specific purposes, such as walking to a friend's house or driving to a hotel.

Whole-class work
- Display the zoo map and discuss presentation – for example, a pictorial layout with animal enclosures, paths, cafés and toilets included.
- Discuss what can be learned from this map – for example, how different types of animals are grouped and where we can buy snacks.
- Pose questions, for example: *How can I get to the toilets from the baboon house?* Encourage children to give full answers, using subordination or coordination to connect ideas: *Go along the path towards the penguins **because** the toilets are just next to them.*

Group work
- Provide similar-ability groups with a copy of the map, individual whiteboards and a list of questions you have devised, for example: *How can I get from the lion house to the penguin enclosure?*
- Ask them to take turns to scribe the group answers on their boards, asking an adult to scribe for those who struggle. Encourage full answers as above.

Review
- Invite the class to share answers to the questions. Invite comments on effective use of information.

Curriculum objectives
- To use subordination (using *when, if, that,* or *because*) and coordination (using *or, and,* or *but*).
- To draw on what they already know or on background information and vocabulary provided by the teacher.

Resources
A selection of different maps, such as road maps, ordnance survey maps, pictorial maps, atlases, street maps, zoo map from visit or downloaded from website; individual whiteboards and pens; large pieces of paper; coloured and black pens

Curriculum objectives
● To listen to, discuss and express views about a wide range of contemporary and classic poetry, stories and non-fiction at a level beyond that at which they can read independently.
● To answer and ask questions.
● To participate in discussion about books, poems and other works that are read to them and those that they can read for themselves, taking turns and listening to what others say.

Resources
Non-fiction books and resources about zoo animals, such as *100 Animals to Spot at the Zoo* (Information Cards published by Usborne); accurate, small zoo animal models; examples of information cards (such as recipe cards and seed growing instruction cards); photocopiable page 'Animals factsheet' from the CD-ROM; computer access; individual whiteboards and pens; paper; card; coloured and black pens and pencils

Week 4 lesson plans

This week children find out facts about favourite zoo animals from a range of sources. They read non-fiction and discuss information before writing fact cards. A favourite zoo animal is chosen and research undertaken, emphasising the importance of non-fiction as an information source. Pictures of the animal are created, with captions that use subordination and coordination. Children identify different forms of sentences and add punctuation. They write for a purpose by planning and writing individual factfiles on a chosen animal.

I: Fact finders

Introduction
● Recall the recent zoo visit and invite the children to list the animals that they saw. Write these as a list on the board, using commas to separate them. Add other zoo animals that the children are familiar with. Save the list for later.

Whole-class work
● Explain that animals in zoos can be sorted into different categories, and describe a *category* as a group of things sharing common features.
● Display photocopiable page 'Animals factsheet' from the CD-ROM and read the headings. Invite children to categorise the animals they saw at the zoo, and others they are familiar with, by writing them in the correct box on this sheet.
● Ask them to read the key features of each category to check that their animal shares these common features.
● Discuss any wording that children find unfamiliar, for example *warm-blooded* and *cold-blooded*, and talk about what these expressions mean.
● Invite children to suggest other sources of information about zoo animals, such as non-fiction books, models and websites. Explain that they are going to use these resources, along with the factsheet, to create fact cards about their own favourite animals.
● Show an example of a fact card (see Resources). Discuss the information contained and the way it is presented.

Group work
● Provide the children with access to computers, individual whiteboards, zoo animal resources, the photocopiable sheet and non-fiction books. Provide each group the photocopiable factsheet and display the animal list from earlier.
● Suggest that mixed-ability groups choose a joint favourite zoo animal they would like to find out more about.
● Show the bank of resources that they can use.
● Encourage them to ask and answer questions about what they read and want to know, and decide the form their fact cards will take, perhaps a labelled drawing followed by facts written as sentences.
● Recall features of effective sentence structure and give examples, for example of an expanded noun phrase that injects interesting information.
● Ask them to allocate tasks to individuals or pairs, for example: making illustrations, gathering facts from books, researching websites.
● Try out some layouts on paper before creating the finished fact cards.

Differentiation
● Help less confident children to write names of very familiar animals.
● Challenge groups of more confident children to find strange animals in books, such as the pink fairy armadillo or clown frogfish, and create a series of cards about them.

Review
● Display the completed fact cards for children to browse. Bring them together to discuss what they have learned by reading book information and cards created by other groups.

2: Focus on a favourite

Curriculum objectives
● To listen to, discuss and express views about a wide range of contemporary and classic poetry, stories and non-fiction at a level beyond that at which they can read independently.
● To be introduced to non-fiction books that are structured in different ways.
● To participate in discussion about books, poems and other works that are read to them and those that they can read for themselves, taking turns and listening to what others say.

Resources
Non-fiction and fiction books about the children's chosen zoo animal, such as *Elephants* by James Maclaine, *The Elephant's Child* by Rudyard Kipling; animal models; internet images and clips of the chosen animal; large sheets of card; creative materials such as paint and collage items

Preparation
● Ask children to write their favourite zoo animal on a piece of paper and put it in a hat. Create a tally on the board and establish the class favourite.
● Prepare information resources about this animal.

Introduction
● Discuss information resources they used in the previous lesson.
● Explain that you have gathered similar resources about the favourite animal decided by the class.

Whole-class work
● Read a fiction book from your resources. Discuss whether the information given could be considered accurate.
● Share pages from a non-fiction book, looking at illustrations and commenting on interesting facts.
● Decide if fiction or non-fiction books provide the most accurate information.

Group work
● Invite each group to create a large, accurate picture of the chosen animal.
● Allow time for exploration of models, books, websites, materials and techniques before creating the picture.
● Discuss and decide upon important facts to add as sentence captions and labels. Write these on paper and stick them to the picture.

Review
● Ask the groups to display their pictures in the style of an art gallery. Share opinions about which provide the most effective information.

3: Sorting and punctuating sentences

Curriculum objectives
● To use subordination (using *when, if, that, or because*) and *coordination* (using *or, and, or but*).
● To use sentences with different forms: statement, question, exclamation, command.
● To read most words quickly and accurately, without overt sounding and blending, when they have been frequently encountered.
● To use and understand the grammatical terminology in Appendix 2 in discussing their writing.

Resources
Children's animal pictures from the previous lesson; photocopiable page 108 'Sorting and punctuating sentences'; interactive activity 'Sorting and punctuating sentences' on the CD-ROM; individual whiteboards and pens

Introduction
● Recall previous lessons involving joining words (subordinations and coordinations), and provide an example of a sentence involving each one.
● Explore the children's pictures from the previous lesson and read some of their sentence captions.
● Decide whether any of these sentence captions could be joined using conjunctions, writing examples on the board.

Whole-class work
● Recall different sentence forms, for example questions, statements, commands and exclamations, and invite children's examples for each one. Identify the different punctuation used at the end.
● Display photocopiable page 108 'Sorting and punctuating sentences' (or use the interactive version on the CD-ROM) and work through the first example. Decide the form of sentence and write this in the column at the side. Invite individuals to complete the punctuation.

Paired work
● Provide pairs with the photocopiable sheet for completion.

> **Differentiation**
> ● Provide less confident children with simpler statements and questions to punctuate.

Review
● Reassemble the class. Display the photocopiable sheet on the board and go through it together, asking pairs to check each other's work.

Curriculum objectives
● To use subordination (using *when*, *if*, *that*, or *because*) and coordination (using *or*, *and*, or *but*).
● To use sentences with different forms: statement, question, exclamation, command.
● To write for different purposes.

Resources
Photocopiable page 109 'Animal factfile'; children's work on animals including their zigzag books, fact cards and pictures; previous non-fiction books and resources related to animals; individual whiteboards and pens

4: Writing a factfile (1)

Introduction
● Recall previous individual and group research and explain that children are now going to compile more detailed factfiles about an animal of their choice.
● Talk about resources already used and establish what children liked best about them. Consider how information should be presented.
● Make a list of features to show how information can be made interesting, for example: colourful pictures, lively sentences joined with conjunctions and so on.
● Emphasise the importance of exploring non-fiction books for this purpose.

Whole-class work
● Display photocopiable page 109 'Animal factfile' and suggest that children use this as a plan to compile facts they wish to include.
● Consider the value of transforming the page headings into questions and then answering them underneath, for example: *Where does a penguin live?*

Paired work
● Divide the class into pairs who have decided to create factfiles about the same animal so that they can pool ideas.
● Provide each child with the photocopiable sheet to fill in.
● Once this plan is completed, suggest that children make notes about how they can make their factfile more attractive.

Review
● Bring children together to discuss this initial planning and exchange ideas.

Curriculum objectives
● To use subordination (using *when*, *if*, *that*, or *because*) and coordination (using *or*, *and*, or *but*).
● To use sentences with different forms: statement, question, exclamation, command.
● To write for different purposes.

Resources
Children's completed versions of photocopiable page 109 'Animal factfile' and their work on animals including their zigzag books, fact cards and pictures; previous non-fiction books and resources related to animals; individual whiteboards and pens

5: Writing a factfile (2)

Introduction
● Recall planning the factfiles. Explain that these plans will help when completing the final factfiles and preparing them for display in this lesson.
● Recap things the children should remember, for example to include sentences with different forms and to join sentences with conjunctions.

Whole-class work
● Revise different sentence forms by asking children about those they plan to include in their factfiles.
● Invite examples of statements of facts, and of questions that introduce sections.
● Talk about the use of commands, such as: *Visit your local zoo to find out more.*
● Consider using exclamations and cartoon-like drawings when emphasising unusual facts, for example, *A lion's teeth work like scissors!*

Paired work
● Provide children with their completed versions of photocopiable page 109 'Animal factfile' and access to other resources. Explain that they are going to produce a neat factfile based on this material.
● Suggest that they finish a section at a time and discuss it with their partner. Allow time to modify sentences after these discussions.
● Ask children to aim to write at least three sentences for each section. Support struggling pairs with this where necessary.
● Invite individuals to compile their work into a book or file with extras, such as illustrations and an attractive cover, before reading them to partners.

Review
● Display the factfiles for class exploration. Discuss how previous lessons have influenced the way the children have presented their files.

Week 5 lesson plans

This week the children plan an imaginary zoo, considering aloud what they will write. They learn to use subordination and coordination when writing sentences about their zoo, and create a zoo map using features of Standard English. Zoo information is planned and written, based on actual zoo literature. Children are encouraged to use expanded noun phrases and suffixes to enhance written work. They revise taught letter formation, start using diagonal and horizontal strokes to join letters, and understand which letters are better left separate. Finally, they set up a role-play version of their zoo, writing building and enclosure labels and using their written information on guided tours. This writing is then evaluated by teacher and peers.

1: Opening a zoo

Introduction
● Recall discussions from previous weeks about zoos and their key features.
● Suggest that the children consider opening a zoo of their own. Ask them to think about the animals and the facilities needed to care for them.

Whole-class work
● Suggest choosing an outdoor space within the school site and imagining how a school zoo could be created within it.
● Display photocopiable page 110 'Our zoo plan' on the board and discuss.
● Ask children to consider the variety of animals to be introduced, perhaps they would like to focus on large animals, or maybe they would like to include pet animals. Invite children to come and write their suggestions in this box.
● Adopt the same approach for the remaining boxes.
● Discuss types of enclosures and animal houses, considering animal needs, such as somewhere to swim, play, burrow or climb.
● Recall *Zoo* and refer to this when deciding essential facilities for visitors, such as toilets and first aid posts. Use past experience of zoo visits to add facilities such as cafés, ice-cream and hot dog stalls.
● Ask children to think of people who work at the zoo, such as keepers, first aid officers and ticket booth supervisors.
● Use research into animal diets to decide the foods that would be needed.
● Discuss how labels, signs, captions, questions and informative sentences created additional learning opportunities during the class and family zoo visits.
● Recall the role of questions on signs, followed by informative answers. Recap the use of conjunctions to extend sentences and explain statements.
● Display photocopiable page 111 'Using subordination' and read through the instructions. Explain that this revision page will help them when they write the sentences for their zoo. Work through the first example together.

Paired work
● Divide children into pairs and provide them with photocopiable page 111 'Using subordination'. Discuss possible ways of making the sentences more interesting.
● Invite individuals to fill in their own pages before reading them to one another to check that they make sense.

> **Differentiation**
> ● Support less confident learners by creating a simplified version of the photocopiable sheet that includes the conjunction, for example: *This lion is in a cage because....* Ask children to finish the sentence orally first and help with spelling as they write.

Review
● Gather the class together to read out their versions of the sentences. Discuss how expanding sentences can introduce and clarify new words and facts.

Expected outcomes
● All children will devise a plan for a real event.
● Most children will generate more than one idea and make a selection, then develop it into information.
● Some children will choose a plan from a selection of ideas, giving reasons for their choice, and develop it into information which they review with the teacher and other children.

Curriculum objectives
● To plan or say out loud what they are going to write about.
● To use subordination (using when, if, that, or because) and coordination (using or, and, or but).

Resources
Photocopiable pages 110 'Our zoo plan' and 111 'Using subordination'; individual whiteboards and pens

Curriculum objectives
● To use some features of written Standard English.
● To plan or say out loud what they are going to write about.

Resources
Zoo map from the class visit or downloaded from website; photocopiable page 110 'Our zoo plan'; individual whiteboards and pens; large pieces of paper; coloured and black pens

2: Zoo maps

Introduction
● Display the zoo map from the class visit (week 3). Recall identifying features and following routes between enclosures.
● Discuss the need for a visitor zoo map. Suggest that groups of children design different versions for their school zoo.

Whole-class work
● Begin a list of things suggested by children to include on the map.
● Point out the displayed map annotations, such as labels and signs. Discuss what the children might include in their maps.
● Comment on the displayed map design. Emphasise the need for clear writing with correct word choices, grammar, punctuation and spelling.
● Display photocopiable page 110 'Our zoo plan'. Suggest children use this to write down possible annotations, such as labels and sentence captions.

Group work
● Provide mixed-ability groups with large pieces of paper and photocopiable page 110 'Our zoo plan'. Display the zoo map for reference.
● Suggest children draw a pencil plan of the zoo, marking key features.
● Once they are happy with this, they can use the photocopiable sheet to write down proposed annotations. Remind them to check that these are presented correctly.
● Allow time for modification before creating their final versions.

Review
● Ask groups to explain their maps and annotations. Encourage class comments on what works and what needs improving.

Curriculum objectives
● To write about real events.
● To use expanded noun phrases to describe and specify.
● To use the grammar for Year 2 in Appendix 2.
● To add suffixes to spell longer words.

Resources
Examples of zoo leaflets, guides and other written information; children's written sources of zoo information such as factfiles, maps and zigzag books; sheets of coloured and white paper; coloured pens

3: Planning visitor information

Introduction
● Explore the zoo information. Recall the need for attractive images and good clear written English.
● Suggest that children provide written information for visitors to their zoo.

Whole-class work
● Discuss the different forms their information might take. Make a list of children's suggestions and some of your own. Leave this list on display.
● Focus on relevant aspects of written English recently explored, for example expanded noun phrases to describe an animal in detail, and use of suffixes such as *excitement, enjoyment, happiness*. Encourage children to give examples of sentences that they might include in their writing using these features.

Group work
● Give groups a written information item from the displayed list. They can then plan how to present this information.
● Show groups the bank of resources for reference and ask them to include proposed sentences in their plan.

> **Differentiation**
> ● Distribute information items according to group ability – for example, challenge a group to create a guide book or ask a group requiring support to compile a menu.

Review
● Ask groups to present their finished plans to the class and read out some of their proposed sentences. Discuss whether information was presented clearly.

4: Writing visitor information

Introduction
● Emphasise the need to present information clearly. Revise basic letter formation, reminding children of the handwriting families. Invite individuals to write examples of letters with different strokes ('j', 'd', 'c', and 'z').

Whole-class work
● Write a short sentence using joined letters on the board. Point out some of the diagonal and horizontal strokes needed to join letters and discuss which letters, when adjacent to one another, are better left separate.
● Encourage confident writers to try using joining strokes in their writing.

Group work
● Return to the same groups as the previous lesson and provide children with their plans and access to the other resources.
● Invite them to begin their information documents, taking turns to write the sentences. Allow time to add modifications, illustrations and decorations.
● When they have finished, ask them to check their work for correct letter formation, spelling and punctuation.

> **Differentiation**
> ● Encourage less confident children to focus on correct letter formation and spelling, for example of items on their menu. Suggest they decorate the menu with suitable designs.

Review
● Display the group written information texts for class exploration. Encourage discussion about clear content and presentation. Praise attempts to join letters.

5: Zoo tours

Introduction
● Recall the class work linked to the imaginary zoo. Remind children of the original concept of a school zoo.

Whole-class work
● Look at the maps created by groups and make a class decision about which map has the most interesting zoo layout.

Group work
● Go outside to the 'zoo area', taking the chosen map. Ask children to work with the groups they were in to write their information documents.
● Allocate the areas on the map to different groups.
● Ask groups to make use of the apparatus to create enclosures and buildings, and to write name labels indicating the purpose, for example: *Lion house, Zoo café*. Emphasise that these labels must be easy to read, with correct letter formation. Suggest that they might like to try joining up some of the letters.
● Hang the labels and information documents in appropriate areas of the zoo.
● Ask group members to take turns to be a zoo guide conducting the rest of the group on a zoo tour. Encourage them to read labels and discuss information on documents along the way.

Review
● Bring the class together to discuss the effectiveness of their written information, including the enclosure and building labels. Encourage them to focus on clarity, content and correct letter formation. Discuss how they could extend the visitor information for future tours.

Curriculum objectives
● To listen to, discuss and express views about a wide range of contemporary and classic poetry, stories and non-fiction at a level beyond that at which they can read independently.
● To continue to build up a repertoire of poems learned by heart, appreciating these and reciting some, with appropriate intonation to make the meaning clear.
● To discuss their favourite words and phrases.

Resources
A range of books containing poems about animals and zoos; fiction books written in rhyme, including one rhyming animal story by Julia Donaldson; CDs of poems for children; internet access; photocopiable page 'Animal poems' from the CD-ROM; individual whiteboards and pens; percussion instruments

Week 6 lesson plans

This week children listen, explore and recite poems, identifying favourite words and phrases and expressing views. Homonyms are introduced, with the meaning of *homophone*, *near homophone* and *homograph* discussed. Children use these kinds of words in sentences. They plan a group poem about a favourite zoo animal, discussing structure and content, and saying what they are going to write. They are encouraged to encapsulate ideas within sentences and verses. The poem is then written, with emphasis on applying recent learning – for example, using new vocabulary and expanded noun phrases. Children develop positive attitudes towards writing, using poetry as stimulus. A class or school performance of these poems is organised, placing emphasis on speaking confidently with clear intonation.

1: Zoo poems

Introduction

● Encourage children to recall familiar stories and poems featuring animals, particularly those found in zoos. Invite volunteers to recite these poems.
● Read a favourite book featuring rhyming text about animal characters by Julia Donaldson. Identify memorable repeated lines children particularly enjoy. Consider the role of rhyme and rhythm in fiction.

Whole-class work

● Visit the Julia Donaldson website to hear clips of Julia singing songs (www.juliadonaldson.co.uk). Discuss which ones the children like best and why.
● Explore websites to find other clips of poets reading their work. Listen to audio readings with closed eyes and discuss images 'in the mind's eye'.
● Display the photocopiable page 'Animal poems (1)' from the CD-ROM and read 'Guess Who!'. Look at the poem shape and discuss the regular structure. Identify words and phrases that provide clues to the animal's identity.
● Circle rhyming words at the end of alternate lines and discuss how they create a strong rhythm. Read the poem together, clapping to accentuate these words. Now clap two beats in every line, saying the word at the end loudly.
● Repeat this as you march in crocodile fashion, beating instruments.

Group work

● Provide photocopiable pages 'Animal poems (1)' and 'Animal poems (2)' from the CD-ROM. Remind children that poems do not always rhyme.
● Suggest that children read 'At the Zoo' together. Invite them to decide whether this poem was written recently or a long time ago. Suggest they look for clues, such as the words *mutton*, *maw*, *mercy* and *a-waving*.
● Ask them to clap the beats of each line. Discuss what happens at the end. Consider why the poet changes the pattern and rhyming structure.
● Suggest children compose alternative last lines on their whiteboards to fit the pattern – for example, finishing with *stunk*. Come to an overall conclusion about whether changing the regular pattern works.
● Following the same approach, ask children to read the excerpts from rhyming stories on 'Animal poems (2)' and discuss the effect of rhyming words.

Paired work

● Provide access to your selection of poetry and rhyming story books.
● Ask each child to find a poem they particularly like and discuss it with their partner, identifying why they made their choice and writing favourite words on their whiteboards.
● Suggest that they read or recite the poem to one another and talk about what they enjoyed about each other's interpretation.

Review

● Share opinions as a class and discuss the words on their whiteboards.

2: Homophone detectives

Introduction
- Use starter activity 11 'Homophone snap'.

Whole-class work
- Display photocopiable pages 'Animal poems (1)' and 'Animal poems (2)' from the CD-ROM. Use this to introduce revision on homophones.
- Focus on the poem 'Guess Who!' on the first sheet. Ask children to circle the word *ground*. Discuss how this word has different meanings that are written and sound the same. Identify the meaning of *ground* in this poem and think of another meaning. Compose a sentence demonstrating this alternative meaning, for example: *Dad added ground pepper to his curry.*
- Underline words in the other extracts that can be written using different letters yet still sound the same: *tail, bears, pairs, to, there.*
- Invite suggestions for alternative graphemes for these phonemes, for example *tale, bares, pears, two, their.*
- Discuss how the words can be paired forming rhymes.
- Distinguish homophones and near homophones. Compose sentences with them, for example: ***Please*** eat your ***peas*** and give me some ***peace***.

Paired work
- Ask children to copy the underlined words from the board onto whiteboards, and then write words with alternative graphemes underneath.
- Suggest they compose pairs of sentences together, using the poem words then those with alternative graphemes.

Review
- Invite pairs to read their sentences to the class. Praise correct matching of spelling and meaning.

Curriculum objectives
- To learn new ways of spelling phonemes for which one or more spellings are already known, and learn some words with each spelling, including a few common homophones.
- To distinguish between homophones and near-homophones.

Resources
A range of books containing poems about animals and zoos; fiction books written in rhyme; internet access; photocopiable page 'Animal poems' from the CD-ROM; individual whiteboards and pens

3: Poetry planning

Introduction
- Suggest children plan a group poem about a favourite zoo animal.
- Discuss previous plans the children have worked on.

Whole-class work
- Display 'At the zoo' from photocopiable page 'Animal poems (1)' from the CD-ROM. Consider how an animal is introduced in every line, and a feature described. Comment that this structure can support poetry writing.
- Display photocopiable page 'I Went to the Farm' from the CD-ROM. Consider the rhyming couplets, with each starting and ending with the same two words. Key information is encapsulated within couplets.
- Draw a grid, two columns down and six rows across. Ask children to write the names of the poem's animals or people in the boxes in the left column, and the verbs describing actions in the right.

Group work
- Ask children to use their new animal knowledge to plan their poem.
- Encourage them to choose a structure and draw a grid on a piece of paper.

> ### Differentiation
> - Less confident children can plan three simple rhyming couplets.

Review
- Share plans as a class and comment on the most effective structures.

Curriculum objectives
- To plan or say out loud what they are going to write about.
- To write down ideas and/ or key words, including new vocabulary.
- To encapsulate what they want to say, sentence by sentence.

Resources
Photocopiable pages 'Animal poems' and 'I Went to the Farm' from the CD-ROM

Curriculum objectives
● To write poetry.
● To use expanded noun phrases to describe and specify.

Resources
Children's group poem plans from the previous lesson; coloured pens

4: From plans to poems

Introduction
● Recall children's poetry planning and talk about how this is providing a strong structure on which to hang words and ideas.

Whole-class work
● Recall discussions in the previous lesson about suitable words, including homophones. Invite examples of such words.
● Talk about how authors and poets sometimes invent amusing words to suit their rhyming structure, for example Lynley Dodd's *flying flapdoodles.*
● Encourage children to consider every word they use and then see if they can think of a better one, real or imaginary. Write a simple noun phrase on the board, such as *small monkey*. Ask children to create an expanded noun phrase that enhances this description, for example *tiny talkative monkey*.

Group work
● Ask each group to follow their plan structure as they draft their poems.
● Invite them to consider how this could be improved, for example with expanded noun phrases.
● Ask each group to write their finished poem on a large sheet of paper and decorate it with an attractive design.

Differentiation
● Support less confident children by asking them to say each line out loud and talk about it before helping them to write it down.

Review
● Bring the class together to talk about using plans, techniques and vocabulary learned in previous lessons to help write their poems.

Curriculum objectives
● To read aloud what they have written with appropriate intonation to make the meaning clear.
● To participate in discussion about books, poems and other works that are read to them and those that they can read for themselves, taking turns and listening to what others say.

Resources
Children's group poems written in the previous lesson; green and brown fabric drapes; images of zoo animals; strips of green curled tissue and brown wool; individual whiteboards and pens

5: Poetry performance

Introduction
● Recall the writing of their group poems and suggest reciting in class or during assembly. Choose a performing area.

Whole-class work
● Decide on a performance title and write this on the board.
● Invite groups to write the titles of their poems underneath.
● Decide on an order for the performance – for example, particular animals grouped together. Number poems in the chosen order.

Group work
● Provide groups with their written version to practise reciting the poem.
● Encourage them to try different approaches – for example, reciting in unison, taking a line each, or asking pairs to read verses.
● Remind them to focus on rhythm, expression and confident delivery.
● Create an attractive performance area using the suggested resources.
Display the children's poems on the drapes.
● Modify after discussion and then put on the performance.

Differentiation
● More confident children can produce a programme for the performance.

Review
● Discuss the success of their recitations and what could be improved.

Curriculum objectives
● To use subordination (using *when*, *if*, *that*, or *because*) and coordination (using *or*, *and*, or *but*).

Resources
Photocopiable page 111 'Using subordination'

Grammar and punctuation: Practising subordination and coordination

Revise
● Recall previous exploration of subordination using familiar examples from photocopiable page 111 'Using subordination'.
● Write down subordination words, for example *when, if, that, because*.
● Ask children to suggest sentences about school routines that include at least one of these words.
● Write down connectives used for coordination (*or, and, but*). Invite children's sentences, such as: *Some of us have a hot dinner **but** others have a packed lunch*.
● Leave the connective words on display. Ask the children to recall things that they know about zoos. Invite them to put these facts into sentences, using connective words.
● Encourage children to write some of their sentences on the board and underline the connectives. Discuss how using connectives helps to make sentences longer and more interesting.

Assess
● Invite children to write four different sentences that show what they have learned about zoos, using a different connective in each sentence.

Further practice
● Give small groups of children requiring support a simple sentence starter. Ask them to add a connective from the list and finish the sentence.
● Challenge pairs of confident children to write the start of sentences for their partners to finish.
● For further practice, see page 197

Curriculum objectives
● To add suffixes to spell longer words.

Resources
Photocopiable page 105 'Adding suffixes'

Spelling: Adding suffixes

Revise
● Recall previous work on suffixes including adding the correct suffixes to photocopiable page 105 'Adding suffixes'.
● Read one or two of the sentences from the photocopiable sheet, asking children to decide which suffix to use so that the sentence makes sense.
● Write the suffixes '-ment', '-ness', '-ful' and '-less' on the board and ask the children to suggest words that end with these. Write the words on the board and then ask the children to circle the suffix.
● Discuss which words are nouns and which words are adjectives and ask the children to use the words orally in sentences.
● Focus on the suffixes '-ful' and '-less' as these were not focused on as much in the original suffix exercises. Write the words *playful* and *careless* on the board and circle the suffixes. Ask children to explain the meaning of these.
● Invite children to think of different words ending in these suffixes and put them in spoken sentences.

Assess
● Ask children to choose four words from the board and use each one in a separate written sentence.

Further practice
● Invite confident children to create a list of emotion words ending in '-ful', describing a range of feelings, for example *sorrowful, gleeful*.
● Ask children needing support to put a selection of words with suffixes (taken from their current reading level) into sentences.
● For further practice, see page 133.

Curriculum objectives
● To make inferences on the basis of what is being said and done.

Resources
Photocopiable page 107 'Zoo thoughts'; multiple copies of *Zoo* by Anthony Browne; Blu-Tack®; a selection of familiar books that the children enjoy; scissors

Reading: Making inferences

Revise
● Recall previous discussions about the story *Zoo* and some of the questions posed – for example, considering whether the animals were watching the humans rather than the other way around. Talk about how the illustrations gave more information about the emotions of both humans and animals – for example, the orang-utan sitting in the corner looking hunched and dejected. Recall how we learned about Dad's character from the attitudes of the family to his jokes and moods, and how the expression of the boys demonstrated whether they felt bored or excited.
● Introduce the word *infer* and explain that hidden clues help us to *infer* the emotions of characters. The thoughts that we have can be termed *inferences*.
● Play a game involving pulling an 'emotion' word out of a hat, for example *worried, frightened, joyful*, and demonstrating this emotion by modifying body language and facial expressions and using different words and sounds, such as sobs, sighs or laughter.
● Talk about the results of this game and how children were able to guess each other's moods by observing their actions and expressions and listening to their words and sounds.
● Ask children: *How do we know what someone is thinking in the story?* Agree that we might be told through the author's words, or we might have to make guesses by exploring what is being said and done and looking closely at illustrations. Explain that being able to make *inferences* is an important skill that will help them to get the most from the books they read.
● Re-read *Zoo* to the children, putting lots of expression into your voice and holding up the illustrations.
● Give groups of similar-ability children a copy of *Zoo*, along with the photocopiable page 107 'Zoo thoughts'. Ask them to read the photocopiable sheet together and cut the thoughts out.
● Invite them to go through the book together, looking for a suitable place for each thought. Explain that there are options for each one and they need to discuss the options before choosing the best one.
● After they have finished, discuss the positioning of the thought bubbles. Identify some thoughts that children agreed on and others that demonstrated differences of opinion. Visit the groups and encourage them to justify their choices.

Assess
● Work with individuals, asking them what they thought of the exercises involving playing the 'mood' game and working in a group to explore the feelings of characters in the book. Discuss whether they agreed easily with group members or had some disagreements. Ask how they resolved these disagreements.
● Go through the book, asking the child to read the text and being ready to support with helpful hints about how to apply their phonic knowledge and skills to decode words they are struggling with.
● Ask the child to find two pages that show clearly what the character is thinking. Question the child to ascertain how much they have inferred from 'hidden clues'.
● Observe children as you work with them, noting any successes and difficulties in interpreting the content.

Further practice
● Explore popular picture books that the children know well.
● Extend the activity by challenging confident children to write thought bubbles and place them in appropriate places.
● Support less confident children by helping them to write and place a thought bubble in the book and then ask them to create an illustration of this, with the thought bubbles included.

Curriculum objectives

● To encapsulate what they want to say, sentence by sentence.
● To plan or say out loud what they are going to write about.
● To use present and past tenses correctly and consistently including the progressive form.

Resources

Fiction books set in zoos and non-fiction books about zoos; coloured pens and pencils

Writing: A zoo adventure

Revise

● Recall fiction and non-fiction books explored throughout the half term.
● Explain that children are going to write stories about a zoo adventure. This could be set in a real or imaginary zoo, such as the one in the book *Zoo*.
● Recall previous discussions about how a story follows a sequence of beginning, middle and end, and discuss possible opening and closing sentences.
● Revise work on using connectives to extend sentences. Recall work on extended noun phrases to add interest and detail to the story.
● Ask children to consider new vocabulary they have learned and encourage them to include these words in their stories.
● Recall sentence writing and remind children about correct punctuation. Recall the use of appropriate suffixes and go through familiar ones together. Perhaps they could use some of the 'feeling' words from the Reading assessment, for example *sorrowful, gleeful, merriment*.
● Consider the importance of continuity, staying in the same tense and consider the appropriate endings for words in these tenses.
● Write the title *A zoo adventure* on the board and invite children to speculate about what this adventure might involve. Talk about the meaning of *adventure*, and discuss how it usually involves excitement and something unknown. With this in mind, consider possible characters that might either live in or visit the zoo, both humans and animals.
● Remind the children of their work on *Zoo*. Encourage them to think 'out of the box' by asking them if they have ever had a day out that did not turn out as they expected, for example someone was sick or got lost. Discuss exciting, funny and scary things that could go wrong with a day at a zoo.
● Consider what the main characters might look like. They may be quite ordinary, like the boys in *Zoo*, or be fantasy visitors from another planet coming to observe zoo animals on Earth.
● Divide into groups so that the children can discuss their story ideas. Encourage them to decide on the appearance of main characters and draw pictures of them. Recall how inferences were made about *Zoo* and consider how clues will encourage readers to make inferences about their stories. Suggest they make notes of interesting suggestions to use in their own stories.
● Write a list on the board, with the children's help, to remind them of things to include in their story, for example: new vocabulary, expanded noun phrases, suffixes, connectives. Write down possible punctuation marks to use such as question marks, exclamation marks or speech marks.

Assess

● Provide paper and writing tools and ask children to write their zoo adventure.
● Invite children to read their finished stories to a partner and discuss features, such as imaginative use of new vocabulary, strong sequence and appropriate sentence structure.
● Choose stories at random to discuss with the class. Give praise for correct inclusion of familiar grammar, spelling and punctuation as well as new features learned in this half term and discussed during revision time. Encourage children to consider how they will improve their writing next time.

Further practice

● Support less confident learners by encouraging them to create a picture of their zoo and main characters. Ask them to tell you the story and help them to compose and write three sentences representing beginning, middle and end. Use correct terminology relating to sentence structure as you draw attention to their completed writing.
● Challenge more confident children to write more complex stories set in an unusual zoo setting of their choice, such as a dinosaur zoo on another planet visited by time travel.

Actions and moods

■ How are the animals in *Zoo* feeling? Write words in the boxes to help you to understand more about them.

Animal	What is this animal doing?	How do you think this animal is feeling?
elephant		
tiger		
baboon		
orang-utan		
gorilla		

I can write words that describe what the animals in the book are doing and feeling.

How did you do?

Adding suffixes

- Read the sentences and change the word in brackets so that the sentence makes sense.
- Choose one of these endings to finish your words:

-ment	-ness	-er	-ing	-ed

The boy was full of _____ (excite) about his zoo visit.

Masses of cars were _____ (move) along the road.

Dad's jokes made the boys _____ (embarrass).

Dad thought his jokes were _____ (amuse).

Tears kept on _____ (roll) down Dad's face.

The orang-utan seemed full of _____ (sad).

I can change the words in brackets by adding a suffix so that the sentence makes sense.

How did you do?

Planning a recount

■ Use the boxes to help you to plan your recount.

When?			
Who?			
What?			
Where?			

I can plan a recount.

How did you do?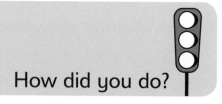

Zoo thoughts

- Cut out the thought bubbles and place them in a hat.

Zoos teach us about wild animals.

Zoos protect rare animals that might die in the wild.

Scientists can learn about animals by observing them in zoos.

Zoos are exciting places to be.

Loud visitors can cause the animals stress.

Zoos have good cafés and gift shops.

Animals should not be kept in cages.

Animals should be left in the wild.

Zoos are boring.

Sorting and punctuating sentences

- Punctuate the sentences correctly.
- Decide whether each sentence is a statement, command, question or exclamation. Write this in the column at the end.

	Type of sentence
Go and feed the giraffes	
All mammals have lungs to breathe air	
How do fish breathe	
That is daylight robbery	
What time do the seals get fed	
The fish is for the penguin enclosure	
You must be joking	

I can sort and punctuate sentences correctly.

How did you do?

PHOTOCOPIABLE

Animal factfile

■ Fill in the boxes with information about your chosen animal.

Animal name: _____

Appearance	Picture
Habitat	**Diet**

Unusual facts

I can create a factfile.

How did you do?

Our zoo plan

■ Fill in the boxes with information about the planned school zoo.

Zoo name: _____

Animals	Animal houses and enclosures
Food for animals	**Facilities for visitors**
People working at the zoo	**Extra features**

I can plan a project.

How did you do?

PHOTOCOPIABLE

■ SCHOLASTIC
www.scholastic.co.uk

Using subordination

- Extend the sentences below using the joining words *when, if, that, because.*
- Consider the questions *Why?* or *When?* to help you.
- Use the empty lines to make up sentences of your own that include joining words.

This fierce lion is in a strong cage _____

_____

This hungry seal will swim to the poolside _____

_____

These giraffes need a tall entrance to their house _____

_____

These penguins hop quickly towards the keeper _____

_____

This elephant uses his trunk to pick things up _____

_____

The zoo café opens at 10 o'clock _____

_____

_____

_____

I can use joining words when answering questions.

How did you do?

Ourselves

This half-term's work is wide-ranging and includes looking at how humans grow, their feelings and the senses. The children read a number of picture books, including Janet and Allan Ahlberg's *Funnybones*, and poems. They predict events, ask and answer questions and consider characters' feelings as well as considering how the senses are used in different settings. They use Standard English and noun phrases to write descriptive sentences, newspaper reports, labelled diagrams, non-fiction reports, poems and character game cards. Spelling focuses on suffixes, using syllables for longer words, words starting with 'kn', and revising contractions. They also work on different sentence types and their associated punctuation.

Expected prior learning
● Can recognise basic story language.
● Can recognise different sentence types.
● Can understand the difference between fiction and non-fiction.
● Can recognise and use noun phrases.
● Can understand basic poetic language, rhyme and rhythm.

Overview of progression
● Children's developing reading skills are enhanced by a greater requirement to use inference and deduction, and they are encouraged to include a wider range of sentence types in their writing.
● The children's writing should also increasingly reflect the wider vocabulary and structure they have identified and discussed in their reading.
● They are expected to be less overt in decoding when reading, and to use with increasing confidence the spelling, punctuation and grammar they have learned so far this year.

Creative context
● 'Ourselves' is a key science subject, linking with the body and healthy living.
● In art the children could make articulated skeletons using split pins or create portraits showing varied facial expressions, expressing the feelings.
● The song 'Dem Bones' can be learned and enjoyed in music, with appropriate percussion accompaniment.

Preparation
Familiarise yourself with the recommended books, noting where the salient elements of spelling, grammar and punctuation occur, such as the use of apostrophes, question and exclamation marks, multi-syllabic and exception words. Ensure you are aware of Top Trumps-style game cards, how characters are described on them, how their characteristics are given values and how they are used to play games. Be informed of any children or their family members who have disabilities involving the senses that you may need to be sensitive towards during work on that area.

You will also need:
Funnybones by Janet and Allan Ahlberg (multiple copies), online recording or video of 'Dem Bones', scissors, a selection of newspapers, a selection of non-fiction books at a suitable level about the body and its growth, a large selection of fiction and non-fiction books – enough for groups to have at least 10 each, *The Tiger Who Came to Tea* by Judith Kerr, a range of picture books that focus on characters' feelings, items with different textures, foods to taste, two boxes, blindfold, recording equipment (optional), individual whiteboards and pens, internet access, sticky notes, flipchart paper, Top Trumps-style cards.

On the CD-ROM you will find:
Media resources 'How are you feeling?', 'Settings'; interactive activities 'Fiction or non-fiction?', 'Which suffix?'; photocopiable pages 'The Magic of the Brain', 'Thanksgiving', 'I Asked the Little Boy Who Cannot See'

■SCHOLASTIC

Chapter at a glance

An overview of the chapter. For curriculum objective codes, please see pages 8–10.

Week	Lesson	Curriculum objectives	Summary of activities	Outcome
1	1	RWR: 7 RC: 5, 13	Introduce Funnybones. Predict what might happen. Discuss language in story. Identify skeleton animals.	• Can predict events in a story and recognise the effects of repetitive language.
	2	RC: 5, 15 WC: 13, 19 WC19	Look at sentence types in *Funnybones*. Discuss effect that using questions and exclamations has. Write conversation between the skeletons.	• Can write a conversation using questions, exclamation and statements, correctly punctuated.
	3	RC: 12, 15	Talk about character of skeletons. Focus on answering and asking questions. Devise own questions, sharing with others to answer.	• Can answer questions about the story with justification. • Can devise own comprehension questions.
	4	RWR: 3, 6 RC: 1, 7	Use starter activity 5 'Syllable count'. Pairs read and play word snap. Share favourite words and phrases from *Funnybones*.	• Can use syllables to decode longer words.
	5	RC: 11	Examine plot of *Funnybones*: how characters' decisions move plot on. Create annotated map.	• Can sequence and annotate events to show how characters' actions move the plot along.
2	1	RC: 11, 14 WC: 6	Children imagine they are in bed, hearing the skeletons. Role play conversations. Suggest interesting sentences which teacher scribes.	• Can role play imagined scene based on known story.
	2	WC: 15, 18	Teacher explains reasons for rules for writing. Find rules in picture books. Write accurate sentences about the dog skeleton.	• Can write sentences using written Standard English.
	3	RC: 11, 14	Gather information for newspaper report about skeletons. Pairs discuss what witnesses heard and found. Complete witness statement sheets.	• Can use inferred events from the story to write about what witnesses may have heard, seen and felt.
	4	WC: 4, 5, 6, 18	Look at newspaper report, list key features. Devise questions for witnesses. Groups share and comment on questions.	• Can devise written questions for imagined characters from story.
	5	WC: 4, 7, 18	Teacher reads newspaper report openings. Use previous work to compose orally and write reports. Pairs share and comment.	• Can compose orally and write a newspaper report with some key features.
3	1	RC: 14 WT: 1	Listen to 'Dem Bones', play 'Simon Says'. Draw labelled diagram of human body, adding descriptive phrases to body parts.	• Can produce labelled diagram with descriptive phrases for labelled items.
	2	WT: 2, 8	Identify links between knees and knuckles. Gather words beginning with 'kn'. Write sentences for 'kn' words. Complete an informal spelling assessment.	• Can list and spell words starting with 'kn', putting them into sentences.
	3	WC: 6	Discuss stages of human growth. Complete 'Sticky note find out' activity. Write sentences for each stage.	• Can suggest ideas for topic and use these to write descriptive sentences.
	4	RC: 4 WC: 5, 6	Sort fiction and non-fiction books. Use interactive 'Fiction or non-fiction?'. Use books to gather information for report.	• Can use non-fiction books to gather and record relevant information.
	5	WC: 7, 18	Oral ideas of sentences for inclusion in report. Write reports using Standard English.	• Can use written Standard English to write a report based on own research.

Chapter at a glance

Week	Lesson	Curriculum objectives	Summary of activities	Outcome
4	1	RC: 11, 14, 15	Starter: 'Saying with attitude'. Introduce book with focus on feelings. Groups read books noticing characters' feelings. Add vocabulary to feelings images.	• Can discuss characters' feelings using inference and deduction.
	2	WT: 4, 9 WC: 12	Recap contractions. Find and list contractions in the books from the previous lesson. Oral sentences with contractions. Teacher dictates sentences including contractions.	• Can identify and write correctly spelled contractions.
	3	RWR: 4 WT: 7 WC: 17	Recap suffixes. Focus on '-ful', '-ness', '-less'. Complete suffix sheet and compare with partner. Use interactive 'Which suffix?	• Can add correct suffixes to root words and use these to write sentences.
	4	RC: 11, 14 WC: 4, 6	Discuss Top Trumps-style game cards and their use. Discuss known stories and choose characters for cards. Plan cards.	• Can create character game cards, with descriptions and character attributes.
	5	WC: 4, 6	Explain how game cards are used. Create finished versions of cards. Play a game with the cards and evaluate.	• Can use created game cards to agree rules, play game and evaluate.
5	1	WT: 8 WC: 17	Describe unseen items. Add 'er', 'ier', 'est' to appropriate adjectives. Write descriptive sentences. Complete an informal spelling assessment.	• Can spell words with 'er', 'ier', 'est' endings and use them appropriately in descriptive sentences.
	2	RC: 11, 14	Read passage from an appropriate text. Imagine what characters can see, hear and so on at relevant points, listing under the senses.	• Can infer how characters might use their senses in specific settings, using adjectives to describe these where appropriate.
	3	WC: 14	Suggest noun phrases to describe image. Pairs list noun phrases using the senses for more images. Write descriptive sentences.	• Can use the senses to write noun phrases to describe a variety of settings.
	4	WC: 4	Discuss body parts linked to senses. Label diagrams of the face, linking senses to body parts.	• Can produce a labelled diagram using appropriate language.
	5	WC: 4, 8	Jointly improve a brief descriptive sentence. Improve a given piece, adding descriptions using the senses. Share and discuss.	• Can use descriptive phrases using the senses to improve a piece of text.
6	1	RC1 RC5 RC8	Read, discuss and perform 'The Magic of the Brain'. Groups read, rehearse, perform and evaluate performance of two other poems.	• Can discuss poems, perform them effectively and evaluate performances.
	2	WT: 1, 8, 10, 11, 12, 13 WC: 3	Introduce acrostics – create one together about 'sight'. Pairs write an acrostic for another sense. Individuals rewrite poems in best handwriting.	• Can write an acrostic poem about one of the senses and write it in legible handwriting.
	3	RC: 5, 7 WC: 3, 14	Choose descriptive language in poems and discuss. Choose structure for poem, note possible vocabulary, share with partner. Seven-word sentence starter.	• Can plan possible descriptive language for use in own poem.
	4	WT: 1, 8, 10, 11, 12, 13 WC: 3	Share words from own notes. Write poems using best handwriting. Share favourite sections of poems.	• Can write a descriptive poem about the senses, using legible handwriting.
	5	WC: 11	Class agree criteria for effective performance. Practise then perform own poems. Feedback and discussion.	• Can read own poems aloud effectively.

Background knowledge

Acrostic: Type of list poem where each line begins with one letter taken from a word written vertically, for example, in the word *SENSES*, the first line would begin with 'S', the second with 'E' and so on.

Encapsulation: The process of thinking and formulating ideas in our head before writing.

Recurring literary language: The deliberate repetition of words and phrases used to create emphasis or dramatic effect.

Suffix: The ending of a root word that modifies its meaning.

Week 1 lesson plans

In the opening week of this half-term's work, the children enjoy reading and working with a modern classic picture book – The Ahlberg's *Funnybones*. They enjoy effects of the repetitive language and predict events in the story. They role play and write a conversation between the two skeletons in the story, including sentences that are correctly punctuated statements, questions and exclamations. They ask and answer questions about the book and plot the events on an annotated map. They learn to read multi-syllabic words from the text.

1: Introducing *Funnybones*

Expected outcomes
● All children can discuss the story with reference to the text. They can role play and write a conversation between the two main characters.
● Most children can make sensible predictions based on what they have read. They can use statements, questions and exclamations, and can read multi-syllabic words.
● Some children can explain clearly how characters' questions and answers move the plot forward and understand the literary effects of the use of repetitive language.

Curriculum objectives
● To read aloud books closely matched to their improving phonic knowledge, sounding out unfamiliar words accurately, automatically and without undue hesitation.
● To predict what might happen on the basis of what has been read so far.
● To recognise simple recurring literary language in stories and poetry.

Resources
Funnybones by Janet and Allan Ahlberg; internet access; individual whiteboards and pens

Introduction
● Play the class a version of the traditional gospel song 'Dem Bones' (available online), or play them an animated version such as 'The Skeleton Song' on Youtube. Ask if any of the children know the song, then show them the front cover of the book *Funnybones*. Who can guess why you played the song? Can they suggest why the book has the title *Funnybones* from looking at the cover illustration?

Whole-class work
● Explain to the class that this half term, the focus for their work will be 'Ourselves', starting by enjoying the book *Funnybones*. Can anyone suggest how this might link with the theme 'Ourselves'? (We all have skeletons like the cover illustration.)
● Enjoy sharing the book, using a multiple copies if possible so the children can join in, pausing at various points, asking them to predict what might happen:
  ● After spread 1 – *What might be in the cellar?*
  ● After spread 3 – *What might happen in the park?*
  ● After spread 5 – *What might happen to the dog skeleton?*
  ● After spread 6 – *Will they be able to put the dog back together again?*
  ● After spread 8 – *Now will they find someone to frighten?*
● After completing the book, ask: *Did you notice the words of the skeleton song?* Find the page with this on and go over it with the children, asking them to point to each body part on themselves.
● Now turn to the page with zoo animal skeletons and enjoy identifying which animals they are. Link this to the work the children did on zoos in Spring 1.
● Re-read the first two pages of text. Ask: *What do you notice about the words?* agreeing that there is a lot of repetition. Ask: *Why do you think the author chose to do this?* (For emphasis, to make it like a poem, to build tension.)

Paired work
● Ask the children to devise a similar opening for a book, changing the word *dark*, perhaps to *high* or *old* for example, changing some or all of the locations, and the characters at the end. They should note their openings on individual whiteboards.

Differentiation
● Mixed-ability pairings would allow less confident writers to contribute equally while the more experienced writer scribes.

Review
● Invite the children to read out their revised story openings. Make a note on the board of the words they used in place of *dark*, discussing these and the effects they have. Do different adjectives suggest different ways of reading the text, or suggest different atmospheres? Would the original story be as effective if *light* had been used in place of *dark*?

Curriculum objectives

● To recognise simple recurring literary language in stories and poetry.
● To use sentences with different forms: statement, question, exclamation, command.
● To explain and discuss their understanding of books, poems and other material, both those that they listen to and those that they read for themselves.
● To use and understand the grammatical terminology in Appendix 2 in discussing their writing.

Resources

Funnybones by Janet and Allan Ahlberg

2: Sentence types

Introduction

● On the board write: *Statements, Questions, Exclamations*. Ask the children to explain what each type of sentence is. Establish the punctuation they need.

Whole-class work

● Look at the opening sentence of *Funnybones*. Ask: *What kind of sentence is this?* (statement). Read the first page and ask: *Are there any other statements?*
● On page 4 identify the questions, exclamations and statements. What happens if you read a statement as a question and vice versa?
● Ask: *What effect do the questions and exclamations have on the story?* (Make it more interesting, give us an idea about the characters, create a sense of mystery and surprise).

Paired work

● Ask the children to role play a conversation between the skeletons, as if they are going shopping or on holiday, including questions and exclamations.

Independent work

● They should then write a section of their conversation, retelling it in story form, using all three sentence types and the correct punctuation

Review

● Ask the pairs to compare their writing. What differences are there? Have they included all three sentence types and used correct punctuation?

Curriculum objectives

● To answer and ask questions.
● To explain and discuss their understanding of books, poems and other material, both those that they listen to and those that they read for themselves.

Resources

Funnybones by Janet and Allan Ahlberg; individual whiteboards and pens

3: Questions, questions

Introduction

● Look together at the front cover of the book. How would the children describe the skeletons? Are they scary or not? The children should justify their responses. Talk about ways in which they don't look like normal skeletons. Ask: *In the story, in what ways do the skeletons behave the same as ordinary people?*
● Look together at the spread where the dog skeleton has been put together wrongly, focusing on the speech bubbles. Ask: *What do you notice about the words?* Agree that the letters are mixed up because the skeleton is too.
● Ask: *Do you have any questions for me about the story?*

Paired work

● Challenge the children to devise comprehension-type questions about the story, referring to the text if possible, writing them on individual whiteboards. They must be confident that they know the answers.
● After five to ten minutes, invite pairs to join up, asking and answering each other's questions.

Differentiation

● Mixed-ability pairings would allow both children to offer suggested questions, the more experienced child being the scribe.

Review

● Bring the class together to discuss the questions. Were there any that were particularly difficult to answer? Ask for examples of some of the questions for the whole class to answer.

4: Word choices

Introduction

- Use starter activity 5 'Syllable count'.

Paired work

- Hand out photocopiable page 136 'Syllable build-up' to each child. Ask the children to work in pairs to read the words, building them syllabically if they don't recognise them immediately. Tell them that all the words are from the story *Funnybones*.
- When they have decoded the words, they should cut them out, making one set of words each with which to play a game of word snap. Ensure all the children understand how to play the game. Each time they call *Snap!* they must read the word they are claiming. Keep the sets for further games.
- Ask the children to recall which parts of the book any of the words on the cards might have come from.

Differentiation
- Children of similar abilities should work together in the paired activity, so the game is fair.

Review

- Hand out copies of the book *Funnybones* to small groups, asking them to share with the class their favourite words or phrases from the book, explaining their choices.

5: Following the plot

Introduction

- Ask the children to recall the events of the story of *Funnybones*, and the order in which they happen. If they are unfamiliar with the term, introduce the word *plot* to describe this.
- Refer back to the questions the skeletons asked in the story. Ask: *How do the questions affect what happens next in the story? For example, what might have happened if the big skeleton hadn't asked 'What shall we do tonight?' for the little skeleton to suggest they take the dog for a walk?*

Whole-class work

- Referring to the book if necessary, ask the children to list the events of the story in order. List these briefly as bullet points on the board. Note that the story moves from the skeletons' home to various locations around the town, and then back home again.

Independent work

- Give the children a sheet of plain paper and ask them to create a simple map or plan showing the skeletons' route around the town, starting and finishing at their home in the cellar. Ask them to annotate the various locations listed on the board, briefly explaining what happened there, for example: *They walked past the houses, shops, police station and zoo. They played on the swings in the park* and so on.

Review

- Invite the children to compare their maps with a partner, noting similarities and differences.

Week 2 lesson plans

The use of inference is a key element of this week's work. Using the story *Funnybones*, the children are asked to imagine how the skeletons' antics might affect townsfolk who overhear their noisy night-time escapades. These characters are only implied by the book's illustrations, requiring the children to use inference and deduction. They will use role play and discussion to gather information which they use to plan and write a newspaper report, having looked at key features needed. After a lesson on the use of written Standard English, they are required to use this in their written reports.

1: Enjoying *Funnybones*

Introduction
● Remind the children of the *Funnybones* story and ask them where and at what time the story happens (in a town, at night). Ask them to imagine they are in bed in the town in one of the houses the skeletons go past, and that they can hear them scaring each other.
● Ask the children to close their eyes and imagine what it would feel like, as you read that part of the book (where the skeletons are going home). Include the speech bubbles.
● Ask the children to open their eyes and tell you what pictures came into their minds, and how they would have felt if that had been really happening. Would they know the noises were being made by skeletons? What might they think was making the noises? What other sounds would they hear as well as the voices, for example dustbins clanking. (They may need to look at the illustrations for this information.)

Group work
● Organise the children into mixed-ability groups of three to four, asking them to take on the role of people who were woken up with the skeletons' noise. They should role play the conversation they have the following morning, describing what they heard, what they thought it was, and how it made them feel, including asking each other questions, such as *What time did it wake you up?* and *What did you think it was?* What did they do about it? Perhaps one of them looked out of their window and saw the skeletons. Maybe they could also hear animal sounds from the zoo.
● Invite some of the groups to re-enact their conversations for the rest of the class.

Whole-class work
● Ask the children for suggestions for interesting phrases and sentences from their role plays, scribing them on the board. Include question and exclamation marks where appropriate.

Review
● Think again about the skeletons scaring each other in the town at night. What do the children think the skeletons thought about the noise they were making? Were they bothered that they might be waking people up, or scaring them? When do they think the skeletons go to sleep?

Curriculum objectives
● To use some features of written Standard English.
● To use present and past tenses correctly and consistently including the progressive form.

Resources
Individual whiteboards and pens; multiple copies of *Funnybones* by Janet and Allan Ahlberg or a selection of picture books

2: Using Standard English

Introduction
● Write on the board: *the skeletons was well scary wasn't they.*
● Ask the children to point out any mistakes they can see, correcting them accordingly. Explain that when we write, there are rules to follow so that our writing can be easily read and understood by anyone. We don't always follow these rules when we speak so we have to learn the rules for writing.

Paired work
● Give the children copies of *Funnybones* or any other picture books and ask them to look through the text to find, and list on their individual whiteboards, all the rules they can find for writing.
● After 10–15 minutes, ask the children to share what they have listed, discussing the points and seeing which ones were found by the majority, listing them on the board. Ensure key elements of punctuation and grammar are listed, including the correct use of verb tenses.

Independent work
● Ask the children to write several sentences about the dog skeleton, using correct language, grammar and punctuation.

Differentiation
● Less confident writers may benefit from being given sentence starters.

Review
● Ask the children to share their sentences with their partners, checking that they have followed the writing rules.

Curriculum objectives
● To participate in discussion about books, poems and other works that are read to them and those that they can read for themselves, taking turns and listening to what others say.
● To make inferences on the basis of what is being said and done.

Resources
Photocopiable page 137 'What they heard'

3: Gathering facts

Introduction
● Remind the children of the role playing they did in lesson 1 and tell them that later this week they will be writing a newspaper report about how the skeletons in *Funnybones* disturbed the neighbourhood.

Paired work
● Ask the children to talk together about things the skeletons might have done that the people discovered in the morning, such as moving washing on the line, hiding the dustbin, leaving gates open at the zoo and so on. How would this have made the people feel, and what would they have done about it?

Independent work
● Hand out photocopiable page 137 'What they heard'. Explain that they will complete the sheet for three different witnesses of the events, writing different things for each. They should use their role-playing experience from lesson 1 and today's paired discussion to help them. Explain that they will be able to use these witness statements when they write their newspaper reports later in the week. Allow time for the children to complete the sheets.

Differentiation
● Less confident children may need more detailed reminders about the role playing from lesson 1 to act as prompts for their writing.

Review
● Ask the children to choose their most unusual or interesting comments and invite them to share these with the rest of the class.

Curriculum objectives
● To plan or say out loud what they are going to write about.
● To write down ideas and/or key words, including new vocabulary.
● To use some features of written Standard English.
● To write for different purposes.

Resources
Examples of appropriate newspapers, including children's papers such as *First News*; individual whiteboards and pens; children's completed versions of photocopiable page 137 'What they heard'; photocopiable page 138 'The five Ws'

4: Planning a report

Introduction

● Give groups of children one of the newspapers to browse through. Ask them to select a story, with a headline. They may find it difficult to separate stories from adverts, so give them some pointers, such as the story gives news of something that has happened, it isn't trying to sell us something.

Whole-class work

● Ask the groups to look at how the report has been organised, noting any features they find on individual whiteboards. After a few minutes ask what they have found, noting key features on the board, adding any you feel are missing. They should include: headlines, subheadings, paragraphs (though the children don't need to know the term), perhaps photos with captions. They may also have noticed quotes in the reports.

Independent work

● Hand out photocopiable page 138 'The five Ws'. Explain that these are the types of question that reporters use to get information for their reports. Ask the children to think of questions they could ask their three witnesses from the previous lesson in order to write their own report of the events. They should complete the photocopiable sheet independently.

Review

● Invite small groups of children to share their questions, each commenting on the others' choices.

Curriculum objectives
● To encapsulate what they want to say, sentence by sentence.
● To use some features of written Standard English.
● To write for different purposes.

Resources
Children's completed versions of photocopiable pages 137 'What they heard' and 138 'The five Ws'; two or three selected newspaper articles

5: Writing a report

Introduction

● Read out the headlines and first sentences from the newspaper articles, demonstrating how to begin the newspaper reports the children will be writing. Draw attention to how they give away a key element at the start – not like a story where we don't know what happens until later on.

Paired work

● Ask the children to use their work from previous lessons to compose their story orally, a sentence at a time, with their partner, offering each other helpful comments as they go along. They should think of a good headline.

Independent work

● After their oral composition, the children should write their finished reports, referring to previous work to help them. Remind the children to use Standard English in their writing. Encourage them to try to include at least one subheading as well as their headline.

> **Differentiation**
> ● You could provide less confident writers with sentence openings such as: *Two nights ago there was..., Mr X said he heard..., The next morning...*
> ● More experienced writers could include speech marks for witness quotes if they already know how to use them (though this is not a requirement for Year 2).

Review

● Back in their pairs, ask the children to swap their reports and read each other's work, making positive comments. Did they change anything from their original oral version?

Week 3 lesson plans

The focus this week is on how humans change as they grow. The children identify body parts using a song and game, using the vocabulary to label and annotate a diagram of the human body. They identify five stages of human growth, suggesting characteristics for each. They classify non-fiction books and use them to find and record information about the human body, using this to write a non-fiction report on how the body changes as we grow. They learn to spell words beginning with 'kn'.

1: Parts of the body

Introduction

● Play the class 'Dem Bones', or show them an animated version, on the internet. Find the song in the book *Funnybones*, and the second song that the two skeletons sing when they have successfully rebuilt the dog.
● Have fun identifying body parts, by playing a quick game of 'Simon Says', asking the children to point to different parts of their body.
● Enjoy singing together the song 'Heads, Shoulders, Knees and Toes', getting progressively quicker as the song goes on. If there are children in the class who are not native English speakers, they could teach the others the song using the words from their language.
● Ask the children for suggestions of the names of other body parts, such as *head, arms, legs, eyes, knees, ankles, ears, toes* and so on. (Be prepared for the inevitable body parts that will raise sniggers and blushes.) Extend the children's vocabulary to include words such as *wrist, forearm, shoulder, elbow, calf, shin, neck, thigh* if they are not suggested.

Independent work

● Ask the children to make a labelled diagram of the human body, with the names of body parts they know. Encourage them to use their spelling and phonic knowledge for words they are unsure of. In addition to the labels, ask them to write a short phrase describing what each part is used for – for example, *eyes for seeing, knees so we can bend our legs, chest where our heart and lungs are, thigh – the top part of the leg*, and so on.

> **Differentiation**
> ● This is a useful lesson for children new to speaking English, as it enables them to learn specific vocabulary in a fun way. Repeating the songs will help to consolidate the words.

Review

● Working in pairs or small groups, ask the children to read out some of the short descriptive phrases they added to their diagrams for the others to guess which body part they are referring to.

Expected outcomes
● All children can use information to write a non-fiction report about the human body.
● Most children can use non-fiction books to research relevant information, make notes from this and use it to write a non-fiction report.
● Some children can divide their reports into relevant sections, using subheadings.

Curriculum objectives
● To participate in discussion about books, poems and other works that are read to them and those that they can read for themselves, taking turns and listening to what others say.
● To segment words into phonemes and represent these by graphemes, spelling many correctly.

Resources
Online recording or video of 'Dem Bones'; multiple copies of *Funnybones* by Janet and Allan Ahlberg, internet access

---

Curriculum objectives
• To learn new ways of spelling phonemes for which one or more spellings are already known, and learn some words with each spelling, including a few common homophones.
• To apply spelling rules and guidelines, as listed in Appendix I.

Resources
Individual whiteboards and pens

2: Knees and knuckles

Introduction
• Ask the children what *knees* and *knuckles* have in common. If they don't suggest that they begin with the same two letters, write them on the board so they can spot it for themselves. Draw attention to the spelling, noting the unsounded letter 'k'. Explain that hundreds of years ago, this would have been sounded, but over the years the pronunciation has changed.

Paired work
• Ask the children to list as many words as they can that they think begin with 'kn'. After about five minutes, gather these in, scribing the correct ones on the board. Check they know the meanings and point out the homophones.

Independent work
• Ask the children to write sentences for as many of the words as they can.

> **Differentiation**
> • For those struggling with this spelling pattern, suggest they sound the initial letter 'k', as would have been the case historically.

Review
• Take some root words such as *knit*, *know* and *knock*, giving these as spellings for the children to write on their whiteboards, then extend them by adding appropriate suffixes, such as '-ed', '-ing'. Ask them to show their boards for informal assessment of the spellings.

Curriculum objectives
• To write down ideas and/ or key words, including new vocabulary.

Resources
Sticky notes; five sheets of flipchart paper; before this lesson, invite the children to bring in photos of themselves as babies

3: Growing up

Introduction
• Ask the children to share the photographs of themselves as babies. How easily can they be recognised? Ask: *In what ways have you changed?*
• Ask the class what stages people go through as they grow, for example *baby*, *toddler*, *child*, *teenager*, *adult*. Do they remember anything about being a toddler?

Whole-class work
• Prepare five sheets of flipchart paper, one for each stage of growth, and ask the children to write what they know about the subject on sticky notes. Then stick these notes on the relevant sheet of paper.
• When the sheets are complete, discuss some of the children's suggestions, drawing attention to useful and specific vocabulary. Retain these sheets.

Independent work
• Ask the children to write at least one sentence, correctly punctuated, for each of the five stages, in the correct sequence.

> **Differentiation**
> • More confident children can be encouraged to write more than one sentence, or include conjunctions to create sentences with more than one clause.

Review
• Invite children to read out one of their sentences, for the rest of the class to suggest which stage is being discussed. What clues gave them away?

4: Non-fiction report

Introduction

- Provide groups of children with a random selection of fiction and non-fiction books, including some relevant to the topic 'Ourselves', without telling them what types of books they are. Ask them to arrange the books into groups according to their own criteria.
- Ask each group to explain their sorting. Did anyone divide the books into fiction/non-fiction? Ask: *What is the difference between fiction and non-fiction?*

Whole-class work

- With the class, use the interactive activity 'Fiction or non-fiction?' on the CD-ROM. What clues did they use in order to decide?

Group work

- Explain that the children will be writing a non-fiction report about 'Ourselves'. Today they will gather information for their reports.
- Hand out the photocopiable page 139 'Ourselves – a non-fiction report about growing'. Explain that they should gather and note information they find for each heading, bearing in mind the five stages from the previous lesson.

Review

- Ask the children to add any further information from their research to the flipchart sheets they used in the previous lesson.

Curriculum objectives

- To plan or say out loud what they are going to write about.
- To write down ideas and/ or key words, including new vocabulary.
- To be introduced to non-fiction books that are structured in different ways.

Resources

Random selection of fiction and non-fiction books – enough for groups to have at least 10 each, some of which should be relevant to the topic 'Ourselves'; interactive activity 'Fiction or non-fiction?' on the CD-ROM; photocopiable page 139 'Ourselves – a non-fiction report about growing'; 'Sticky note find out' sheets from the previous lesson

5: Writing a report

Introduction

- Remind the children that today they will be using their research from the previous lesson to write a non-fiction report about 'Ourselves'.
- Explain that the focus for their report is about how humans grow through the five stages they have identified, and how they change during that time. Their notes will have information they can use in their reports – for example, they might write about our bodies growing gradually, perhaps giving average sizes. They could write about how we eat different foods as we grow and that our changing bodies enable us to do different things, both physical and intellectual, including learning and developing language.
- Ask for some oral examples of sentences they might use for different elements of the report.

Independent work

- The children will spend the majority of the lesson writing their non-fiction reports. Remind them to use Standard English, including correct punctuation.

Curriculum objectives

- To encapsulate what they want to say, sentence by sentence.
- To use some features of written Standard English.

Resources

Children's completed versions of photocopiable page 139 'Ourselves – a non-fiction report about growing'; 'Sticky-note find out' sheets from the previous lesson

> **Differentiation**
> - Less experienced writers may need support to develop their notes into a report. Sentence starters may help, such as *When we are babies we can only...*, *When we are toddlers we learn to...* and so on. Suggest they refer to the flipchart sheets for further assistance.
> - More confident writers can be encouraged to use subheadings to divide their reports.

Review

- Invite children to read out sections of their reports, without referring to any particular stage of growth, for the rest of the class to guess which stage is being discussed.

Expected outcomes
● All children can discuss characters' feelings and make a set of character game cards. They can spell some contractions and words with suffixes.
● Most children can describe characters' feelings using appropriate vocabulary and use this to describe characters on their game cards. They can spell many contractions and words with suffixes.
● Some children can use a wider range of vocabulary to discuss feelings and create characters. They are confident in spelling contractions and words with suffixes.

Curriculum objectives
● To participate in discussion about books, poems and other works that are read to them and those that they can read for themselves, taking turns and listening to what others say.
● To make inferences on the basis of what is being said and done.
● To explain and discuss their understanding of books, poems and other material, both those that they listen to and those that they read for themselves.

Resources
A range of picture books that focus on characters' feelings, such as *Little Beaver and the Echo* by Amy MacDonald, *"Let's Get a Pup!" Said Kate* by Bob Graham, *Meerkat Mail* by Emily Gravett, *Dogger* by Shirley Hughes, *Hue Boy* by Rita Phillips Mitchell, *Elmer* by David McKee – if possible, two or more copies of each title; media resource 'How are you feeling?' on CD-ROM

Week 4 lesson plans

Using a range of picture books in which the feelings of characters are the focus, this week the children look at how these can change in a story, and add appropriate words to their descriptive vocabulary. The focus on characters is the basis for creating game cards based on stories the children know, and using these to play a game. They revisit contractions and use the suffixes '-ness', '-less' and '-ful' to create words that can be used to describe feelings or characteristics.

1: Characters' feelings

Introduction
● Use starter activity 6 'Saying with attitude'. After each phrase, ask: *What is the speaker feeling here?* Write the feelings on the board.
● Explain that how we feel changes the way we speak. Carry out the starter activity again, but this time, ask the children to choose an inappropriate emotion to use before reading the phrase. Enjoy how silly many of the phrases now sound.

Whole-class work
● Choose one of the books from the resources and share it with the class, asking them about how different characters are feeling at various points in the story. How do we know?

Group work
● Provide each group with two or more copies, if possible, of different books from the resources list or your own choice of books that deal with characters' feelings. These could include books the children will be familiar with from Year 1, such as *Elmer*, *The Rainbow Fish* and *Amazing Grace*.
● Ask the children to read the books together and look for places where we are aware of the characters' feelings, noticing how we know that. Ask them to see if any of the characters' feelings change during the course of the story, and if so what makes that happen. Typically, sadness changes to happiness because of events or the actions of others.
● When they have read the books, ask for feedback on each title, asking what feelings they found and what changes they noticed.
● Ask children to select short sections of the books to read aloud to the class, with suitable intonation, for them to suggest how the character speaking or being described might be feeling. Add any new feelings words to those already on the board from the introductory activity.

> **Differentiation**
> ● The groups should be of similar ability and the books appropriate to their levels of reading.

Review
● Display the media resource 'How are you feeling?' on the CD-ROM which show faces with different emotions. For each image, ask the children to suggest words to describe how the characters might be feeling. Extend this to ask for suggestions to what they also might be thinking.

2: Contractions

Curriculum objectives
● To learn to spell more words with contracted forms.
● To learn how to use both familiar and new punctuation correctly (see Appendix 2), including full stops, capital letters, exclamation marks, question marks, commas for lists and apostrophes for contracted forms and the possessive (singular).
● To write from memory simple sentences dictated by the teacher that include words using the GPCS, common exception words and punctuation taught so far.

Resources
Books used in lesson 1; individual whiteboards and pens

Introduction
● Ask the children to suggest some of the contractions they remember from previous work, and write them on the board. As you do so, ask the children to check your work, making deliberate mistakes by either missing out or misplacing the apostrophe, for the children to correct you.

Group work
● Working in the same groups and with the same books as in lesson 1, ask the children to go through the text, looking for contractions and listing them on their individual whiteboards. Where words appear more than once, they should keep a tally of their occurrence. Warn the children not to include words where the apostrophe is being used to indicate possession.
● After a few minutes, ask which words they found and list them on the board. Add the tally totals to see if some words occur more than others overall.
● Ask the children to suggest sentences for characters in the stories, using any of the contractions, or others they feel would be more appropriate, for example, *Sunny the Meerkat wasn't very happy, Elmer didn't want to feel different from the other elephants, Hue Boy wasn't growing at all.*

Review
● Dictate similar short sentences for the children to write on their whiteboards, showing you their results for informal assessment.

3: Suffixes

Curriculum objectives
● To read words containing common suffixes.
● To add suffixes to spell longer words.
● To use the grammar for Year 2 in Appendix 2.

Resources
Photocopiable page 140 'Choose the suffix'; interactive activity 'Which suffix?' on the CD-ROM

Introduction
● Ask the children what a suffix is. What suffixes do they remember from previous work?
● Tell the class that today they will be concentrating on three suffixes that can be added to make words useful for describing feelings or telling us more about characters. Write on the board the three suffixes '-ful', '-ness' and '-less'. Draw attention to the spelling of 'ful'. Ask the children what they notice about it (it isn't spelled in the same way as the word *full*, although it means the same thing). Ask for examples of words using the suffix 'ful', and use them to demonstrate its meaning. Select several to write on the board, choosing only those where the suffix is added to the root word without changing its spelling, for example *playful* rather than *beautiful*.

Independent work
● Hand out photocopiable page 140 'Choose the suffix' for the children to complete independently.

Paired work
● As they complete the sheet, ask the children to find a partner to share and compare their results, changing any where they feel they have chosen wrongly.

Differentiation
● Offer support to any children whose knowledge of language means that they may be unfamiliar with the word choices.

Review
● Use the interactive activity 'Which suffix?' with the class. There may be some new vocabulary for many of the children, such as *ruthless*, to be explained.

Curriculum objectives
● To participate in discussion about books, poems and other works that are read to them and those that they can read for themselves, taking turns and listening to what others say.
● To make inferences on the basis of what is being said and done.
● To write for different purposes.
● To write down ideas and/or key words, including new vocabulary.

Resources
A set or more of Top Trumps-style cards – the children may be able to bring some in to school; photocopiable page 141 'My game cards'

4: Game cards

Introduction

● Ask the class whether any of them have played with 'Top Trumps' game cards. Ask a child to explain them, or tell the class yourself that they are sets of cards, each representing a character from a story or theme. Each character is given scores for certain characteristics, and they are used to play games with. Look at some of the characteristics on the cards.
● Explain that they are going to create their own set of cards for characters from a story they know well. They will need at least four characters, who should differ from each other in some way.

Paired work

● Ask the children to talk together about possible stories. They must then choose one and decide on the characters for their cards.

Independent work

● Hand out photocopiable page 141 'My game cards'. Explain that the children will draw a picture of each character in the box, write a short description of them beside it including their feelings in the story, and choose four characteristics that each could have, awarding points for these for each character. Ask for some suggestions for characteristics, such as *size*, *strength*, *bravery*, *friendliness*, *intelligence*, *kindness*. The children plan their cards, using extra sheets if necessary.

Review

● Ask partners to share and compare their cards, making changes if they wish.

Curriculum objectives
● To write for different purposes.
● To write down ideas and/or key words, including new vocabulary.

Resources
Children's game card plans from the previous lesson; photocopiable page 141 'My game cards' printed on card

5: Playing the game

Introduction

● Tell the children that today they will make the finished versions of their character game cards, and use them to play a game.
● Ask children familiar with game cards to explain to the class how they play with them, explaining the rules they use.
● Tell the children to bear this information in mind as they make their finished cards, so that they can make any changes they think might be needed.

Independent work

● The children use their plans from the previous lesson to create their finished cards, in neat handwriting.

Group work

● When the cards are complete, the children should work in pairs or groups to play a game with them. They must agree on how they will play the game and on the rules before beginning.

Review

● Ask the children how well their game cards worked when they played with them. Would they make any changes to the cards or the game itself, to improve things?

Week 5 lesson plans

This week the children investigate how to improve their descriptive writing by making use of the senses. They use picture books to suggest what characters might see, hear and so on. within particular settings and use noun phrases to describe a variety of settings using as many senses as possible. This culminates in improving a given description to make it more interesting for the reader. They learn to spell words with the suffixes '-er', '-ier' and '-est', using the resultant words to describe objects and food items.

1: What's it like

Introduction

● Prepare the two boxes so that one contains items to feel and the other conceals a few food items for the children to taste. Explain to the class that there are various items hidden in the boxes and ask for volunteers to feel and/or taste them to guess what they are. (Ensure there are no potential food allergy problems.)

● Blindfold a child, who then selects and describes the feel, taste and – for the food – smell of the object, to the class, before suggesting what the item is. Encourage them to describe the shape, size and weight as well as the texture. Scribe on the board some of the words used.

Whole-class work

● Read through the list of words on the board, and ask the children to suggest which could have the suffixes '-er', '-ier' and '-est' added to them, for example *sweet, tasty, juicy, smooth, rough, soft, hard, round, small, heavy*. Ask: *What kind of words are these?* (Adjectives)

● Select one word at a time and ask the children to write on their whiteboards the new words they can make by adding one or more of the endings, for example *sweeter* and *sweetest*, *juicier* and *juiciest*. Ask them to show you their spellings. Ensure some of the words end in the letter 'y', and ask the children what they notice about the spelling when the suffixes are added. (The 'y' changes to an 'i'.)

● Give the children several descriptive words ending with the letter 'e', such as *nice, white, pale, rare, brave*. Ask them to see what happens to these words when the suffixes '-er' and '-est' are added. (The final 'e' is dropped.)

Independent work

● Display all the objects from the two boxes. Ask the children to select some to write sentences about, using words with the suffixes '-er', '-ier' and '-est'. Their sentences will be about comparing the objects with others – for example, if they chose an apple they might write *The apple is juicy, but I think oranges are juicer* or *The fabric is rough, but the roughest thing I know is sandpaper*. Ask for some oral examples before the children begin to write.

Differentiation

● Less confident learners could work with an adult, composing their sentences orally before writing.

● Encourage confident writers to try to use two comparisons in their sentences, for example: *The apple is juicy, but strawberries are juicier and oranges are the juiciest.*

Review

● Ask the children to write several words with the suffixes on their whiteboards, and show them to you for informal assessment.

● Use starter activity 10 'Add a suffix' to reinforce adding suffixes.

Expected outcomes

● All children can use the senses to write descriptive sentences. They can spell some words with the suffixes '-er', '-ier' and '-est'.

● Most children can improve a given text by adding descriptions using the senses. They can spell many words with the suffixes '-er', '-ier' and '-est'.

● Some children can substantially improve a piece of given text with descriptions using all of the senses. They confidently spell words with the suffixes '-er', '-ier' and '-est'.

Curriculum objectives

● To apply spelling rules and guidelines, as listed in Appendix 1.

● To use the grammar for Year 2 in Appendix 2.

Resources

Items with different textures; foods to taste; two boxes; blindfold; individual whiteboards and pens

Curriculum objectives
● To make inferences on the basis of what is being said and done.
● To participate in discussion about books, poems and other works that are read to them and those that they can read for themselves, taking turns and listening to what others say.

Resources
The Tiger Who Came To Tea by Judith Kerr, or one of the books already used in this half term; a selection of picture books for pairs of children to use; individual whiteboards and pens

2: Stop and think!

Introduction

● Use starter activity 3 'Why say one word', starting with the sentence *I ate a cake.*
● Discuss the use of the senses in the chosen descriptive adjectives.

Whole-class work

● Read the class several passages from *The Tiger Who Came To Tea*, or another book of your choice, pausing at various points to ask the children to imagine what the characters can see, hear and so on.
● Ask: *Which of the five senses were used the most?* Discuss responses.

Paired work

● Give each pair a picture book to use – they can include those already used in this term's work. Ask them to go through the book in the way you have demonstrated, finding passages where they can suggest what characters can see, hear and so on. and discussing these together.
● Ask them to write the five senses as headings on their individual whiteboards, and to note the things they find using adjectives when they can. For example, when Hue Boy is eating pumpkin soup they might write *tasty and sweet* under the heading *Taste*, and *warm* under the heading *Touch*. When Sunny the Meerkat is in the desert he may feel *hot* and see *sand*.

Review

● Discuss which of the senses they have the longest list for. Has everyone found the same? Why do they think this might be?

Curriculum objectives
● To use expanded noun phrases to describe and specify.

Resources
Media resource 'Settings' on the CD-ROM; photocopiable page 142 'Describe the setting'

3: Using the senses

Introduction

● Show the class the first photograph in media resource 'Settings' on the CD-ROM (of a beach). Ask them to suggest noun phrases that could be used to describe it, scribing them on the board.
● Look at the phrases and ask which of the senses the children have used. It is likely that most will have to do with sight. Ask the children to think of the other senses and add to the list under headings for each of the senses.

Paired work

● Show the children the other four settings, one at a time, for just two minutes each. Challenge them to imagine they are in the setting, and to write at least one phrase, using a descriptive adjective, for each of the senses for each image. If there are any that stump them, allow them to be missed out – for example, taste may be particularly difficult.
● Run through the images again, asking for some of the noun phrases the children have written. Which senses were the most difficult to think of?

Independent work

● Hand out photocopiable page 142 'Describe the setting'. Using their lists, the children should use as many of the senses as possible to write descriptions, avoiding over-using the same adjectives.

Review

● Invite children to read out their descriptions for the class to suggest which settings are being described.

4: Senses and the body

Curriculum objectives
● To write for different purposes.

Resources
Media resource 'How are you feeling?' on the CD-ROM

Introduction
● Select one face to display from the media resource 'How are you feeling?' on the CD-ROM. Ask: *Which parts of the face do we use for our senses? What about the sense of touch? Is there one part of the body that deals with that in the same way as the other senses?* They will probably suggest the hands, so discuss how we can feel with all our body, as our skin is the sensory organ for touch and it covers us all over.

Independent work
● Ask the children to draw a face, including the key features for the senses. They should leave enough room around the edge to label the face, indicating which sense relates to which feature, including the skin for the sense of touch. The annotations should briefly explain how each feature and sense are linked. Take this opportunity to explain the difference between prose writing and the language used for labelling diagrams, for instance label writing is usually in note form, not sentences, and would not include noun phrases. For example, we might write *Eyes – used for seeing* rather than *We use our eyes for seeing things with.*
● Allow enough time for the children to draw and label their face pictures.

Review
● Discuss which sense the children would least like to lose, and why. (Be sensitive to individual personal circumstances.)

5: Making sense of the senses

Curriculum objectives
● To write for different purposes.
● To evaluate their writing with the teacher and other children.

Resources
Photocopiable page 143 'I can do better than that!'

Introduction
● Write on the board the sentence *On the beach I could see sand, rock pools and seagulls.* Ask the children to help you improve the sentence by adding descriptive words and phrases including those which use the senses. Take ideas and agree on the best ways of improving the sentence, for example: *On the windswept beach I could see golden sand. I felt tingling cold water in the clear rock pools and heard the loud cawing of seagulls.*

Independent work
● Hand out photocopiable page 143 'I can do better than that!', telling the children that, as with your example, they are to re-write the piece to make it more interesting. Explain that it is fine to add sentences – they can use their imagination to paint a picture that includes all the senses. They should look for opportunities to use more than one sense when describing one thing, for example the cows could be heard as well as seen, the flowers could be smelled.
● After making initial notes on the sheet, the children should re-write the description on a separate piece of paper.

> **Differentiation**
> ● Some children may need adult support with reading the text and discussing potential ways of adding description to the scene.

Review
● Invite children to read out parts of their descriptions and compare ways in which the text has been improved.

Week 6 lesson plans

Poems about the senses are read, discussed and performed to start the week's poetry focus. All can be found in the book *Sensational!*, compiled by Roger McGough (Macmillan Children's Books), where you will find many more if you wish to share others with the class. The children go on to compose their own acrostics and descriptive poems, considering the most effective language before writing. They then read their own poems aloud, aiming for an engaging performance.

1: Poetry about the senses

Introduction

● Display photocopiable page 'The Magic of the Brain' from the CD-ROM. Allow the children a little time to scan quickly through the poem before reading it to them, asking them to follow the words as you read.
● Afterwards, ask: *Why do you think it is called 'The Magic of the Brain'?* discussing responses. Ask the class if there are any words they don't understand. Focus on these, asking if they can work out their meaning from the context. Supply definitions for any that remain unfamiliar.
● Ask a series of differentiated questions, such as *Which sense is being described in each verse? How can a smell take you to places? What patterns of language can you see? What kind of animal do you think is in verse 4? Why does starlight lift the head? Why is the tree described as being empty?* (verse 2).

Group work

● Organise the class into six mixed-ability groups, giving them copies of the poem and assigning each group one verse. Appoint a confident child as group leader and give them 10 minutes to practise reading their verse aloud together. Tell them to take note of punctuation and to agree the speed and volume of their performance. Ensure they know how to pronounce all the words.
● After 10 minutes bring the class together to read the poem, each group contributing their verse. Afterwards, discuss the different ways each group has chosen to read their verse.
● Ask the groups to read their verses again, if possible this time recording the performance and playing it back for them to listen to. Discuss the second performance – had it improved, and if so how?
● Next, give half of the groups photocopiable page 'Thanksgiving', and the other half 'I Asked the Little Boy Who Cannot See', both from the CD-ROM. Ask them to read through the poems quietly to themselves, then in pairs within the group, then together as a whole group. Explain that the groups will come together to read their poems later, so they should practise reading them ready for a performance. Those with the second poem will need to pay particular attention to the punctuation. Encourage them to use appropriate intonation in their reading. They should bear in mind the discussion following their earlier performances.

> **Differentiation**
> ● As they read, provide help to children who are stuck with decoding or pronouncing any unfamiliar vocabulary.

Review

● Bring the two sets of groups together to perform their poems, each half offering comments after listening to the readings. Finally, ask the children which poem they liked the most from the three heard today, and why.

2: Writing an acrostic

Introduction

● Write the word *SIGHT* vertically on the board. Explain that you will be composing a poem together about sight, each letter of the word giving you the start of each line. Explain that poems like this are called *acrostics*. They do not have to rhyme.
● Begin the poem yourself by thinking aloud about the opening line, modelling the composition process for the children. Begin with, for example, *Seeing everything around me*, or *Such amazing things I can see*.
● Carry on composing the rest of the poem with the class, editing as you go along to achieve the best lines possible.

Paired work

● Ask the children to choose one of the other senses and write an acrostic on individual whiteboards so that they can edit as they work together.

Independent work

● When the poems are finished, each child should make a copy on paper using their best handwriting. If there is time they can add illustrations.

Differentiation
● Guide less confident writers to choose a sense with fewer letters, for example *TASTE*.
● More experienced writers could use *HEARING* or perhaps write more than one acrostic.

Review

● Ask pairs of children to read their poems together to other pairs, each offering positive comments on both poems and performance.

Curriculum objectives
● To write poetry.
● To segment words into phonemes and representing these by graphemes, spelling many correctly.
● To apply spelling rules and guidelines, as listed in Appendix 1.
● To form lower-case letters of the correct size relative to one another.
● To start using some of the diagonal and horizontal strokes needed to join letters and understand which letters, when adjacent to one another, are best left unjoined.
● To write capital letters and digits of the correct size, orientation and relationship to one another and to lower-case letters.
● To use spacing between words that reflects the size of the letters.

Resources
Individual whiteboards and pens

3: Writing descriptive poetry

Introduction

● Display the photocopiable pages 'The Magic of the Brain', 'Thanksgiving' and 'I Asked the Little Boy Who Cannot See' from the CD-ROM. Looking at them individually, ask the children to select phrases they think use descriptive language particularly well, giving reasons for their choices.
● Explain that it is unlikely that the poets chose all of these effective words when the poems were first written, they will have gone over the poems several times, making changes until they felt they had chosen the best words.

Paired work

● Focus on 'The Magic of the Brain' and 'Thanksgiving', identifying the repetition in the structure of each poem.
● Ask the children to choose one of the poems to copy the structure for writing their own poem about the senses.
● Working with a partner, they should share ideas for their poems, thinking about their reasons for valuing and appreciating their senses.

Independent work

● Ask the children to make notes to use when writing their poems. Suggest they use headings for the senses, writing possible words and phrases under each heading. Remind them to use noun phrases and powerful verbs.

Review

● Ask the children to work again with their planning partners, discussing their potential word choices, each offering comments and possible alternative suggestions.

Curriculum objectives
● To use expanded noun phrases to describe and specify.
● To write poetry.
● To recognise simple recurring literary language in stories and poetry.
● To discuss their favourite words and phrases.

Resources
Photocopiable pages 'The Magic of the Brain', 'Thanksgiving', 'I Asked the Little Boy Who Cannot See' from the CD-ROM

Curriculum objectives
● To write poetry.
● To segment words into phonemes and representing these by graphemes, spelling many correctly.
● To apply spelling rules and guidelines, as listed in Appendix 1.
● To form lower-case letters of the correct size relative to one another.
● To start using some of the diagonal and horizontal strokes needed to join letters and understand which letters, when adjacent to one another, are best left unjoined.
● To write capital letters and digits of the correct size, orientation and relationship to one another and to lower-case letters.
● To use spacing between words that reflects the size of the letters.

Resources
Children's poem planning notes from the previous lesson

Curriculum objectives
● To read aloud what they have written with appropriate intonation to make the meaning clear.

Resources
Children's acrostic poems from lesson 2 and descriptive poems from lesson 4; recording equipment (optional)

4: Writing a descriptive poem

Introduction
● Invite the children to share some of the words and phrases they noted in the previous lesson for possible inclusion in their poems. Ask the rest of the class to identify which senses are being described.

Independent work
● Tell the children that they will use their notes to write their poems, using the structure they selected from the two poems you read together. Explain that they may think of other words or phrases to use as they are writing, and that this is fine – they do not have to just use their ideas from the previous lesson if they think of something better today. Remind them to use their spelling and phonic knowledge and to use their best handwriting, so that others can read and enjoy their finished poems.
● Allow the children time to write their poems, illustrating them if there is time.

Review
● Ask: *Did anyone think of new words or phrases that you didn't think of in the previous lesson?* Share examples. Invite the children to share their favourite parts of their poems.

5: Poetry performance

Introduction
● Explain that in today's lesson, the children will have the opportunity to share the poems they have written this week, by reading them aloud. Ask them to suggest what they should bear in mind in order to give a good performance, noting their ideas on the board. Ensure all relevant points are covered, such as using a loud, clear voice, not reading too quickly, using punctuation to pause in the right places, and using intonation to engage listeners.

Independent work
● Give the children a few minutes to read through their poems quietly, practising in their heads how they will read them aloud.

Group work
● Organise the class into groups and place them sufficiently apart from each other that there is as little disturbance as possible between groups when the children are reading aloud.
● The children take turns to read first their acrostics then their descriptive poems to their group, taking up the majority of the lesson.

Review
● Ask children from each group to feed back on how it felt to read their own work aloud. Invite positive comments from the children as listeners, referring to the content and performance, and using the criteria listed on the board at the start of the lesson. The lesson could be followed up by inviting children to record their poems to be listened to in the future.

Grammar and punctuation: Writing questions

Revise

● Recap the three different sentences forms: statements, questions and exclamations. Give the children examples of each type about the human body, for example: *What sense do our eyes give us? We all have a skeleton. The human body is amazing!* Ask them to write in the air the correct punctuation for the end of each sentence. Then ask them to suggest other similar sentences.

Assess

● Ask the children to write three sentences of each type about 'Ourselves'. These could be on a mixture of topics, such as the growth of the human body, feelings and the senses (all areas they have worked on in the half term). Remind them to punctuate the sentences correctly, according to the sentence type.

Further practice

● Periodically carry out the same activities as those above for other topics you are studying, including lessons in other subject areas, reinforcing for the children that the skills they learn in English should be transferred to all of their writing. When they learn about commands, add these to the sentence types.

Curriculum objectives
● To add suffixes to spell longer words.
● To use the grammar for Year 2 in Appendix 2.

Resources
Interactive activity 'Which suffix?' on the CD-ROM

Spelling: Suffixes '-ness', '-less', '-ful'

Review

● Write the three suffixes – '-less', '-ness', '-ful' – on the board. Ask the children for examples of words describing feelings or characteristics that end with each suffix, and for a sentence containing each word. Remind the class of the spelling of the suffix '-ful' – that it has only one 'l'.
● Write on the board: *dark, harm, end,* asking which suffixes can be added to them. (*Darkness, harmful/harmless, endless.*) Ask: *Are these also words that describe feelings or characteristics?* Establish that the suffixes can be added to words that describe other things. Note also that some root words can have more than one suffix added to form new words, often creating opposites as in the example above.

Assess

● Read out a series of words with the suffixes '-less', '-ness', '-ful' for the children to write. Also give them some root words, asking them to add an appropriate suffix. Some suggestions are: *boldness, successful, careless, cheerful, loudness, breathless, kindness, truthful, thoughtless, cold, delight, harm, gentle, point, play.*
● From their list of words, ask the children to write a sentence for each, spelling the suffix correctly.

Further practice

● Children who are still unsure, could use the interactive activity 'Which suffix?' on the CD-ROM independently.
● Challenge the children to create three long lists, one for each of the suffixes. As they find a new word, they should add it to the list which is displayed on the wall.
● Add the suffix '-ment' to the collection when this has been introduced to the class.
● For further support, see page 101.

Curriculum objectives
● To be introduced to non-fiction books that are structured in different ways.
● To listen to, discuss and express views about a wide range of contemporary and classic poetry, stories and non-fiction at a level beyond that at which they can read independently.

Resources
A pile of non-fiction books; a pile of fiction books; photocopiable page 'Fiction or non-fiction?' from the CD-ROM; interactive activity 'Fiction or non-fiction?' on the CD-ROM

Reading: Comparing fiction and non-fiction

Revise

● Use the interactive activity 'Fiction or non-fiction?' on the CD-ROM.
● Ask each child to choose a non-fiction book from the pile and compare it with the book of a partner.
● Tell them to make a list of all the organisational and language features they find in their books.
● Make a class list of all the features the children have found in their non-fiction texts: glossary, index, contents page, pictures, captions, subheads, facts and so on.
● Discuss which of these features are also found in story books.
● Talk about which books need to be read in order and which can be dipped in and out of. Discuss the difference between reading a story and looking up information.
● Ask the children to work with a partner. Tell one of the partners to get a fiction or a non-fiction book from the pile without their partner seeing what it is. Ask them to describe the features of the book they have chosen to their partner. How quickly can the partners guess whether the book is fiction or non-fiction?

Assess

● Hand out photocopiable page 'Fiction or non-fiction?' from the CD-ROM and ask the children to carry out the task.

Further practice

● Give a child a story book and a non-fiction book and ask them to tell you the difference between them.
● Remind the children to keep the class or school library organised properly, ensuring that when they use books they go back into the right section, either fiction or the correct non-fiction section.

Curriculum objectives
● To re-read to check that their writing makes sense and that verbs to indicate time are used correctly and consistently, including verbs in the continuous form.
● To proofread to check for errors in spelling, grammar and punctuation.

Writing: Checking, proofreading and correcting

Review

● Ask the children to find some examples of their own recent writing where they have made corrections to their first drafts (their poems in week 6 perhaps, or their re-write of 'A walk in the country' in week 5). When they have looked through both pieces of work, ask them what sort of changes they made, listing these on the board.

● Go through the list with the class, asking if there could be other things that might be checked when proofreading their work, adding any that are obvious omissions. Ensure that language use is included as well as technical points – for example, changing a word or sentence structure to improve the quality of the writing, avoiding repetitions and so on.

Assess

● This assessment is in two parts, over two lessons. In order for the children to proofread and change their own writing they first have to do a draft, and then have the opportunity to proofread and change it.

● Ask the children to write a descriptive piece about the sense of taste. They should think of different taste sensations, such as sweet, sour, salty, bitter, and different foods or drinks that can be described in different ways. More experienced writers might include less obvious ideas, such as the taste of salty sea air. They can also include textures in their descriptions. Encourage them to begin their sentences in a variety of ways.

● Allow the children time to write their descriptive pieces independently, explaining that in the next lesson they will have the opportunity to proofread and change their writing.

● In the second lesson, remind the children about the list you compiled together of things that should be considered when checking and proofreading writing. Explain that they will now go over their descriptive writing about taste, using those criteria and making any changes they feel are necessary either to correct or to improve their writing. They should re-write their piece with the corrections and amendments. If you wish, you could add a handwriting requirement to this stage of the assessment.

● To assess the writing, you will need both pieces of writing – the drafts and the final copies – in order to see where and how the children have made changes and how effective they are.

Further practice

● Encourage the establishment of writing partners who get used to helping each other proofread and re-draft their work.

● Encourage newly learned elements of writing to be included in proofreading and amending work, in order to further develop the children's writing skills.

Name: _____ Date: _____

Syllable build-up

■ Cut out your own set of words and use them to play word snap with a partner.

✂

skeleton	staircase
houses	station
frighten	tennis
happened	together
connected	finished
funny	properly
another	reminds
animals	awake
elephant	parrot
crocodile	better

Name: _____   Date: _____

What they heard

■ Think about the night the skeletons were making a noise. Write some ideas for what people in the town heard and thought.

Witness 1 Name _____

What they heard _____

What they found _____

How they felt _____

What they did _____

Witness 2 Name _____

What they heard _____

What they found _____

How they felt _____

What they did _____

Witness 3 Name _____

What they heard _____

What they found _____

How they felt _____

What they did _____

> I can suggest ideas for what characters said and felt based on the story.
>
> How did you do?

The five Ws

■ Think of your three witnesses to the skeletons' noisy night in the town. Write a question for each of the Ws that you would ask them to find out more about what happened.

 When _____

_____

 What _____

_____

 Where _____

_____

 Who _____

_____

 Why _____

and one extra...

 How _____

_____

I can ask questions of characters in a story.
I can use question marks.

How did you do?

PHOTOCOPIABLE   **SCHOLASTIC** www.scholastic.co.uk

Ourselves – a non-fiction report about growing

■ Write down notes for each heading to help you gather ideas for writing your non-fiction report.

How we change _____

_____

_____

_____

_____

What we eat and drink _____

_____

_____

Things we can do/what we learn _____

_____

_____

_____

I can use non-fiction books to find information.

How did you do?

Choose the suffix

■ Choose the suffix '-ful', '-less' or '-ness' to complete each of the words below, then write a sentence for each new word.

sad_____   joy_____   friend_____

play_____   cheer_____   fear_____

peace_____   rest_____   wonder_____

_____

_____

_____

_____

_____

_____

_____

_____

_____

I can use suffixes to make new words and use them in sentences.

How did you do?

My game cards

■ Use this sheet to plan your character game cards.

Name
_____
_____
_____
_____
_____
● _____
● _____
● _____
● _____

Name
_____
_____
_____
_____
● _____
● _____
● _____
● _____

Name
_____
_____
_____
_____
● _____
● _____
● _____
● _____

Name
_____
_____
_____
● _____
● _____
● _____
● _____

I can create characters with different characteristics.

How did you do?

Describe the setting

■ Write descriptions for each of the settings, using as many senses as you can. Try to use as many different adjectives as you can.

A wood   A street in town

A busy kitchen   A river and waterfall

I can use my senses to choose good words to describe settings.

How did you do?

I can do better than that!

■ Use what you know about using the senses to describe things. Rewrite this piece making it more interesting for the reader. As you read it, note your ideas for words and phrases on the lines underneath.

A walk in the country

As I walked down the lane I could see trees and hedges. One of the fields was full of flowers while in another there were some cows. I could hear birds in the trees and I drank some water from a nearby stream. The air was fresh even though there was traffic in the distance. There was a little breeze. I felt the grass brush against my legs and a spider crawling along my arm. The sky was blue with some clouds

Write your ideas here:

_____

_____

_____

_____

I can add words and phrases to improve a piece of descriptive writing.

How did you do?

Habitats

From looking at hot and cold places and the animals and people who live there, the concept of habitat is extended from the local area to locations that provide the settings for stories. The children use a range of non-fiction texts, including the internet, to find out about creatures of polar lands and deserts. They read a poem by Thomas Hardy about the snow and use the popular *Katie Morag* to see how characters and events are linked to their settings. Reading *Katie Morag and the Two Grandmothers*, the children interrogate the text and use the idea of island life to plan and write their own story. Spelling, punctuation and grammar elements covered include possessive apostrophes, contractions, noun phrases and subordinate clauses.

Expected prior learning
- Can understand what a setting is.
- Can use the senses to describe a setting.
- Can understand what a habitat is.
- Can understand that stories take place in particular settings.

Overview of progression
- The children will move from looking at and describing their local area, to finding out about and describing unfamiliar habitats and locations.
- They will develop their understanding of how characters and events are affected by their setting.
- By using noun phrases and subordinate clauses they will improve the quality of description and language construction in their writing.
- They will gain confidence in using the apostrophe, for singular possession and contractions.

Creative context
- This half-term's work would fit in well with the study of habitats in science.
- There are clear links to basic geographical vocabulary, the use of maps and looking at characteristics of a small area of the UK.
- In art, the children can create representations of a wide variety of habitats using drawing, painting, collage or 3D. They could also draw or paint characters showing how what they wear is affected by their location.
- The Scottish setting for the Katie Morag stories could link to listening to and learning some traditional Scottish songs, and maybe even dances.

Preparation
Gather together a range of books, suitable for the reading levels of the class, about hot and cold places and the animals that live there. It will also be useful to have copies of several of the *Katie Morag* titles. Familiarise yourself a little with the geography of the part of Scotland where the Katie Morag stories are set – the north-west coastal area. Check out the suggested websites about animals and habitats (week 1, lesson 2), adding more if you wish.

You will also need:
Multiple copies (if possible) of *Katie Morag and the Two Grandmothers* by Mairi Hedderwick, a selection of other *Katie Morag* stories, large map of the world, sunhat, winter hat, information books about hot and cold places and animals in their habitats, internet access, scissors, glue sticks, sticky notes, a selection of fiction, non-fiction and poetry books, photos of snow, map of a local park, nature reserve or school grounds, leaflets about rural locations, leaflets about local walks, a map of Scotland showing the island of Coll, a map of Struay that you have created showing the main locations, dice.

On the CD-ROM you will find:
Media resources 'Habitats', 'Living at the extreme', 'Island versus mainland'; interactive activities 'Get it right', 'Which /j/?', 'Possessive apostrophes'; photocopiable pages 'Katie Morag and the Two Grandmothers', 'Animal homes', 'Sam Sparrow gets lost', 'The strange room'

■ SCHOLASTIC

Chapter at a glance

An overview of the chapter. For curriculum objective codes, please see pages 8–10.

Week	Lesson	Curriculum objectives	Summary of activities	Outcome
1	1	RC: 12	Define the term *habitat*. Identify habitats on map of the world. Formulate questions on given habitats.	• Can understand what habitats are. • Can answer and ask general questions about habitats.
	2	RC: 9, 12	Choose wild animal to research using books or websites. Choose and justify key words to describe animal's habitat.	• Can answer own questions through research.
	3	WC: 16	Connectives of subordination explained and examples shared. Sentences about animals linked using suggested connectives.	• Can use researched facts about animals in written sentences using subordinate connectives.
	4	RC: 12 WC: 4, 16	Explore and describe hot and cold places for humans to live. Write descriptive paragraph.	• Can identify characteristics of hot and cold places, assigning appropriate vocabulary. • Can write, share and ask questions about descriptive paragraph.
	5	WC: 4, 16	Recap on habitats and animals that live there. Discuss and write about one animal.	• Can use writing frame to explain why one animal survives in its habitat, either hot or cold.
2	1	RC: 1, 7	Listen to and discuss 'Snow in the Suburbs' by Thomas Hardy.	• Can identify unfamiliar words. • Can choose favourite parts of poem, reading aloud and commenting on them. • Can choose section of poem to learn by heart.
	2	RWR: 4 WT: 8, 9 WC: 17	Recap suffixes learned this year. Find examples in Hardy poem and other book. Create sentences with root and suffix words.	• Can identify words with suffixes. • Can use correct spellings in dictated sentences.
	3	RC: 1, 7	Re-read poem for descriptive purposes, highlighting adjectives.	• Can work as a text detective looking for language features in the poem.
	4	WC: 3, 14	Describe different types of snow using noun phrases.	• Can write noun phrases about snow for each of the senses and share favourite ones.
	5	WC: 3, 11, 14	Use notes and imagination to write snow poem, including noun phrases.	• Can write and read aloud snow poems using interesting vocabulary including noun phrases. • Can offer comments on partner's work.
3	1	RC: 15 WC: 6, 14	List wildlife that might be seen locally. Go on a nature walk and map flora and fauna.	• Can create annotated map showing and describing locations of flora and fauna. • Can link creatures seen to habitats noted.
	2	RC: 4 WT: 1 WC: 6, 8	Investigate leaflets and identify key features and descriptive vocabulary. Write leaflet on habitat from recent walk.	• Can begin to make own simple leaflet on a habitat chosen from recent walk.
	3	WC: 4, 11, 18	Recap instructions. Identify vocabulary for directions. Write instructions for own walk.	• Can write directions for a walk based on map from earlier in the week.
	4	WT: 1 WC: 4, 14	Describe a pond. Write descriptive phrases for habitat in own leaflet.	• Can add descriptive phrases to leaflet, share and evaluate.
	5	WC: 2, 8, 16, 18	Recap visit to nature area. Check leaflet contents and add information under subheadings and extra fun facts.	• Can use all required elements of content and language to complete leaflet. • Can read and comment on partner's work, with explanations.
4	1	RWR: 3, 4 RC: 1, 2, 11, 12, 13	Listen to *Katie Morag and the Two Grandmothers*, predicting events, discussing setting and characters.	• Can offer ideas about differences between the two grandmothers based on own home location and write some of these in speech and thought bubbles.
	2	RWR: 5 WT: 3, 4, 5, 8, 9	Identify words with possessive apostrophes and common exception words and learn to spell them.	• Can find and learn to spell words with possessive apostrophes and those that do not follow phonic rules.
	3	RC: 1, 9, 12	Compare island and city life. Hot seat the two grandmothers. Discuss how where the grandmothers live affects their relationship.	• Can offer suggestions for how location affects how a character behaves.
	4	RC: 2, 3, 9, 15	Compare map of Struay with the *Katie Morag* stories and the end-papers from the books. Label map with events. Role-play, freeze-frame and thought-track characters.	• Can connect events and characters' actions and thoughts with locations on Struay.
	5	WT: 5 WC: 1, 5, 16	Listen to oral model of creating a recount. Select character to write recount for.	• Can write recounts of character in a particular setting taken from role play in previous lesson.

Chapter at a glance

Week	Lesson	Curriculum objectives	Summary of activities	Outcome
5	1	WT: 5 WC: 5, 6	Discuss familiar story settings. Annotate a story map.	• Can produce annotated maps with location names, characters and brief descriptions.
	2	WT: 5, 8 WC: 5, 6, 14	Listen to oral model of expanding descriptions of settings on maps. Expand descriptions of settings with a partner, then write own descriptions.	• Can write an expanded description of a setting from the annotated map.
	3	WC: 1	Listen to explanation of how to use the story map as a board game. Choose characters from cards, and select locations on island map. Play the game, building a story as they go.	• Can develop a story in role using setting to influence actions and dialogue.
	4	WC: 1, 5, 6	Recap interpretations of characters from board game. Choose three to discuss with a partner and develop. Write brief biographies.	• Can develop different types of character in discussion and writing.
	5	WC: 5, 6	Recap week's work. Partners discuss plots for stories and note down ideas.	• Can develop ideas for a story using existing settings and characters.
6	1	WC: 5, 7	Listen to explanation of how storyboards are made and their purpose. Create island storyboards and use to tell story to partner, each offering advice.	• Can create a storyboard and use it to tell own story aloud.
	2	WT: 8, 9	Listen to explanation of ways /j/ sound is spelled. Indicate spelling choice for given words.	• Can spell words with /j/ sound in the correct way.
	3	WT: 5 WC: 1, 12, 14, 16	Watch model of how to write a draft using a storyboard, including elements of spelling, grammar and punctuation. Write first draft of island story.	• Can use storyboard to write draft story.
	4	WC: 10	Watch model of proofreading and editing process using interactive activity 'Get it right'. Proofread and edit own story, then share work with a partner for further suggestions.	• Can proofread and edit own writing, understanding that this is a vital part of the writing process.
	5	WC: 12, 14, 16	Read through own story, finding examples of subordinate clauses, noun phrases, contractions and possessive apostrophes, which are shared.	• Can identify, share and discuss subordinate clauses, noun phrases, contractions and possessive apostrophes. • Stories collated into class book.

Background knowledge

Report: A text that tells about a certain subject. In this half term, the reports studied are non-chronological reports which are written in the present tense.

Sequence: The order in which events take place.

Subordination: A clause that is less important than the main clause, often introduced by *when*, *if*, *that* or *because*. In this half-term's work, subordination is used for reasoning and sentence extension.

Week 1 lesson plans

This week the children identify and discuss different large-scale habitats. They describe hot and cold habitats and find out about animals that survive there. They use a writing frame to explain why one animal can live in either a hot or cold habitat. Connectives for subordination are introduced as a technique for extending sentences and providing more detail.

1: What is a habitat?

Introduction

- Explain to the class that you are going to spend the next few weeks investigating habitats. Ask: *What is a habitat?* Establish that it is the place where living things live.
- Ask the children to think of different animals and together decide what sort of habitat each one lives in.

Whole-class work

- Display the media resource 'Habitats' on the CD-ROM. Talk about the main features as you look at each one – they might be very cold, dry, wet and so on.
- Display a map of the world (see screen 2 of the media resource). Establish what is land and what is water and determine which parts the children can identify as hot, cold and in between. Use this information to decide together which parts of the world might contain the habitats you have been looking at.

Paired work

- Ask the children to share with their partner some questions about habitats. Encourage half of the class to focus on questions about very cold places – for example, Is all the water frozen? Is it cold all year round? How do animals keep warm?
- The other half of the class can think of questions about very hot places, such as deserts or tropical rainforests, for example, Is there any water to drink? How do the animals keep away from the sun? What do they find to eat? and so on.
- Provide the children with slips of paper. Ask them to write down three questions from their paired discussion that they would most like to know the answers to or that they thought were the most interesting. Remind them to use capital letters and question marks.
- Invite the children to bring their questions to the front of the class. Place the questions about hot places in the sunhat and those about cold places in the winter hat.

Whole-class work

- Gather the class together. Select a number of questions from the hat and discuss possible answers to the questions with the children.
- Make a note of any fresh questions that the discussions throw up.

> **Differentiation**
> - Less confident learners can formulate questions as a group.

Review

- There will be some questions in this lesson that no one knows the answer to, or where responses are uncertain. Ask how we could find out what the answers are, and discuss responses. Can we always be sure that answers about factual information are correct? How could we check up on the answers we are given? What makes us confident that someone is giving us the right answer?

Expected outcomes
- All children can explain some differences between hot and cold places and can use the subordinate conjunction because.
- Most children can explain why particular animals are adapted to survive in either a hot or cold habitat. They can use more than one subordinate conjunction.
- Some children can make further comparisons between habitats, using a greater vocabulary and clearer explanations both orally and in writing. They can use several subordinate conjunctions confidently.

Curriculum objectives
- To answer and ask questions.

Resources
A large map of the world; media resource 'Habitats' on the CD-ROM; a sunhat and a winter hat; small slips of paper

Curriculum objectives
● To draw on what they already know or on background information and vocabulary provided by the teacher.
● To answer and ask questions.

Resources
Habitat questions from the previous lesson; information books about animals and habitats at the correct reading level; access to child-friendly websites about habitats, such as World Wildlife Fund (WWF) and National Geographic

2: Habitat vocabulary

Introduction
● Revisit the questions that the children wrote in the previous lesson.
● Focus on potential research topics about animals that live in the habitats, such as where they live, what they eat, what they drink and how they cope with the extreme temperatures.

Group work
● Working in groups of three, ask the children to choose one wild animal to research using the books and websites made available. They should find out where the animal lives, what the habitat is like, and why the animal is good at living in that environment.
● Suggest headings to guide their search, such as the animal's name, and key words such as *habitat*, *food*, *description*.
● When they've finished, ask them to write ten words that describe the habitat their animal lives in.
● Next, ask them to put their ten words in order of importance and then to cross out all the words apart from the top three.

Review
● Encourage the different groups to share their words and explain why they think these words are the most important.
● Ask: *If you could only teach someone learning about habitats three words, what would they be?*

Curriculum objectives
● To use subordination (using *when, if, that* or *because*).

Resources
Word lists from the previous lesson

3: When, if, that

Introduction
● Taking an example such as polar bears living in the Arctic, ask the children to suggest some sentences about the animal – for example, *Polar bears can live where it is very cold, Polar bears have thick fur, Polar bears eat seals* and so on.
● Recap on how we use connectives to link sentences and ideas. Write the words when, if, that and because on the board. Explain that these connectives are useful when we want to explain something in more detail.
● Ask the children to help you to combine some of these sentences – for example, *Polar bears can live where it is very cold because they have thick fur. Polar bears catch seals when they come to up to breathe.*

Group work
● Ask the children to return to their groups of three from the previous lesson and to look at the notes they made about an animal and its habitat, and at the three words that they thought were the most important.
● Ask them to write three sentences about their animal and its habitat, each of which uses *when, if, that* or *because* to provide more information.

> **Differentiation**
> ● Ask less confident learners to focus on sentences using because and when.

Review
● Invite the groups of three to read their sentences aloud, with one child reading the first part, another saying the connective and a third saying the second part.
● Discuss which connective was used most frequently.

4: Living at the extreme

Curriculum objectives
● To answer and ask questions.
● To write for different purposes.
● To use subordination (*when, if, that* or *because*).

Resources
Media resource 'Living at the extreme' on the CD-ROM; photocopiable page 168 'Hot or not?'; scissors; a range of information books, and/ or suitable websites about hot and cold places (where people can live)

Introduction
● Display the images of houses in hot and cold places, in media resource 'Living at the extreme' on the CD-ROM. Ask: *If you had to live in one of these two locations, which would you choose?* Invite children to explain their choice, including the word *because* in their replies.

Paired work
● Give pairs of children the photocopiable page 168 'Hot or not?' to cut into word cards. Ask them to sort the words into hot words and cold words.

Whole-class work
● Go through the words as a class and discuss which category each pair put them into. Could some words fit in both categories?
● Use information books and/or websites to explain any words that the children weren't sure of and clear up any misconceptions. Point out, for example, that some hot places are very cold at night.

Independent work
● Ask the children to write a descriptive paragraph about what it is like to live somewhere hot or cold, using descriptive phrases, interesting facts and the connectives *when, if, that* and *because* to build in explanations.

> **Differentiation**
> ● Encourage less confident learners to write two descriptive sentences using the words from the photocopiable sheet.

Review
● Working in pairs, ask the children to read each other's descriptive paragraphs and ask their partner questions about it.

5: A good place to live

Curriculum objectives
● To write for different purposes.
● To learn how to use subordination (*when, if, that* or *because*).

Resources
Photocopiable page 169 'A perfect home'; a map of the world

Introduction
● Display a map of the world and explain that they will be choosing one animal to write about, explaining why it survives in its habitat.

Paired work
● Ask the children to recap on the different animals they have been finding out about, linking them to hot or cold places. They should help each other to select one animal that they feel they know most about.

Independent work
● Hand out photocopiable page 169 'A perfect home', and explain that this shows sentence starters to help the children organise their thoughts and guide their writing about their chosen animal.
● Go briefly through an example that they are unlikely to have chosen, and work through the writing frame orally, referring to the availability of food relative to the animal's size and diet, the animal's fur or skin in relation to temperature, its characteristics such as speed, stealth or camouflage.
● Draw attention to the subordinates, inviting the children to use more if they can. Guide children how to use the sheet before they do their writing independently.

Review
● Invite several children to read out part of their explanations, missing out the animal's name for the rest of the class to guess.

Expected outcomes

● All children can engage with and discuss the poem. They can write some descriptive noun phrases for different types of snow.
● Most children can choose favourite words and phrases. They can identify and spell suffixes they have learned this year.
● Some children can incorporate new language learning into their own poems, making effective use of noun phrases.

Curriculum objectives

● To listen to, discuss and express views about a wide range of contemporary and classic poetry, stories and non-fiction at a level beyond that at which they can read independently.
● To discuss their favourite words and phrases.

Resources

Photocopiable page 170 'Snow in the Suburbs'

Week 2 lesson plans

This week the children read 'Snow in the Suburbs' by Thomas Hardy. The poem is at a higher reading level than the children are able to read themselves, but by the end of the week they should be able to understand it and comment on it. The poem is used to look at how we can use extensive vocabulary for a small subject matter, and further revision is done on using suffixes. At the end of the week, the children write their own snowy poem.

I: Snow in the suburbs

Introduction

● Display photocopiable page 170 'Snow in the Suburbs' (by Thomas Hardy). Read the poem to the children, using expression in your voice and actions to bring out as much of the meaning as possible. Did they notice where you paused for the punctuation?

Paired work

● Now hand out individual the photocopiable sheet and encourage the children to follow the words as you read.
● Tell the children to turn to their partner, and together to pick out any words they don't understand and underline them.

Whole-class work

● Share the words that the children don't understand, which will probably include *palings* (wooden railings), *waft* (move gently), *mute* (without speech), *inurns* (to bury in an urn), *nether* (lower), *blanched* (turned white). Explain what the lines that include these words mean. Point out Thomas Hardy's dates and explain that this old poem uses old-fashioned language and phrases, but that we can understand it if we think about it carefully.
● With these words explained, go through the poem asking the children what they think is happening in each line. Help them to see where each individual sentence or phrase begins and ends.
● Read the poem again, this time asking the children to close their eyes and picture the tree covered in snow, the silent street, the snow-filled fence, the snow billowing about, the ball of snow landing on the little sparrow, the cascade of snow falling off the tree, and the black cat looking for someone to let him in.

Paired work

● Tell the children to turn back to their partner and to have a go at reading the poem together.
● Encourage them to tell each other what their favourite pair of lines is. They should explain why they like it, and what the lines are about. Challenge them to describe what's happening in the line in their own words.
● Invite the pairs of children to choose a set of four lines to learn to recite by heart.

> ### Differentiation
> ● Some children will need extra support with this poem. If possible, spend time reading it with them before the lesson. Go through it line by line, explaining the meaning so that they can participate in the class discussion.

Review

● Ask the children to tell you which favourite lines they have chosen, what they mean and why they like them. Correct any misconceptions.
● Choose children who have chosen different lines to recite the poem, filling in any unloved lines yourself if necessary.

Curriculum objectives
● To read words containing common suffixes.
● To write from memory simple sentences dictated by the teacher that include words using the GPCs, common exception words and punctuation taught so far.
● To apply spelling rules and guidelines, as listed in Appendix 1.
● To use the grammar for Year 2 in Appendix 2.

Resources
Photocopiable page 171 'Practising suffixes'; a large selection of fiction, poetry and non-fiction books

2: Revisiting suffixes

Introduction
● Ask the children what a suffix is and to offer some examples.
● Give each pair the photocopiable page 171 'Practising suffixes'.
● Tell them to cut out the roots and suffixes and to use them to create nine words, trying out all the options.
● Challenge them to say which words can be found in 'Snow in the Suburbs'. (*pavement, meeting, blanched, meandering* and *immediately*.)

Paired work
● Give each pair a fiction, a poetry and a non-fiction book and challenge them to find as many words as they can ending in the suffixes '-ing', '-ly', '-ed' and '-ment'. They should note them down and also attempt to write the root word.

Whole-class work
● Share the words that the children have found, and discuss how they have spelled the root word, correcting any errors.
● Choose some of the most useful words and create some sentences using both the root and root-and-suffix versions of the word.

> **Differentiation**
> ● Invite less confident learners to focus on finding words ending in '-ing'.

Review
● Dictate the new sentences as a short spelling test, asking the children to check their partner's work before giving the correct spellings for them to see.

Curriculum objectives
● To listen to, discuss and express views about a wide range of contemporary and classic poetry, stories and non-fiction at a level beyond that at which they can read independently.
● To discuss their favourite words and phrases

Resources
Photocopiable page 170 'Snow in the Suburbs'

3: Fleecy fall

Introduction
● Display photocopiable page 170 'Snow in the suburbs'. Re-read the poem to the children and then focus on the description of how flakes move. How many ways can they spot? (*grope back upward, meandering down, descend again, fleecy fall, showers, volley.*)

Whole-class work
● Read the poem once more and ask the children to listen for how these four words are described: *fall, size, slope, hope*.
● Highlight the adjective used in each case (*fleecy, slight, blanched, feeble*) and ask pairs to think of a different noun this adjective could be used to describe.
● Say: *So, Thomas Hardy uses 'wow' words in his poem. He describes the same thing in different ways, and he uses adjectives and nouns together instead of just a noun. What else does he do?*

Paired work
● Challenge the children to be text detectives to find a place in the poem where Thomas Hardy uses repetition, where he uses rhyme, where he paints a picture in our heads and where he brings in feeling.
● Ask the children to decide now on their favourite part of the poem. Can they remember the favourite lines they learned in the previous lesson?

Review
● Share the children's finds, checking that they have understood the different techniques that Thomas Hardy has used.
● Ask: *Has anyone's favourite line changed now we know the poem better?*

Curriculum objectives
● To write poetry.
● To use expanded noun phrases to describe and specify.

Resources
Photos of snow – ask the children to bring them in from home, use your own or look on local news websites (optional); A4 paper; photocopiable page 170 'Snow in the Suburbs'

4: Some snowy words

Introduction

● Ask the children to turn to their partners and describe how snow falls and what it looks like. Tell them to think about different types of snow they've come across: *slow and big, thin and wind-blown, almost rain* and so on. Challenge the children to create as many different noun phrases as they can to describe how the snow moves.
● If they are in need of inspiration, show the class a selection of snowy photographs.

Independent work

● Ask the children to spend a little time picturing a snowy scene they have experienced: their garden, their street, building a snowman and so on.
● Tell them to divide a piece of paper into six sections and write a heading for each section: *What I see, What I hear, What I touch, What I taste, What I smell* and *What I feel.* Tell them to note some adjective/noun phrases, using the poem or their classmates' ideas to help them. Ask: *How does the snow change the landscape? How does the snow change the sounds around us – is it quieter or noisier? How does the snow make us feel?*

> **Differentiation**
> ● With less confident learners, discuss each sense in turn.

Review

● Ask children to read out their best phrases. Write these as a list to create an impromptu poem.

Curriculum objectives
● To write poetry.
● To read aloud what they have written with appropriate intonation to make the meaning clear.
● To use expanded noun phrases to describe and specify.

Resources
Snow scene notes from the previous lesson

5: My snowy poem

Introduction

● Ask the children to close their eyes and picture again the snowy scene they made notes about in the previous lesson.
● Now tell them to turn to their partner and describe their scene.

Independent work

● Tell the children to look at their notes from the previous lesson and to circle the parts that are most successful.
● Are there any words that could be improved by adding a suffix to them?
● Encourage the class to write a poem with six or eight quality lines about snow. Tell them to focus on creating phrases with interesting vocabulary – using adjectives to create noun phrases – that really capture their thoughts on snow, rather than worrying about using rhyme or making the lines all the same length.

> **Differentiation**
> ● For less confident learners, create a group poem using the words that the children gathered in the previous lesson, perhaps with a repeating start to each line such as *Snow moves..., Snow is..* or *When it snows every..*

Review

● Organise the children into groups and ask them to read their poems aloud to each other. Remind them to speak clearly and to try to use their voice to show the meaning in the poem.
● Ask the other children to tell the reader what they liked about their poem. Invite them to try to say how it made them feel.

Week 3 lesson plans

This week the children investigate their own local habitat. At the beginning of the week they go on a local nature walk, noting down the habitats they find and the animals they find in them. This walk will then feed into a week-long project to create a leaflet for your area, building up noun phrases to use, practising previous work on connectives and writing instructions for a walk.

I: Going on a walk

Introduction

- Before this lesson, ask the children to hunt for animals in their garden or near their house (snails, birds, cats and so on) and to note down where they found them.
- Create a class list of all the animals that the children have seen and where they saw them.
- Display images of garden wildlife from the internet and discuss which the children have seen in the past. Sound out the names of the animals and talk about the animals the children are unlikely to see, even though they might be around – for example, foxes, bats and moles.
- What types of plants did the children see?

Whole-class work

- Go on a class walk to a local park or nature reserve, or use the school grounds, and give each child a map which covers the area they're going to be looking at.
- Ensure that the children can understand what the map represents, and that they know where they are located on it.
- Tell the children to put a star on the map where they find a plant or animal of interest and write the name of what they find – pet, snail, moss, cherry tree and so on.
- Discuss that they won't be able to write down all the plants they find so they will need to choose the ones they thought were most interesting. They will probably be able to note all the animals they see.

Paired work

- Back in the classroom, give each child a piece of A3 paper and tell them to stick their map in the middle of the paper. Encourage them to use the space around their map to record the different types of habitat they found – for example, logs, grass, pond, bird house, wall, wood, dry area under a hedge. They can draw lines linking the labels to the locations on the map.
- Can they add an adjective to describe each location? (*Damp bog*, *dry leaves* and so on.) Tell them to discuss options with their partner before adding the adjectives to their map.

Whole-class work

- Using an enlarged version of the map, gather together all the locations the children have found and choose the best adjective to describe each one. Add notes on the animals and plants they found in each location.
- Help the children to make links between the locations and the needs of the animals and plants that the children found in them.

> **Differentiation**
> - Give less confident learners a list of example adjectives that they can choose from to describe their locations.

Review

- Using the map, follow the route that you took on your walk, asking different children to describe the locations, animals and plants they found.

Expected outcomes

- All children can add simple annotations to a local map. They can identify some of the features of a leaflet and use this to make their own. They use some noun phrases.
- Most children can add annotations with greater detail and identify and include all key features of a leaflet.
- Some children can critically reflect on their own and others' leaflets, taking all key features into account including language use.

Curriculum objectives

- To write down ideas and/ or key words, including new vocabulary.
- To use expanded noun phrases to describe and specify.
- To explain and discuss their understanding of books, poems and other material, both those that they listen to and those that they read for themselves.

Resources

An A4 map of a local park, the school grounds or a nature reserve (a simple black and white map that will be easy for the children to annotate is best); one enlarged copy of the map; a website displaying garden wildlife, such as the Royal Society for the Protection of Birds (RSPB); internet access

Curriculum objectives
● To be introduced to non-fiction books that are structured in different ways.
● To write down ideas and/ or key words, including new vocabulary.
● To segment words into phonemes and represent these by graphemes, spelling many correctly.
● To evaluate their writing with the teacher and other children.

Resources
Leaflets about rural locations (such as a wood, a lake, canal area or park) showing animals and plants to look out for on a walk through the area; photocopiable page 172 'A local walk'; annotated maps from the previous lesson; A4 paper; sticky notes

2: Reading leaflets

Introduction
● Give groups of children a selection of different leaflets. Say a range of non-fiction features (headings, lists, pictures, captions, maps) and ask the children to put their hand up when they've found it in one of their leaflets.

Paired work
● Distribute photocopiable page 172 'A local walk' to each pair and ask them to find three key facts about the area. Tell them to then find three descriptive phrases, which make the area sound worth visiting.
● Invite the children to choose one of the leaflets and to find the same elements on there.

Independent work
● Explain to the class that they are now going to make their own leaflets. Give each child a piece of A4 paper folded in half and ask them to write the name of your nature area across the top of the first page.
● Now ask the children to look at their annotated maps and pick out three different habitats that a visitor might enjoy seeing.
● Encourage the children to write the names of these habitats down the left-hand side of the cover. They can then write brief notes about each one on sticky notes and stick them under the headings. (They will return to this later.)

Review
● Tell the children to swap their work with a partner. Each child should offer comments about the headings chosen and how well the notes match them.

Curriculum objectives
● To write for different purposes.
● To use some features of written Standard English.
● To read aloud what they have written with appropriate intonation to make the meaning clear.

Resources
A range of walking leaflets: a local walk, a city walk and so on; photocopiable page 172 'A local walk'; annotated maps and A4 leaflets from the previous lesson; A5 versions of the nature area map that you used in the first lesson

3: Our nature walk

Introduction
● Ask a child to come to the front, look at the classroom and decide on a route around it. Tell them to instruct another child to go round the classroom, pointing out things to look at on the way – for example, *Walk forward to the display board, admire the paintings of the teacher, turn right towards the sink....*

Whole-class work
● Recap on the features of instructions that you worked on earlier in the year. Hand out the leaflets and photocopiable page 172 'A local walk'. Ask different children to read out some of the instructions.

Independent work
● Tell the children to plan a walk through their annotated map, drawing on a dotted line. They can add the numbers one to four at key points.
● Now ask them to prepare a simple set of instructions for their walk, telling the walker what to look out for at each point and where to turn. Tell the children to ensure they use clear, Standard English to make things easy for their readers to follow.
● Suggest that they go through what they want to write a couple of times, following their own instructions on the map with their finger. Then they can write their instructions on the second page of their leaflet.
● Give each child a fresh A5 map of the nature area. Tell them to mark their walk on this smaller map and then stick it on the third page of their leaflet.

Review
● Working in pairs, ask the children to read their instructions to each other, evaluating the clarity of the instructions and suggesting improvements.

Curriculum objectives
- To use expanded noun phrases to describe and specify.
- To write for different purposes.
- To segment words into phonemes and represent these by graphemes, spelling many correctly.

Resources
Leaflets from previous lessons; coloured pens or pencils

4: A beautiful area

Introduction
- Write *The pond* on the board. Give the children five minutes to work with a partner to write the longest, most glorious sentence about a pond that they can. Say they can go as over the top as they like, but the sense needs to be there – for example, *You will find an enchanting, miniature lake where motionless frogs, shoals of fish and brightly coloured dragonflies can be spotted in and around its clear water.*
- Share the sentences, noting the children's use of subordinate clauses, noun phrases and other descriptive language. Ask: *Who thinks this pond sounds interesting to visit?*

Paired work
- Ask the children in their pairs to revisit the map page in their leaflet.
- Tell them to look at all the habitats, including the three they want to focus on in their leaflet, and try to come up with phrases to describe them. They should think about the animals they found there and why the animals live in that location.
- Encourage the pairs to try out different phrases for each of their habitats – for example, *colourful snails, in the damp, hidden soil; local birds in high, safe branches; shy woodlice under secret, damp stones* and so on.
- When they've practised a few and checked on the spelling, tell them to write their phrases in coloured pencil on their leaflet map.

Differentiation
- Help children who need support to break down the task: first they need to remember the animal and the location, then they should think of an adjective for each.

Review
- Ask the children to share their maps with another child. Tell them to check together for the best phrase and to decide if any commas are needed.

Curriculum objectives
- To write about real events.
- To use subordination (using *when, if, that* or *because*) and coordination (using *or, and* or *but*).
- To use some features of written Standard English.
- To evaluate their writing with the teacher and other children.

Resources
The children's leaflets as completed so far

5: Putting it all together

Introduction
- Ask the children to tell you the best bits about the trip to the nature area. Model how you could change their thoughts into an exciting phrase that you might find on a leaflet. For example: *We chased each other across the grass* becomes *Run and play!* or *We found a frog* becomes *Be a nature detective.*

Independent work
- Ask the children to look at their leaflets. So far they should have: a main heading, three subheadings, an annotated map and instructions for a walk.
- Tell them to now write a sentence under each of their subheadings, describing what can be found in each habitat. Remind them of their work in the previous lesson on writing noun phrases. Also encourage them to use their sentence-extending skills of using the connectives *because, that, if, when, or, and* and *but.*
- Finally, ask the children to add some fun facts to the back page of their leaflet, or other reasons why visitors might want to visit the nature area. They can also put on the address, and telephone number and website address.

Review
- Invite the children to share their leaflets with a new partner and to tell each other three things that are successful and explain why. Tell them to locate two good descriptive phrases in their partner's writing.

Expected outcomes
● All children can discuss contrasting settings and write a recount of one character in a particular setting. They can identify singular possessive apostrophes.
● Most children can link characters' thoughts and actions with their setting. They can use singular possessive apostrophes and identify common exception words.
● Some children can give reasons for characters behaving in ways dictated by their setting. They are confident in their use of singular possessive apostrophes and can spell many common exception words.

Curriculum objectives
● To listen to, discuss and express views about a wide range of contemporary and classic poetry, stories and non-fiction at a level beyond that at which they can read independently.
● To discuss the sequence of events in books and how items of information are related.
● To answer and ask questions.
● To make inferences on the basis of what is being said and done.
● To predict what might happen on the basis of what has been read so far.
● To read words containing common suffixes.
● To read accurately words of two or more syllables that contain the graphemes taught so far.

Resources
Katie Morag and the Two Grandmothers by Mairi Hedderwick; photocopiable page '*Katie Morag and the Two Grandmothers*' from the CD-ROM; a map of Scotland showing the island of Coll

Week 4 lesson plans

This week the children enjoy sharing the story of Katie Morag and the Two Grandmothers. They will use the island setting to consider how this habitat affects the actions of the inhabitants and the grandmother who comes to visit. They will place events and characters into their settings and use their discussions and role play to write a recount of one of the events. They learn to recognise singular apostrophes of possession and identify some common exception words.

I: Welcome to Struay

Introduction
● Tell the class that this week they will be sharing the book *Katie Morag and the Two Grandmothers*. Ask whether anyone knows any of the other *Katie Morag* books. Explain that the stories are set on a fictional island called Struay, off the Scottish coast, but Mairi Hedderwick lives on Coll, and this gives us a sense of where Struay might be and what it is like. Point out Coll on the map of Scotland. Introduce the term *mainland* and ask the children where this might be. Follow the ferry route to Coll.

Whole-class work
● Read the book to the class, using multiple copies if possible for them to see the illustrations more clearly and follow the text. Begin by looking at the front cover and asking the children to describe each grandmother to a partner. *How are they different? Would they get on together?* Turn to the illustrated title page. Does this picture confirm their ideas? Explain that Katie Morag calls her grandmothers *Grannie Island* and *Granma Mainland*. Which do they think is which, and why? Ask: *Why has Katie Morag given them these names?*
● Continue reading the book, pausing at various places for the children to predict what might happen next, for example after spreads 3, 6, 7, 9, 10 and 11. Draw attention to words with the suffixes '-ed', '-ing' and '-ment'.

Group work
● Hand out photocopiable page '*Katie Morag and the Two Grandmothers*' from the CD-ROM, distributing one set to each group. Ask the children to imagine the conversations that could take place between the characters in the illustrations on these spreads, showing their different points of view. They should also talk about what the characters might be thinking. Ask them to write these in speech and thought bubbles, linked to the appropriate character, on their sheet.

Review
● Ask each group to feed back to the class. They could role play short impromptu conversations using their annotated copy, to illustrate what their ideas were. Compare the different versions.
● Remind the children of the setting of the story, and that the two grannies live in different places. Ask: *Do you think this has any effect on how they feel about each other? What does Granma Mainland think about being on Struay? What might Grannie Island think about visiting the mainland? What might each of them like and dislike about their own home areas and the opposite one?*

Curriculum objectives

● To apply spelling rules and guidelines, as listed in Appendix 1.
● To read further common exception words, noting unusual correspondence between spelling and sound and where these occur in the word.
● To learn to spell more words with contracted forms.
● To learn to spell common exception words.
● To write from memory simple sentences dictated by the teacher that include words using the GPCs, common exception words and punctuation taught so far.
● To learn the possessive apostrophe (singular).

Resources

Multiple copies of *Katie Morag and the Two Grandmothers* by Mairi Hedderwick otherwise one to share with the whole class; individual whiteboards and pens

2: Some tricky words

Introduction

● Look again together at the view of the Isle of Struay on the inside front cover of *Katie Morag and the Two Grandmothers*. Bring the children's attention to the apostrophe in *Grannie's*, *The Lady Artist's* and *Mrs Bayview's*. Ask: *What has it been used to show?* (Possession)
● Encourage the children to work in pairs to find other examples of this sort of apostrophe in the story.

Paired work

● Ask the children to go through the text again, this time writing on their individual whiteboards any words that they think are difficult to decode because they don't fit the usual phonic patterns. These are likely to be: *Mr, Mrs, Alecina, Beag, Liam, ewe, loch, fury, furious, early, could, would, everyone, beauty, secret*.
● Ask the children to feedback the words they underlined and talk together at ways in which they could be pronounced, ensuring the children know the correct versions. Note that several are names, including *Beag* which, being Scots Gaelic, follows different phonic rules and is usually pronounced /b/e/k/ or /b/e/g/.

> ### Differentiation
> ● Less confident readers may need adult support in choosing the tricky words. Guide them towards those listed above.

Review

● Call out some short sentences for the children to write including possessive apostrophes and some of the exception words, for example *Alecina was Grannie Island's ewe*.

Curriculum objectives

● To draw on what they already know or on background information and vocabulary provided by the teacher.
● To answer and ask questions.
● To listen to, discuss and express views about a wide range of contemporary and classic poetry, stories and non-fiction at a level beyond that at which they can read independently.

Resources

Media resource 'Island versus mainland' on the CD-ROM; multiple copies of *Katie Morag and the Two Grandmothers* by Mairi Hedderwick

3: Island or mainland?

Introduction

● Display the media resource 'Island versus mainland' on the CD-ROM, explaining that these locations are similar to where Kate Morag's two grandmothers live.
● Organise the children into groups of four and ask half the groups to discuss what it's like to live in a city and the other half to discuss what it's like to live on an island. What are the advantages and disadvantages of each location?
● Share the children's thoughts. Ask: *Who would like to live in the city? Who would like to live on an island? Why?*

Paired work

● Look at illustrations of the two grandmothers in the book. Ask the children to discuss how where they live influences what they do. Give them five to ten minutes to consider how the two grandmothers dress, shop, spend their time and get around.

Whole-class work

● Choose two confident children to sit in the hot seat in role as the two grandmothers. Invite the class to ask them questions about their lives, where they live and what they feel about the other grandmother's home area.

Review

● After the question and answer session, talk with the class about how the two grandmothers' different lifestyles might affect how they react to each other. How well do they seem to understand each other in the story?

Curriculum objectives
● To discuss the sequence of events in books and how items of information are related.
● To draw on what they already know or on background information and vocabulary provided by the teacher.
● To become increasingly familiar with and retell a wider range of stories, fairy stories and traditional tales.
● To explain and discuss their understanding of books, poems and other material, both those that they listen to and those that they read for themselves.

Resources
Several copies of an A3 map of Struay you have created showing main locations; a selection of *Katie Morag* stories

4: The island of Struay

Introduction

● Arrange the class into groups and give each a copy of the map of Struay. Give them a few minutes to familiarise themselves with it, noting the places they recognise from the story.

Group work

● Give the children copies of any *Katie Morag* book and ask them to look at the opening and final end-papers which depict Struay in daytime and at night. Ask them to compare this with the map, identifying and linking the locations. Can they work out where the Show Field is? (Look at spread 5 in *Katie Morag and the Two Grandmothers* for clues).
● Ask the children to annotate their copies of the map with events from any of the *Katie Morag* stories, adding any other locations they know about.
● Ask the children to select several of the locations and their associated events to briefly role play, considering what the characters in the scene would say to each other.

Review

● Show the children spread 5 from *Katie Morag and the Two Grandmothers* – the preparations for the island show. Ask them to select a character from the scene to freeze frame, copying their stance and facial expression. Explain that you will be coming round to tap some of the children on the shoulder, which is a signal for them to speak aloud their thoughts as that character. Afterwards discuss each character's thoughts.

Curriculum objectives
● To write narratives about personal experiences and those of others (real and fictional).
● To use subordination (using *when*, *if*, *that* or *because*) and coordination (using *or*, *and* or *but*).
● To plan or say out loud what they are going to write about.
● To learn the possessive apostrophe (singular).

Resources
Annotated maps from the previous lesson; *Katie Morag and the Two Grandmothers* by Mairi Hedderwick

5: Stories in their place

Introduction

● Choose a spread from *Katie Morag and the Two Grandmothers* (not spread 5) and use it to model orally retelling the story of that scene as a recount.
● Remind the children of the role plays and freeze frames they completed in the previous lesson. Explain that they are going to choose one of those characters and write their story in the scene in the same way that you have just done.

Paired work

● Give the children five to ten minutes to go over the scenes, select their character and outline their story to each other.

Independent work

● Allow the children enough time to write their recounts, either from the character's own point of view or as a third person narrative (they do not need to know the term *third person*). Remind them to use subordinate clauses and to be aware of the need for possessive apostrophes as they write.

Differentiation
● Less confident writers may benefit from working with an adult to continue to compose orally a sentence at a time before writing them down.

Review

● Ask the children to read through their work, selecting what they feel are their best sentences and invite some to share these with the class.

Week 5 lesson plans

Using what they have learned about an island setting, this week the children add their own details to a map of a fictional island. They use the island as the basis for a board game where characters they have chosen journey around the island, building a story as they go. The children go on to choose three of the characters to write extended biographies for. They then use a storyboard to begin to plan a story based on their chosen settings and characters.

1: Planning a story setting

Introduction

● Remind the class how different locations on the island of Struay provided the background for story events. Ask the children to name books, television programmes or films that they know with different settings in which key events of the story take place, for example, *Peter Pan*, 'Cinderella', the *Milly Molly Mandy* stories or *Winnie the Pooh* books (these last two also include maps as end-papers). Do they know of any other story books that include maps?

Paired work

● Give each child photocopiable page 173 'Story map'. Give them a little time to look at the map, discuss it with their partner and identify the features on it. Ask the children what features they have found. Explain that each of these features would provide a different habitat for animals and humans to live in.

Independent work

● Explain that they will be using the map as the setting for a story of their own, in the same way as Mairi Hedderwick invented the island of Struay and its inhabitants.
● Ask the children to invent names for the island and the features on it. They might include names such as *Black Jake's cave*, which need possessive apostrophes. As well as naming the features, they should annotate their map with ideas for who might live in some of the places, for example, *a mysterious woman lives here*. They can also add short descriptions for some of the features, such as: *the beach is stony and steep*, or *the mountain always has snow at the top*.
● Encourage them to think about how the different habitats might provide perfect homes for wild animals, such as fish in the river or sea, crabs on the beach, birds in the trees and hedges.

> #### Differentiation
> ● Children with poorly developed fine motor skills would benefit from having the map enlarged to A3.
> ● Any children who might struggle to come up with enough ideas working on their own could continue to work with a partner to generate ideas.

Review

● Tell the children that later in the week they will be choosing settings and characters to write about in a story. Ask them to spend a few minutes studying their annotated map, giving them the opportunity to add extra features that they think they might use in their story, and beginning to think of some ideas for which settings they will use and who their main characters will be. Encourage them to make brief notes on the reverse of their map as reminders.

Expected outcomes
● All children can produce annotated maps and use them to start to plan a story. They can select characters for a story and write brief descriptions of them.
● Most children can write expanded descriptions of settings from their annotations and more detailed biographies of their chosen characters. They can discuss and outline a plot.
● Some children can write more detailed descriptions of settings and develop characters who are very different from each other and who fit well with their locations. Their plots are well defined.

Curriculum objectives
● To plan or say out loud what they are going to write about.
● To write down ideas and/ or key words, including new vocabulary.
● To learn the possessive apostrophe (singular).

Resources
Photocopiable page 173 'Story map'

Curriculum objectives

● To apply spelling rules and guidelines, as listed in Appendix 1.
● To plan or say out loud what they are going to write about.
● To write down ideas and/ or key words, including new vocabulary.
● To use expanded noun phrases for description and specification.
● To learn the possessive apostrophe (singular).

Resources

Annotated maps from the previous lesson

2: Setting the scene

Introduction

● Briefly share one or two of the annotated maps from the previous lesson, pointing out some of the names and interesting comments. Explain that today the children will be using their maps to help them begin to plan their stories.
● Choose a setting of your own and provide a vivid oral description. Use some noun phrases and include descriptions of any animals that live there. Ask the children what noun phrases they noticed.

Paired work

● Using their annotated maps, ask the children to tell each other more about the settings, in the same way that you did. Encourage them to give expanded descriptions with several sentences. Tell them that as they will be moving on to write their descriptions, the more ideas they come up with at this stage, the easier and more effective it will be.

Independent work

● The children now write their descriptions. Remind them to use their spelling and phonic knowledge and include noun phrases and possessive apostrophes where appropriate.

Differentiation

● Encourage less confident writers by guiding them to use their senses when writing their descriptions. Ask: *What can you see there? What else can you see? What is in the distance? What kind of animal might live there?* and so on.

Review

● Ask the children to swap their writing with their partner, each commenting on how it compares to their oral descriptions earlier.

Curriculum objectives

● To write narratives about personal experiences and those of others (real and fictional).

Resources

Photocopiable page 173 'Story map' enlarged to A3 to use as a game board for each group; dice; photocopiable page 174 'Island characters'; scissors

3: An island game

Introduction

● Ask the class to name some board games, and choose several children to briefly describe how their own favourites are played. Establish that players take turns, follow the rules and often a dice is used. Explain that they will be using the story map today as a board game. They will use their journey round the island to build into a story.

Group work

● Arrange the class into mixed-ability groups of four to six. Give each group a game board, a die and the photocopiable page 174 'Island characters', which one child should cut out. Ask them to select one character card each (as there are nine, there is room for choice) and to choose six settings on the map for their game, numbering them 1 to 6.
● Explain that to play the game they take turns to throw the dice, placing their character in the location that matches the number thrown. As their character arrives they must tell part of the story. They can begin by describing their surroundings, thoughts and feelings. As they move around the board, they build the story, based on where they are and where they have just come from. When more than one character is in a location, they should include some dialogue, so that two or more players would be building the story together.

Review

● Ask the groups to share their stories with the class.

4: Building a story

Curriculum objectives
- To write narratives about personal experiences and those of others (real and fictional).
- To plan or say out loud what they are going to write about.
- To write down ideas and/ or key words, including new vocabulary.

Resources
Photocopiable page 174 'Island characters'

Introduction
- Display photocopiable page 174 'Island characters'. Ask the children to raise their hands to indicate which of the characters they chose in the previous lesson's game. Ask several to tell the class something about the character as they saw them. How do the interpretations of similar characters compare?

Paired work
- Explain that each child will be choosing any three of the characters to use in a story. Ask them to discuss all the characters, before choosing those they will be using. Advise them to select different types of character in order to make their stories interesting.
- When they have chosen, ask them to fill out more details through discussion with their partner. If they choose any of the same characters, they don't need to develop them in the same way.

Independent work
- Ask the children to write brief biographies of each of their characters, giving them a name, describing their appearance and personality and saying where they live on the island. They should sum each character up in three or four words, for example, *strong*, *powerful*, *evil*.

Review
- Invite several children to read out one of their descriptions for the rest of the class to suggest which character they are.

5: Planning the plot

Curriculum objectives
- To write down ideas and/ or key words, including new vocabulary.
- To plan or say out loud what they are going to write about.

Resources
Annotated story maps from lesson 1; setting descriptions from lesson 2; character biographies from lesson 4; photocopiable page 173 'Story map'

Introduction
- Display photocopiable page 173 'Story map'. Remind the children that they have described settings on the island, used it as a game to build a story and developed some characters who live there. Explain that today they will start to plan a story that involves the characters and which takes place on the island.

Whole-class work
- Remind the children of the series of events in the *Katie Morag* story. Talk about how the events move from one setting to another and that what the characters do fits in with where they are. Ask the children to give examples of this from what they remember from the story.

Paired work
- Allow the children time to think about and discuss the plots for their stories. Ask them to work with their partner and list plot ideas that could only happen on an island. Where will their stories begin? What events cause the story to move between settings? What will the characters do and what might they say to each other? How might their stories end? Tell them to make brief notes of their best story idea to use next week.

Review
- Ask for feedback on their discussions. How easy was it to fit a story around the settings and characters?

Week 6 lesson plans

During this final week on habitats, the children use their planning ideas to create a storyboard, write and proofread their stories. They will be encouraged to include subordinate clauses, noun phrases, contractions and possessive apostrophes in their stories. They find examples of these in their completed stories to share with the class. They work on the different ways of spelling the /j/ sound, which includes using words from *Katie Morag and the Two Grandmothers*.

1: Creating storyboards

Introduction
● Explain that today the children will create a storyboard of the stories they began to plan last week. If they are not familiar with the idea of a storyboard, briefly explain to the class that it is a way of planning the events in a story in the order in which they happen. Use a well-known tale, such as 'The Three Little Pigs', demonstrating how that would look in storyboard form. Ensure the children understand that the drawings for each box are very basic, so they don't spend too long on them. Give each box a brief written outline underneath.
● Ensure the children understand that they are not writing the story at this stage, but creating an outline plan to work from. This means that when they are doing their writing they already know what is going to happen, so they are able to concentrate on the words to use and their spelling and punctuation.

Independent work
● Give each child a sheet of plain A4 paper, which they should fold into quarters, giving them eight boxes to work in, using both sides of the paper. Tell them to number the boxes so the events are in order. Then, using the notes from their partner discussions last week, they write their storyboards.
● Remind them again that their drawings are there as a guide; they should not spend a lot of time on them.

Paired work
● As the children finish their storyboards, ask them to find a partner and use the storyboards as a prompt to tell their stories orally to each other.
● Encourage the children to listen respectfully and then respond to the story, saying what they thought worked well and what not so well.
● Tell the children to make useful suggestions as to how the plot could be improved.
● The children can make notes around their storyboards, capturing the advice they've been given.

> **Differentiation**
> ● Help less confident children to formulate their ideas so they are able to contribute and make suggestions about their partner's story.

Review
● Ask the children to describe what they found useful about telling their story aloud. Ask: *Did you find that the story had some gaps when you told it out loud? What was the best piece of advice your partner gave you?*

Curriculum objectives
- To apply spelling rules and guidelines, as listed in Appendix 1.
- To write from memory simple sentences dictated by the teacher that include words using the GPCs, common exception words and punctuation taught so far.

Resources
Photocopiable page 175 'Just like a /j/'; interactive activity 'Which /j/?' on the CD-ROM; scissors; individual whiteboards and pens

2: Just like a /j/

Introduction
- Explain that the /j/ sound can be spelled 'j', 'g', 'ge' or 'dge'. Designate one corner of the room for each spelling. From *Katie Morag and the Two Grandmothers*, say the word *just* and ask the children to stand in what they think is the corresponding corner of the room. Write the word on the board, so they know if they were correct. Repeat with other words from the book: *engine*, *judging*, *managed* and *age*. Ask the children to suggest other words and use them similarly.
- Write the words on the board in different clusters.

Paired work
- Hand out photocopiable page 175 'Just like a /j/'. Working with their partner, ask the children to practise spelling words using the /j/ sound on the photocopiable sheet.

Review
- Ask the children to choose words from the photocopiable sheet, to create sentences that could relate to either *Katie Morag* or their own planned story, and share these with the class.
- Use the interactive activity 'Which /j/?' on the CD-ROM with the class.
- Create some sentences yourself, asking the children to write them from memory on their individual whiteboards. Ask them to compare their results with their partner, making any changes they think are needed before showing you for your assessment.

Curriculum objectives
- To write narratives about personal experiences and those of others (real and fictional).
- To use expanded noun phrases to describe and specify.
- To learn how to use both familiar and new punctuation correctly (see Appendix 2), including full stops, capital letters, exclamation marks, question marks, commas for lists and apostrophes for contracted forms and the possessive (singular).
- To use subordination (using *when*, *if*, *that* or *because*) and coordination (using *or*, *and* or *but*).
- To learn the possessive apostrophe (singular).

Resources
Children's story boards from lesson 1; your own prepared example of a storyboard for a story based on the island

3: Drafting stories

Introduction
- Show the children your own example of part of a storyboard (you only need two or three boxes). Use this to demonstrate how to turn the storyboard into a first draft of a story. Talk through your thinking and what you are writing, modelling the process for the children. Ensure you include noun phrases, subordinate clauses and other elements of spelling and punctuation you have covered with the class.

Independent work
- Tell the children that they will write the drafts of their stories, using their storyboards in the same way that you have demonstrated. Remind them to use the spelling, grammar and punctuation elements they have learned so far this year. Briefly recap subordinate clauses and noun phrases. Remind the children about using apostrophes to show possession and for contractions. They may also use words that include the /j/ sound from the previous lesson. Allow them enough time to write their stories. Encourage them to use their phonic knowledge for words they are unsure of.

Differentiation
- Challenge more confident learners to be bold in their choice of descriptive language. Encourage them to include small details as well as describing the broad scene. These will really bring their writing to life.

Review
- Ask the children how useful their storyboards were as a guide for their writing. Did anyone make changes to their original plans as they wrote?

Curriculum objectives
● To proofread to check for errors in spelling, grammar and punctuation.

Resources
Draft stories from previous lesson; interactive activity 'Get it right' on the CD-ROM

4: Proofreading and editing

Introduction

● Display the text from interactive activity 'Get it right' on the CD-ROM.
● Explain that there are some mistakes in the text and some places where the story would be better if the words were changed. Ask the children to help you to proofread and edit the text. The punctuation and spelling errors are obvious, but other changes are up to your discretion.

Independent work

● Allow the children time to go through their stories, looking for places where they can change and improve their work, covering change of language use, punctuation, spelling and grammar.

Paired work

● Ask the children to swap their work, each proofreading the other's work, and offering suggestions that they feel would improve their partner's story.

Differentiation
● Pairings will work best if they are of a similar ability. Less confident learners may need adult support in this activity, particularly when reading another child's work.

Independent work

● Allow time for the children to start writing their final drafts in their best handwriting.

Review

● Talk with the class about proofreading their work. Who made changes and what sort were they? How do they think this has improved their stories?

Curriculum objectives
● To use expanded noun phrases to describe and specify.
● To learn how to use both familiar and new punctuation correctly (see Appendix 2), including full stops, capital letters, exclamation marks, question marks, commas for lists and apostrophes for contracted forms and the possessive (singular).
● To use subordination (using *when, if, that* or *because*) and coordination (using *or, and* or *but*).

Resources
Children's stories from the previous lesson; large sheets of flipchart paper with the headings: *Subordinate clauses, Adjectives describing nouns, Possessive apostrophes, Contractions*

5: The finished stories

Introduction

● Congratulate the children on completing their island stories. Tell them that, when they have finished writing their final versions, they will be collated into a class book, together with the maps the children created in earlier lessons.

Independent work

● Allow time for the children to finish final drafts in their best handwriting.

Whole-class work

● Before the class book is made, the children now have the chance to go through their stories to find examples of some of the things they have been learning, and to share them with the rest of the class.
● Pin up the headed flipchart paper in different parts of the classroom. Explain that as they read through their stories, they should look for examples of these four elements. When they find one, they should write it on the appropriate sheet of paper. Ask for one or two examples of each category to ensure the children understand what they are looking for. The *Adjectives describing nouns* heading refers to noun phrases.
● Allow the class sufficient time to complete the task.

Review

● Go through each of the lists that the class have made, commenting on their choices. Ask: *How do you think subordinate clauses and adjectives help to improve your writing?*
● Ensure the stories and maps are collated into a book all to enjoy.

Curriculum objectives
● To write sentences with different forms: statement, question, exclamation, command.

Resources
Photocopiable page 'Animal homes' from the CD-ROM

Grammar and punctuation: Writing different types of sentences

Revise
● Discuss the different animals that the children know about. Ask: *Where do they live?*
● Ask the children to imagine that they are able to visit one of the animals, shrinking if necessary. What questions would they like to ask about the habitat? What might they exclaim? What instructions would they give someone who wanted to look after the animal?
● Scribe the sentences for the children, discussing the different punctuation needed.
● Give pairs of children the photocopiable page 'Animal homes' from the CD-ROM and ask them to fill it in together, remembering how to punctuate each type of sentence appropriately.

Assess
● Ask the children to imagine that they find themselves in the middle of a lions' den – and these are talking lions.
● Tell them to write: an exclamation, a question, a statement and an instruction by the lions.
● Tell them to write: an exclamation, a question, a statement and an instruction that they might say.
● What do they imagine saying about the den when they get back?

Further practice
● Ask the children to create a simple 'How to look after your pet' poster.
● Use starter activity 16 'Knowing terminology'.

Curriculum objectives
● To learn the possessive apostrophe (singular).

Resources
Interactive activity 'Possessive apostrophes' on the CD-ROM; computer access for the children if possible; multiple copies of *Katie Morag and the Two Grandmothers* by Mairi Hedderwick; individual whiteboards and pens

Spelling: Possessive apostrophes

Revise
● Use the interactive activity 'Possessive apostrophes' on the CD-ROM with the class, or ask them to do this on their own if there is sufficient computer access.
● Ask the children to re-read *Katie Morag and the Two Grandmothers*, noting on individual whiteboards all the examples of the use of the possessive apostrophe, including the opening end-paper.

Assess
● Dictate the following short sentences for the children to write on paper, so that you can assess them later. (You may wish to write the names, without the apostrophes, on the board for the children to use, as the spellings of those are not being assessed and may be difficult for some children.)
  ● *Alecina was Grannie Island's prize sheep.*
  ● *Katie rode on Grannie Island's tractor.*
  ● *They used Granma Mainland's hair stuff.*
  ● *The judges liked Alecina's shiny coat.*
  ● *There was a party at Grannie Island's.*
  ● *The lady artist's house was round the bay.*
  ● *Katie passed Mrs. Bayview's.*
  ● *They went on Neilly Beag's boat.*

Further practice
● Challenge the children to find other examples of the possessive apostrophe being used in books they are reading independently.
● Use starter activity 9 'This belongs to...'.

Curriculum objectives
● To read most words quickly and accurately, without overt sounding and blending, when they have been frequently encountered.
● To discuss the sequence of events in books and how items of information are related.
● To check that the text makes sense to them as they read and to correct inaccurate reading.

Resources
Photocopiable page 'Sam Sparrow gets lost' from the CD-ROM; scissors; glue sticks

Reading: Sequencing stories

Revise

● Recap on how stories are built up event by event. Retell stories that the children have recently read.
● Write the following events from *Katie Morag and the Two Grandmothers* on the board and together reorder them. Remind children about stories told in sequence:
   ● Alecina wins the trophy at the Isle of Struay Show.
   ● Katie Morag and Grannie Island take Alecina to the Post Office.
   ● Granma Mainland arrives.
   ● Alecina is in a bog.
   ● Katie Morag and Grannie Island use Granma Mainland's lotions to clean up Alecina.
   ● Katie Morag goes to help Grannie Island.
● Ask the children to see how the different events are connected. Ask: What would Grannie Island have done if Granma Mainland had not come to stay with her lotions? Would Katie Morag have thought of Granma Mainland's lotions if she hadn't watched her unpack?

Assess

● Hand out the photocopiable page 'Sam Sparrow gets lost' from the CD-ROM and ask the children to cut out the elements and reorder the story.
● Encourage the children to discuss their decisions with you. Can they understand that if the mother says 'Don't fly too far', Sam will have first said that he is going to fly? Do they have the confidence to see that the rabbit and horse are interchangeable?

Further practice

● Give the children an event from a story or fairy tale they know well – for example, *Cinderella gets into the coach*, *Jack climbs the beanstalk* – and ask the children to tell you what happens before and after the event.

Curriculum objectives
● To write narratives about personal experiences and those of others (real and fictional).

Resources
Photocopiable page 'The strange room' from the CD-ROM

Writing: Writing about real events

Revise

● Ask the children to turn to a partner and tell them a story about something that really happened to them. This might be an event from a holiday, a memory from a special event such as a birthday, a time when they were anxious about something such as being lost, or perhaps their first day at school.

● Ask the children to compare their story to *Katie Morag and the Two Grandmothers*. Ask them to consider: whether the stories are real or made up and whether the story is written in the first or third person.

● Ask: *If a story is going to be set in our own life, how are we going to make it interesting? What can it have instead of fantastical events?* (Perhaps emotion or humour.)

● Ask the children to discuss all the things that make an event seem very real. Remind the children about the work you've done on: including specific details using descriptive language, including information about smells, sights, sounds, tastes and touch, including description about how we feel and so on.

● Ask the children to retell their stories to their partner adding extra humour or extra emotion and extra detail following their discussion.

Assess

● Hand out the photocopiable page 'The strange room' from the CD-ROM and ask the children to plan and write a short story about sleeping somewhere new. They should use their notes from the sheet as a guide for writing the complete story.

Further practice

● Challenge the children to take a very straightforward event – such as getting ready for school, or eating a meal – and challenge them to make the event seem as interesting and real as possible by adding great description and emotion.

Hot or not?

■ Cut out these cards and sort them into words to do with hot places and words to do with cold places.

dune	freezing	drought
glacier	iceberg	desert
ice	hot	dry
cold	snow	oasis

A perfect home

■ Use this page to write about why your chosen animal can survive in its habitat.

_____ is a good place for _____

to live because _____

_____.

Another reason why this is a good place for the _____ to

live is _____

_____

because _____.

If the _____ didn't have _____

then _____.

The _____ survives well here because _____

_____

_____

_____

_____

_____.

I can explain why an animal lives in a particular habitat.

How did you do?

Snow in the Suburbs

Every branch big with it,
Bent every twig with it;
Every fork like a white web-foot;
Every street and pavement mute:
Some flakes have lost their way, and grope back upward when
Meeting those meandering down they turn and descend again.
The palings are glued together like a wall,
And there is no waft of wind with the fleecy fall.

A sparrow enters the tree,
Whereon immediately
A snow-lump thrice his own slight size
Descends on him and showers his head and eye
And overturns him,
And near inurns him,
And lights on a nether twig, when its brush
Starts off a volley of other lodging lumps with a rush.

The steps are a blanched slope,
Up which, with feeble hope,
A black cat comes, wide-eyed and thin;
And we take him in.

by Thomas Hardy (1840–1928)

Practising suffixes

■ Cut out these roots and suffixes to make a set of words. Some of the suffixes will work on more than one word, but every word needs a suffix so you might need to try different options.

pave	ing
meet	ing
blanch	ly
care	ed
meander	ment
immediate	ment
enjoy	ful
play	ful
sad	ness

A local walk

Begin your walk by going through the gate at the top of the free car park and walk towards the church, whose huge stone tower you can see in the distance. Follow the footpath beside the river. You may be lucky enough to spot swans or ducks gliding by. Look closer and you could see shoals of silvery fish swimming in the clear water.

As you reach the traffic-free town centre, you will have plenty of coffee shops to choose from if you want something to eat or drink and a wide variety of shops to tempt you. From the High Street turn left into Church Lane and pause to admire the beautiful old houses here. The Miller's House on your right gives you a clue about who lived here in the past and the Old Hall opposite was once the home of Sir David Barton a wealthy local landowner.

Spend time looking at the church, with its fine stained glass windows. And don't forget the churchyard to the west of the church, which has areas set aside to encourage wildlife.

The land behind the church was once a derelict area but it has been transformed into an exciting children's play park, with swings, slide, roundabout and large climbing frame. Follow the lane back to the car park, passing the well-stocked fishing lake.

We hope you enjoy your walk.

Name: _____   Date: _____

Story map

Island characters

■ Cut out these character cards. Use them in your board game, with the story map as the board.

a dog	a boy	a girl
an eagle	a king	a dragon
a wizard	an old woman	a fairy

Just like a /j/

■ Use these cards to practise spelling the /j/ sound when it's spelled with a 'g'. Test your friends. Can you see any spelling patterns?

badge	badger
edge	hedge
fridge	bridge
dodge	judge
age	cage
huge	change
charge	bulge
village	gem
giant	magic
giraffe	energy

PHOTOCOPIABLE

Pirates!

This half-term's pirate theme begins with children exploring pirate stories and discussing common features shared by these books. They explore real and fictional pirate characters and talk about how they dress and speak. Children read, learn, recite and enjoy poems about pirates, and create group performances. This leads to writing their own pirate poems and performing them. Finally, children write their own pirate adventure stories using all the expected features of grammar, punctuation and spelling.

Expected prior learning
- Familiar with the terms *plot*, *character* and *setting*.
- Know what is meant by a contraction.
- Familiar with clauses and conjunctions.
- Know the days of the week.
- Have experience of sequential writing.
- Able to spell some rhyming words.
- Know some pirate features.
- Understand some features of an adventure story.
- Have experience of planning a story structure.
- Able to learn about a character from what they say and do.

Overview of progression
- During this half term, children learn to compare stories and draw conclusions. Their appreciation of stories is enhanced as they use discussion to understand difficult stories and express their opinions about a character's behaviour.
- They attempt to read difficult words and contractions, and to read new words and find out their meaning.
- They learn to use the language of instruction and ask questions to find out more about a subject. Sentence writing is developed further use a range of sentence types, writing compound sentences and writing recounts in the first person. They can plan and write a story with growing confidence. They use expected features of grammar, spelling and punctuation with growing confidence.
- During poetry explorations they find and spell rhyming words, write poems and read them aloud, and further develop their ability to recite poems.

Creative context
- Express ideas creatively using paint and collage, drama, music and role play.
- Increase their knowledge of historical figures and their lifestyles.
- Enhance their appreciation of music through sea shanties.

Preparation
Before the topic begins, ask the children to complete internet searches for pirate information. This chapter focuses on pirates and any age-appropriate pirate titles could be used, we suggest *The Pirate Cruncher* by Jonny Duddle.

You will also need:
Individual whiteboards and pens; fiction (inc rhyming fiction) and non-fiction books about pirates; blue drapes; pirate accessories and costumes; internet access; recycled materials to build a pirate ship; examples of diaries; ship's logs; tea-aged paper; coloured pens; audio clips of sea shanties; scissors; pirate poems; large sheets of paper; collage materials; simple adaptation of *Treasure Island*; old sheets; items of treasure; treasure chest; treasure maps; *We're Going on a Bear Hunt* by Michael Rosen and Helen Oxenbury; model pirate; .

On the CD-ROM you will find:
Interactive activities 'Pirate story spellings', 'Sequencing events', 'Matching homophones'; photocopiable pages 'Famous pirates', 'Pirate poems', '*Treasure Island* summary', 'Pirate's treasure island map', 'Pirate appearance', 'Subordination and coordination', 'Common exception words', 'Ole' Blackeye question sheet'

Chapter at a glance

An overview of the chapter. For curriculum objective codes, please see pages 8–10.

Week	Lesson	Curriculum objectives	Summary of activities	Outcome
1	1	RC: 1, 10, 11	Explore range of pirate stories. Make inferences based on group discussions. Read aloud, checking that text makes sense and correcting inaccuracies.	• Can listen to and discuss pirate stories. • Can make inferences based on reading and following discussions. • Can read for inaccuracies and correct them.
	2	RWR: 2 RC: 6 WT1	Explore features of pirate stories. List these and read them by blending sounds. Complete exercise involving choosing from alternative graphemes.	• Can read words containing alternative graphemes accurately. • Can segment words and apply spelling rules.
	3	RWR2 RC: 1, 11	Discuss pirate characters. Fill in chart about characteristics of pirates in book. Make inferences from discussion and book content. Read by blending.	• Can discuss stories through character exploration and make inferences. • Can read by blending sounds in words with taught graphemes.
	4	RWR: 5 WT: 1	Explore pirate language and sounds in books. Match cards denoting meaning. Find common exception words. Discuss spelling before writing.	• Can read common exception words and segment words to support reading and writing.
	5	WT: 4 WC: 12	Revise meaning of contraction. Count contractions in books. Learn to spell and use contractions in sentences.	• Can find and spell contractions, using apostrophes correctly.
2	1	RC: 4 WC: 1, 6, 12	Read non-fiction books to find out about life on a pirate ship. Write short narratives about different aspects in role as famous pirate.	• Can read books matched to phonic knowledge when exploring non-fiction. • Can use punctuation, key words and ideas correctly.
	2	RC: 9, 12 WC: 6	Use information to help perform a drama about life on a pirate ship.	• Can draw on what they know to plan drama.
	3	RC: 9 WT: 1 WC: 5, 7	Use information provided to explore and create group plans for ship's log pages written by famous pirate. Encapsulate in sentences.	• Can write sentences based on known information, spelling words correctly.
	4	WT: 10, 12 WC: 12, 16	Write up ship's log using plans. Focus on including joining words, checking punctuation, and forming letters correctly.	• Can use conjunctions in sentences. • Can punctuate correctly. • Can form letters correctly.
	5	WT: 11, 13 WC: 9, 10	Re-read ship logs for sense and proofread for grammatical errors. Create ship's logs on 'old paper', using some joined letters.	• Can re-read writing for sense and proofread for errors. • Can join letters.
3	1	RC: 1, 8 WC: 11	Read pirate poems together. Group discussions of features of a humorous poem. Read views to class. Read poem with intonation to clarify meaning.	• Can listen to poems and discuss views. • Can participate in group discussion, and reading of chosen poem, with intonation to clarify meaning.
	2	RC: 1, 8	Explore given pirate poems and shanties. Choose one to learn in a group and one individually. Recite by heart.	• Can listen to, discuss and express views on pirate poems and shanties. • Can recite favourite poem by heart.
	3	WT: 2, 6	Explore pirate poems and learn new ways of spelling phonemes. Focus on homophones.	• Can distinguish between homophones and near-homophones.
	4	WT: 2, 6 WC: 3	Explore poems to find new ways of spelling phonemes. Write own poems.	• Can write poetry with appropriate spelling of new words.
	5	RC: 8 WC: 11	Recall previous poems learned. Rewrite and recite own poem with appropriate intonation. Display poems for appreciation by class.	• Can read poem aloud with intonation. • Can recite own poem by heart. • Can appreciate poems by peers.
4	1	RC: 1, 6, 13, 14	Read Treasure Island and discuss adventure story features. Make predictions about future events based on what is seen and heard.	• Can discuss an adventure story including making predictions based on what is said and done.
	2	RWR: 1, 2 RC: 2	Read sentences by decoding and blending sounds in words. Arrange sentences from story into correct sequence.	• Can develop decoding skills further until automatic decoding becomes embedded. • Can discuss story event sequencing.
	3	RC: 11, 12	Ask and answer questions about the behaviour of a character using hot-seating. Make inferences.	• Can make inferences based on what is said and done in group and class activities. • Can ask and answer questions in groups.
	4	RWR: 2, 3	Read a given text, blending sounds in words containing taught graphemes. Read text to identify words of two and three syllables.	• Can read text by blending sounds in words, recognising alternative sounds for graphemes. • Can read words of two and three syllables.
	5	RC: 7, 11	Identify group's favourite event and re-enact, using favourite words and phrases. Make inferences based on what is said and done.	• Can discuss favourite words and phrases. • Can make inferences based on what is said and done in class and group work.

Chapter at a glance

Week	Lesson	Curriculum objectives	Summary of activities	Outcome
5	1	RC: 9 WC: 1	Discuss features of adventure story prior to planning and writing. Play game involving choosing appropriate pirate adventure words.	• Can use information provided and own knowledge to choose appropriate words. • Can plan a narrative.
	2	RC: 2 WC: 5	Create treasure map with annotations to link 'journey' to sequence of story events. Say aloud what they plan to write.	• Can use journey maps to discuss sequence of events in books and how they are related. • Can say aloud what they plan to write.
	3	RC: 2 WC: 6	Create story map showing events and discussing how they are related. Write down ideas and key words for own story.	• Can write down ideas and key words for own story.
	4	RC: 9 WC: 5	Discuss proposed story characters. Draw pictures and label character from information known and provided.	• Can say what they are going to write about. • Can use information provided and known to create character plan.
	5	WC: 1, 5	Create final story plan, saying aloud what they plan to write to partner. Plan narrative about fictional experiences.	• Can plan for written narrative about fictional experiences of others.
6	1	WT: 1, 3, 5, 6, 8	Recall previous work on grammar, spelling and punctuation when writing first draft of own story. Read common exception words and recall homophones.	• Can write story draft involving: applying spelling rules and guidelines, spelling common exception words and distinguishing homophones.
	2	WC: 7, 9, 13	Find examples of sentences with different forms in books. Re-read writing for sense.	• Can use sentences of different forms. • Can re-read writing for sense.
	3	WT: 7 WC: 14, 15, 17, 18	Consider changes to draft story after revising previous knowledge of grammar through written examples of suffixes, noun phrases, subordination and coordination.	• Can use suffixes, noun phrases, subordination and coordination.
	4	WT: 4, 5 WC: 12, 13	Focus on punctuation learned and find new punctuation in books. Discuss and spell contractions found. Discover different sentence forms in books.	• Can use new and familiar punctuation correctly in writing. • Can spell contractions.
	5	WC: 8, 9, 15, 19	Re-read draft story to check for sense. Use grammatical terminology when recalling past learning. Evaluate final story with class.	• Can re-read writing to check for sense. • Can use verbs correctly. • Can use grammatical terminology in discussions. • Can evaluate writing with teacher and peers.

Background knowledge

As this is the final half term, no new terms are introduced for the first time. The focus is on revision of terms learned throughout the year. Please refer to previous half terms for specific definitions.

SCHOLASTIC

Week 1 lesson plans

This week children explore a range of pirate stories. They read sections aloud, check that text makes sense and correct inaccuracies. They express their views, and make inferences based on discussions. As features of pirate stories are discussed, focus is on reading words with alternative graphemes and choosing the correct ones to suit the context. Pirate characters are identified, and children make inferences about them. They explore pirate language and sounds and create matching cards denoting the meaning of 'pirate' words. Focus is on reading and writing common exception words. Children learn to spell words with contracted forms as they read and write pirate language, with focus on using familiar and new punctuation correctly.

Expected outcomes
● All children can compare stories and draw conclusions.
● Most children can attempt to use both familiar and new punctuation correctly.
● Some children can read difficult words and contractions.

Curriculum objectives
● To listen to, discuss and express views about a wide range of contemporary and classic poetry, stories and non-fiction at a level beyond that at which they can read independently.
● To make inferences on the basis of what is being said and done.
● To check that the text makes sense to them as they read and correct inaccurate reading.

Resources
Range of pirate stories, such as *Captain Flynn and the Pirate Dinosaurs* by Giles Andreae, *The Night Pirates* by Peter Harris, *The Pirate Cruncher* by Jonny Duddle, the *Pirate School* series by Jeremy Strong; individual whiteboards and pens

1: Discovering pirates

Introduction
● Write the word *pirate* on the board and ask the children what they already know about pirates. Make notes on the board using key words they mention.
● Establish that lots of pirate stories arise from legends of real pirates.

Whole-class work
● Hold up some pirate story books and suggest that reading them might help children to learn some pirate language and to imagine how pirates might look. They can then explore non-fiction books with greater understanding of vocabulary and discover more about real pirates.
● Explore the covers of two or three books and note common features in the illustrations. Write some of these on the board.
● Invite volunteers to read the blurb on the books. Discuss what can be learned about the stories and characters from these blurbs.

Group work
● Invite similar-ability groups to choose a pirate book to read and discuss.
● Suggest that individuals practise reading aloud by taking turns to read a page while the rest of the group listen and check whether what they hear makes sense. Encourage readers to correct any inaccuracies.
● Once they have read the story, encourage children to discuss things they have discovered about pirates through the content. They can then make inferences about common pirate features, such as lifestyle and appearance, and make notes of these inferences on their whiteboards.
● Ask each group to sit with another group and share their notes about the pirates in the books they have read. Suggest that they underline vocabulary they have both used . Identify features that are different – for example, the pirates might be good characters in one book and villains in another.
● Invite groups to visit one another for discussion as time allows.

Independent work
● Ask individuals to write notes about the book they enjoyed the most and why. Suggest that they include things that they have discovered through reading the story and discussing with others. Save these notes for review.

> **Differentiation**
> ● Provide a book at an appropriate reading level for children requiring support. Ask them to read it with a partner.
> ● Challenge confident readers to choose a favourite pirate book to read to the class.

Review
● Invite the groups to present their stories to the class, referring to their notes to describe memorable features and vocabulary. Invite individuals to describe their favourite story and notable things about it.

Curriculum objectives
● To read accurately by blending the sounds in words that contain the graphemes taught so far, especially recognising alternative sounds for graphemes.
● To segment words into phonemes and represent these by graphemes, spelling many correctly.
● To discuss and clarify the meaning of words, linking new meanings to known vocabulary.

Resources
Pirate books explored in lesson 1; photocopiable page 200 'Pirate story spellings'; interactive activity 'Pirate story spellings' on the CD-ROM

2: Features of pirate stories

Introduction
● Recall reading and listening to pirate stories.
● Discuss how these books can help to discover common story features.

Whole-class work
● Invite individuals to write examples on the board of story features, for example *treasure islands, maps, gang planks, fights*.
● Explain new vocabulary encountered, such as *skirmishes* and *doubloons*.
● Read each word in turn, identifying children's incorrect spelling attempts and praising them for trying.
● Work together until all words are spelled correctly. Segment each one into separate phonemes. Discuss graphemes used and comment on alternative graphemes representing the same phoneme, for example in *desert **island**, **fly** the Jolly Roger* and ***eye** patch*.
● Display photocopiable page 200 'Pirate story spellings' (or use the interactive version on the CD-ROM). Explain that this sheet was written by older pirates to help young pirates learning to spell.
● Complete a sentence as an example, segmenting words into phonemes and identifying graphemes.

Paired work
● Provide pairs with the photocopiable sheet to complete. Suggest that they read the sentences together and discuss the word options before completing.

Review
● Work through the photocopiable sheet on the board as a self-correcting exercise. Discuss whether this lesson has increased their ability to blend words.

Curriculum objectives
● To listen to, discuss and express views about a wide range of contemporary and classic poetry, stories and non-fiction at a level beyond that at which they can read independently.
● To make inferences on the basis of what is being said and done.
● To read accurately by blending the sounds in words that contain the graphemes taught so far, especially recognising alternative sounds for graphemes.

Resources
The Pirate Cruncher by Jonny Duddle; range of pirate stories with interesting characters as suggested in lesson 1; photocopiable page 201 'Pirate characters'; individual whiteboards and pens

3: Pirate characters

Introduction
● Recall pirate story explorations, memorable characters and their features.

Whole-class work
● Read *The Pirate Cruncher*. Ask who or what children think The Pirate Cruncher is.
● Display photocopiable page 201 'Pirate characters'. Discuss the book characters, including the monkey, parrot, fiddler and monster, and ask children to write the pirate characters in the boxes. Suggest inventing names for the pirate crew, for example *Ben* and *Ken* the twins, *Blackbeard*.
● Take one character as an example. Discuss appearance, such as scars, clothing, hairstyle, and consider character words, such as *brave, wimpish, funny, strong*. Decide the role a character plays by exploring the story events. Write words on the board.

Group work
● Invite groups to select a pirate story.
● Suggest they begin by naming the pirates on the photocopiable sheet, agreeing invented names if necessary.
● Ask them to take each pirate in turn, exploring the book and recording inferences based on what they see, read and discuss on the photocopiable sheet.

Review
● Invite groups to describe the pirates in their book, showing the book illustrations and referring to their completed written work. Discuss the range of characters, and words chosen to describe them.

SUMMER 2

WEEK 1

4: Pirate language

Introduction
- Read *The Pirate Cruncher*, emphasising words spoken by pirates.
- Ask the children to listen for words and phrases that only pirates would speak, for example *ALL ABOARD ME HEARTIES!* Write these on the board.

Whole-class work
- Focus on sounds made by pirates, such as *Ooh Aah!, Ha-HaRRR!* Invite children to say them aloud.
- Note 'lazy words' such as *Yeh* and *Yeah* instead of *Yes*, and *gotta, betta*. Consider how these words might be spelled.
- Ask children to write the words and sounds discussed, using existing knowledge of phonemes and graphemes. Ask whether their spellings match.
- Display photocopiable page 202 'Pirate language'. Ask children to help find common exception words, such as *friend, the, pull, doors, my*. Discuss why they are exceptions to rules they know.

Paired work
- Hand out the photocopiable sheet and ask them to complete it in pairs.
- Invite them to choose a pirate story, search the book for examples of similar pirate language and note these down.

> **Differentiation**
> - Challenge confident children to search books and make extra matching cards.

Review
- Gather groups together to compare card matches and share the pirate language they have discovered. .

Curriculum objectives
- To read further common exception words, noting unusual correspondence between spelling and sound and where these occur in the word.
- To segment words into phonemes and represent these by graphemes, spelling many correctly.

Resources
Photocopiable page 202 'Pirate language'; scissors; *The Pirate Cruncher* by Jonny Duddle; range of pirate stories as suggested in lesson 1 (particularly those with good examples of pirate language); individual whiteboards and pens

5: Contraction competition

Introduction
- Recall words spoken in *The Pirate Cruncher*. Talk about how we often use shortened forms for words when we speak – for example, *I've* instead of *I have* – and that this is called a contraction.
- Say a sentence that includes contraction/s. Ask children to identify shortened words, for example: ***I'd*** *like to make a pirate book if* ***there's*** *time.*

Whole-class work
- Read passages from *The Pirate Cruncher* that include a range of contractions, such as *ain't, couldn't*. Ask children to put up a hand when they hear one.
- Emphasise that apostrophes are not always used just to shorten words, and can sometimes be used to show possession. Read examples from the book, such as *Pirate's Point, fiddler's last song*.

Group work
- Challenge children to discover which pirate book has the most contractions.
- Remind children to avoid apostrophes denoting possession.
- Use a tally to count the contractions and agree the total.

Independent work
- Ask individuals to choose two contractions from those they have written on their whiteboards and write each one in a sentence. Support if necessary.

Review
- Bring the class together to compare group totals, decide the 'contraction champion' book and share their contraction sentences.

Curriculum objectives
- To learn to spell more words with contracted forms.
- To learn how to use both familiar and new punctuation correctly (see Appendix 2), including full stops, capital letters, exclamation marks, question marks, commas for lists and apostrophes for contracted forms and the possessive (singular).

Resources
The Pirate Cruncher by Jonny Duddle; range of pirate stories as suggested in lesson 1 (particularly those with good examples of contractions); individual whiteboards and pens

Expected outcomes
● All children can ask questions about a subject.
● Most children can attempt to read new words and find out their meaning.
● Some children can use a range of sentence types.

Curriculum objectives
● To be introduced to non-fiction books that are structured in different ways.
● To write down ideas and/ or key words, including new vocabulary.
● To learn how to use both familiar and new punctuation correctly (see Appendix 2), including full stops, capital letters, exclamation marks, question marks, commas for lists and apostrophes for contracted forms and the possessive (singular).
● To write narratives about personal experiences and those of others (real or fictional).

Resources
Photocopiable page 'Famous pirates' from the CD-ROM; non-fiction books about pirates showing examples of information presented in different ways, such as *Pirate's Handbook* by Sam Taplin, *Hot Topics: Pirates* by Peter Riley, *Project X: Pirate Blackbeard's Ship* by Mick Gowar; blue drapes; pirate accessories for children to handle, such as telescopes, Jolly Roger flag, weapons, treasure chest, small wooden chairs; access to internet; individual whiteboards and pens

Week 2 lesson plans

This week children read non-fiction books and explore internet information to learn about life aboard a pirate ship. They write short narratives about different aspects of a pirate's life, focusing on punctuation and using key words and ideas correctly. They perform dramas about pirate life and plan and write a ship's log, drawing on what they have learned. Emphasis is given to segmenting words and using appropriate graphemes in writing. They encapsulate sentences, check punctuation and form letters correctly. They read their logs for sense and proofread for grammatical errors. Finally, ship's logs are rewritten on 'old paper', with emphasis on lettering skills.

I: Pirate life

Preparation
● Set up two 'pirate research stations' for exploring non-fiction books and websites. Create the book area, draping the background with blue fabric and arranging wooden seating and boxes to house books. Provide the photocopiable page 'Famous pirates' from the CD-ROM. Include pirate accessories to make the area authentic. Display a list of suitable websites with allocated computers.

Introduction
● Discuss previous books explored and that most of these were fiction.
● Consider what children know about real pirates and discuss where to find more information.

Whole-class work
● Ask children to imagine that a real pirate has come to visit. Invite them to write questions they want to ask the pirate on the board.
● Read through the questions together and try to group them under common headings, such as *Meals, Clothes, Jobs, Leisure time, Punishments* and so on.
● Write the headings as a list along the board, noting the commas.
● Suggest groups each research a heading from the list.
● Discuss how they will find the answers to questions – by searching the contents list or index in a non-fiction book, or by clicking on website links.
● Remind children that some pirates lived before still and video cameras were invented, so they could not be photographed or filmed, but that information has still been passed down through legends, drawings and written documents.

Group work
● Divide children into groups and allocate an aspect of pirate life from your list to each one. Suggest they take turns to visit the research stations to make notes on their whiteboards.
● When children have sufficient information, invite them to write a short group piece as if they are the pirate visitor talking. Remind them that this should be in the first person and present tense, and compose a sentence to clarify this, for example: *I am Anne Bonny speaking from the pirate ship 'Revenge'.*
● Visit the groups to encourage them to include new words they have discovered and to make sure that they spell them correctly. Recap on the use of clauses and conjunctions, and give examples of how these might be included. Emphasise correct punctuation.

> **Differentiation**
> ● Support children to find information in books that reflect their reading levels.

Review
● Invite groups to read their work to the class, and talk about new things that they have learned. Present the work as a display about pirate life.

Curriculum objectives
● To draw on what they already know or on background information and vocabulary provided by the teacher.
● To answer and ask questions.
● To write down ideas and/ or key words, including new vocabulary.

Resources
Resources and children's group written work from lesson 1; pirate costumes with accessories (such as eye patches, scarves, hats, bandanas); appropriate recycled materials to build a role-play ship

2: All at sea

Introduction
● Transform the book area created in lesson 1 into a role-play area, displaying children's written work on the drapes, building a pirate ship from recycled materials, such as large packing cases, and adding pirate costumes.
● Recall the previous lesson's work. Suggest they role play events that might have happened to create a drama.

Whole-class work
● Discuss everyday routines that happen on a pirate ship, such as mealtimes, leisure time, keeping watch for ships to attack and other pirate ships.
● Contrast these with exciting events that happen less frequently, such as attacks on other ships and searching for treasure on desert islands.
● Decide whether everyday routines or exciting events make the best dramas.

Group work
● Divide into groups and ask children to role play their ideas. Encourage them to ask and answer questions as they decide which one to perform as a drama.
● Suggest that they read books and other available information to make sure they use the correct language and dress appropriately.
● Encourage them to write a short plan of action, including key words and new vocabulary.

Review
● Invite groups to use the role-play area to perform their dramas to the class. Discuss how these dramas accurately reflect their research into pirate life.

Curriculum objectives
● To draw on what they already know or on background information and vocabulary provided by the teacher.
● To plan or say out loud what they are going to write about.
● To segment words into phonemes and represent these by graphemes, spelling many correctly.
● To encapsulate what they want to say, sentence by sentence.

Resources
Non-fiction books used in previous lessons this week; examples of diaries (such as a diary for recording daily personal thoughts and events, a weekly appointment diary and a desk diary used by a business); images of ship's logs; photocopiable page 'Famous pirates' from the CD-ROM; individual whiteboards and pens

3: Ship's log plans

Introduction
● Use diaries to stimulate discussion – for example, about how they can be used to record thoughts, events, important dates and appointments.

Whole-class work
● Write *Ship's log* on the board. Explain that this is a kind of diary usually written by the captain.
● Discuss ship's log images on the internet or in books.
● Suggest creating a ship's log page written by a famous pirate.
● Display photocopiable page 'Famous pirates' from the CD-ROM and discuss how logs written by these characters might differ.
● Invite children to ask questions about what they might include in a log, for example ship's position, times of day, weather.
● Use a heading, for example names of ship and captain, and date.

Group work
● Invite groups to start planning their log page.
● Ask them to decide on the pirate writing it. They should read the photocopiable sheet, segmenting words and using appropriate graphemes to write the chosen name on their plan.
● Encourage individuals to say aloud what they want to include in the log.
● Suggest arranging the page in time slots with possible sentences in each one. Remind children to encapsulate key facts within sentences.

Review
● Ask groups to read and explain their plans to the class. Discuss whether using the information, and working as a group, has created effective plans.

Curriculum objectives
● To use subordination (using *when, if, that* or *because*) and coordination (using *or, and* or *but*).
● To form lower-case letters of the correct size relative to one another.
● To write capital letters and digits of the same size, orientation and relationship to one another and to lower-case letters.
● To learn how to use both familiar and new punctuation correctly (see Appendix 2), including full stops, capital letters, exclamation marks, question marks, commas for lists and apostrophes for contracted forms and the possessive (singular).

Resources
Non-fiction books from previous lessons this week; ship's log plans written in the previous lesson; images of ship's logs; photocopiable page 'Famous pirates' from the CD-ROM; individual whiteboards and pens

Curriculum objectives
● To re-read to check that their writing makes sense and that verbs to indicate time are used correctly and consistently, including verbs in the continuous form.
● To proofread to check for errors in spelling, grammar and punctuation.
● To start using some of the diagonal and horizontal strokes needed to join letters and understand which letters, when adjacent to one another, are best left unjoined.
● To use spacing between words that reflects the size of the letters.

Resources
Photocopiable page 203 'Instructions for making paper look old'; prepared tea-aged 'old paper'; children's group ship's logs written in the previous lesson; images of ship's logs and old parchment documents; black pens; backing paper

4: Writing a ship's log

Introduction
● Recall the previous lesson's plans for writing a ship's log.

Whole-class work
● Revise sentence structure, emphasising that each should be complete and make sense. Model an incomplete sentence and invite children to complete it.
● Recall using joining words to extend sentences. Write two sentences and ask children to add a joining word to make them into a longer sentence.
● Focus on letter formation. Invite individuals to take turns to write each word in a dictated sentence, ensuring that lower- and upper-case letters are formed correctly and at the same size and orientation as others.
● Briefly revise punctuation, emphasising relatively new features, such as contractions and apostrophes.

Group work
● Provide groups with their plans in order to write their finished logs, taking turns to write each sentence.
● Encourage them to discuss each sentence, particularly focusing on letter formation relative to other sentences.

Review
● Ask children to read their logs to the class and focus on the points made during class discussion. Praise effective presentation and handwriting.

5: Ship's log display

Introduction
● The children should prepare some 'old paper' using photocopiable page 203 'Instructions for making paper look old'. Ensure plenty is made.
● Discuss the importance of checking writing to make sure it makes sense.
● Introduce the term *proofreading*. Explain how editors do this to check for mistakes before printing newspapers, books and magazines.

Whole-class work
● Explore images of old parchment documents. Discuss how they look old because of their faded colour and ragged edges.
● Question whether children's finished logs look like this.
● Suggest using 'old paper' (made earlier) to make their logs look real.
● Discuss writing on old manuscripts. Note how the letters are often joined and attractive. Suggest children try to make their writing look older by joining some letters using strokes they have practised.

Group work
● Provide groups with individual copies of their log. Ask them to proofread for mistakes in spelling, grammar and punctuation and check it makes sense.
● Suggest that they mark their copies with changes needed.

Independent work
● Ask individuals to rewrite their corrected logs using a sheet of 'old paper'.

Differentiation
● Encourage more confident children to try joining some letters with appropriate strokes.
● Help those requiring support to choose three sentences to copy.

Review
● Bring the class together to explore a display of their logs.

Week 3 lesson plans

This week children enjoy exploring a range of pirate poems together. They discuss the features of a humorous poem, and then read it with intonation to clarify meaning. Children expand their repertoire of poems learned by heart by exploring different pirate poems and shanties before choosing a favourite one to learn to recite. Through close observation of vocabulary used in pirate poems they learn new ways of spelling phonemes, find homophones and near-homophones, and use them in sentences. Children use some of the new words, and new ways of spelling, encountered to write their own poems.

Expected outcomes
● All children can learn a poem.
● Most children can find and spell rhyming words.
● Some children can write a poem and read it aloud.

Curriculum objectives
● To listen to, discuss and express views about a wide range of poetry (including contemporary and classic), stories and non-fiction at a level beyond that at which they can read.
● To read aloud what they have written with appropriate intonation to make the meaning clear.
● To continue to build up a repertoire of poems learned by heart, appreciating these and reciting some, with appropriate intonation to make the meaning clear.

Resources
Photocopiable page 'Pirate poems' from the CD-ROM; individual whiteboards and pens

1: Pirate poetry

Introduction
● Recall previous work involving exploring poems and stories in rhyme and considering their features. Invite children to talk about their particular favourites and what makes them memorable.

Whole-class work
● Suggest exploring poems about pirates and discuss the possible content of such poems – some might be about fearsome encounters and battles in the high seas whereas others might be about individual pirate characters.
● Display 'Meanest Pirate' from photocopiable page 'Pirate Poems (1)' from the CD-ROM. Read the poem to the children and ask for their personal opinions. How did they find the poem...frightening, boring, exciting, funny? How well can they picture the characters from hearing the poet's words?
● Write the character names on the board and comment on the effective use of the same sound for both adjective and noun. Ask whether the adjectives chosen create an instant picture of each character. Repeat the names together, with appropriate intonation when saying the adjectives.
● Discuss the poem structure, commenting on how it has four regular verses of four lines. Discuss the pattern of rhyme and listen carefully to words that 'almost' rhyme, such as *Dan/hand, Lance/hands*. Do they help the flow?
● Discuss important features to look out for when exploring a poem. Write these on the board, for example *title, character/s, structure, rhyme/no rhyme, word choices*. Write a separate heading, *opinions*, to motivate children to consider their personal thoughts.

Group work
● Provide groups of four with 'Ole' Blackeye' from the photocopiable page 'Pirate Poems (2)' from the CD-ROM. Ask them to explore it together, using the headings on the board and recalling class discussions of 'Meanest Pirate'.
● Ask them to allocate one child to write group notes for each heading.
● Invite them to read the poem aloud, changing the tone of their voices to emphasise important words and make the meaning clear. They can do this as a group, or have individuals read a verse each.
● Suggest children discuss their reading together and modify their expression and intonation if necessary until they are happy that they have captured the meaning of the poem.

Differentiation
● Focus on the first verse with children who require support, encouraging them to read the words they can and helping them to build others. Suggest they draw a picture of how they think Ole' Blackeye looks from what they have read.

Review
● Bring groups together to listen, discuss and share opinions of 'Ole' Blackeye'. Ask each group to read the poem to the class and discuss the most effective interpretation of the meaning of the words.

Curriculum objectives
• To listen to, discuss and express views about a wide range of poetry (including contemporary and classic), stories and non-fiction at a level beyond that at which they can read.
• To continue to build up a repertoire of poems learned by heart, appreciating these and reciting some, with appropriate intonation to make the meaning clear.

Resources
Books about pirates told in rhyme, such as *The Pirate Cruncher*, and pirate poetry books, for example *Pirate Poems* by David Harmer; internet audio clips of familiar sea shanties, such as 'What Shall We Do With the Drunken Sailor?', 'Blow the man down' and copies of the words; photocopiable page 'Pirate poems' from the CD-ROM; individual whiteboards and pens

2: Pirate poems and shanties

Introduction
• Recall the importance of sea shanties sung by pirates for pleasure or to help them to keep time when pulling the oars or hauling the ropes.
• Suggest that children choose a favourite pirate poem or song to learn.

Whole-class work
• Display the verses sung by the fiddler in *The Pirate Cruncher* – photocopiable page 'Pirate poems (3)' from the CD-ROM.
• Read the first verse, stamping a foot in time to the catchy rhythm and pretending to play a fiddle.
• Invite the children to join in, clapping and joining in where they can.
• Play a sea shanty clip and ask children to join in, perhaps with the chorus of 'What Shall We Do With the Drunken Sailor?' Suggest children change the word *sailor* to *pirate* if they choose to learn this one.
• Show children the range of books, photocopiable pages 'Pirate poems (1), (2) and (3)' and print outs of sea shanties for them to choose from.

Group work
• Invite groups to choose a pirate poem or song to learn.
• Once the children are familiar with the words, focus on intonation.

Review
• Gather groups to recite/sing their chosen poems/songs to the class. Encourage positive comments on the most effective performances.

Curriculum objectives
• To learn new ways of spelling phonemes for which one or more spellings are already known, and learn some words with each spelling, including a few common homophones.
• To distinguish between homophones and near-homophones.

Resources
Photocopiable page 204 'Matching homophones'; photocopiable page 'Pirate poems' from the CD-ROM; scissors

3: Helpful homophones

Introduction
• Stimulate children's recollections of homophones by writing examples on the board, such as: When I **write** a list of numbers I always put them in the **right** order, This **light** bulb is very **light**.
• Discuss the differences in the spelling of these words. Note how the word **light** looks exactly the same but has two different meanings.

Whole-class work
• Display the poem 'Meanest Pirate' from photocopiable page 'Pirate poems (1)' from the CD-ROM. Ask children to identify any rhyming pattern. They will probably comment that two lines in each verse rhyme. Ask them to say pairs of rhyming words aloud and consider each in turn, *Dan/hand*, *Lance/hands*, *Pete/feet*. Decide which ones end with exactly the same sound and which ones are nearly the same.
• Give examples of near-homophones, for example *peas* and *peace*.
• Talk about how knowing some homophones might help when children write rhyming poetry.

Paired work
• Provide pairs of children with photocopiable page 204 'Matching homophones'. Ask them to create pairs of homophones.
• Ask them to identify the two pairs of near homophones (*peas/peace, clothes/close*) and write these at the end.

Review
• Bring the class together and invite pairs to write a pair of homophones on the board while others tick them off their lists. Praise the listening skills of children who identified the near-homophones.

■SCHOLASTIC

4: Pirate poems

Introduction
- Recall previous lessons exploring pirate poems and homophones.
- Suggest that children write their own poems about an imaginary pirate.

Whole-class work
- Discuss pirate characters children have come across.
- Ask them to write adjectives to describe these characters on the board.
- Explore the words, focusing on graphemes used, for example in *cut-throat*. Think of alternative graphemes used in words to denote the phoneme /oa/, for example in *bone*, *rowed*.
- Explain that you would like the children to make up their imaginary character using some of the new words and spellings they have learned.

Paired work
- Show the class the range of resources. Encourage pairs to spend time exploring these together, discussing their imaginary pirate.
- Provide them with their list of homophones and suggest that they might use some in their own poem.
- Ask individuals to draw their proposed pirate character, and make notes about them.
- Share ideas with partners for comments.

Independent work
- Invite individuals to write their poems, re-reading for sense and checking spelling of phonemes. Support where necessary. Allow time for modifications.

Review
- Encourage individuals to read their poems to the class. Encourage comments about word choices, especially the introduction of new vocabulary.

Curriculum objectives
- To learn new ways of spelling phonemes for which one or more spellings are already known, and learn some words with each spelling, including a few common homophones.
- To distinguish between homophones and near-homophones.
- To write poetry.

Resources
Books about pirates told in rhyme, such as *The Pirate Cruncher* by Jonny Duddle; pirate poetry books, for example *Pirate Poems* by David Harmer; children's lists of homophones from lesson 3; photocopiable page 'Pirate poems' from the CD-ROM

5: Meeting new pirates

Introduction
- Explain that children will introduce their imaginary pirates to the class by reciting their poems.
- Suggest creating a display of the new pirate poems.

Whole-class work
- Spend a short time discussing ideas for the display to house the written poems – for example, creating a large three-dimensional ship on the wall using brown paper stuffed with newspaper balls and mounting the poems inside porthole frames along the side.
- Suggest that children take turns to work on this with the teacher while the rest of the class rewrite their poems.

Independent work
- Talk about how children could improve the appearance of their poem for display, perhaps by adding an illustration and an attractively designed background, or by writing on aged paper they have made. Emphasise the importance of clear letter formation. Provide the necessary resources.
- Once the poem is written and ready for display, ask individuals to spend time learning it.

Review
- Add the finished poems to the display. Invite individuals to recite them to the class. Discuss the children's use of effective intonation to clarify meanings.

Curriculum objectives
- To read aloud what they have written with appropriate intonation to make the meaning clear.
- To continue to build up a repertoire of poems learned by heart, appreciating these and reciting some, with appropriate intonation to make the meaning clear.

Resources
Children's pirate poems written in lesson 4; large pieces of paper; coloured and black pens; aged paper (see instructions in week 2, lesson 5); paint; coloured paper and tissue; collage materials

Expected outcomes
● All children can use discussion to understand a difficult story.
● Most children can have an opinion about a character's behaviour.
● Some children can ask relevant questions and give appropriate answers.

Curriculum objectives
● To predict what might happen on the basis of what is being said and done.
● To participate in discussion about books, poems and other works that are read to them and those that they can read for themselves, taking turns and listening to what others say.
● To listen to, discuss and express views about a wide range of poetry, including contemporary and classic), stories and non-fiction at a level beyond which they can read independently.
● To discuss and clarify the meanings of words, linking new meanings to known vocabulary.

Resources
Photocopiable page 'Treasure Island summary' from the CD-ROM; simple book adaptations of Treasure Island by Robert Louis Stevenson, such as Treasure Island (Young Reading) by Angela Wilkes, Favourite Classics: Treasure Island by Sasha Morton, Oxford Reading Tree, Tree Tops Classics: Treasure Island by Alan MacDonald; individual whiteboards and pens

Week 4 lesson plans

This week, children read the story Treasure Island, and discuss adventure story features. They make predictions about future events based on what they see and hear. Focus is on reading sentences by decoding and blending sounds in words containing taught graphemes, and arranging story sentences into the correct sequence. Children ask and answer questions about the behaviour of characters using hot seating and make inferences based on responses and discussions. They read a given text, blending sounds in words containing taught graphemes and identifying words of two and three syllables. Finally, they identify a favourite group event and re-enact this, using favourite words and phrases and making inferences based on what is said and done.

1: *Treasure Island*

Introduction
● Explain that you are going to read an adventure story to the children.
● Ask them to think of words that describe an adventure, for example *exciting, dangerous, thrilling.*
● Write these on the board and add some of your own, such as *escapade, wild, daring, risky, extraordinary.*

Whole-class work
● Choose a simple adaptation of Treasure Island and show children the cover. Invite them to predict what the story might be about, having been told that it is an adventure.
● Discuss any illustrations, for example a vast ship, pirates, a sea captain, a treasure chest. Consider what predictions we can make from these illustrations.
● Talk about the time that the story might be set. Ask children to find clues in illustrations such as an old galleon or clothes worn by the captain. Is it usual to go searching for buried treasure chests nowadays?
● Read any blurb and consider things that can be predicted about the story from the words used.
● Read the story to the children, pausing at significant points to ask them for predictions about what comes next, for example after Jim finds the map.
● Explain new vocabulary as you encounter it, writing the word on the board and putting it in another sentence to assist understanding.
● Discuss how recalling such a long adventure story might be difficult and display photocopiable page 'Treasure Island summary' from the CD-ROM on the board. Before closing it, explain that children will be able to refer to a copy in their group discussions.
● Define a summary as a short version of a story that includes key events and characters.
● Recall how children usually explore and write stories by considering characters, setting and events. Write these three words on the board.

Group work
● Provide groups of six with the photocopiable sheet to share.
● Remind them that this is an adventure story and ask them to discuss how the characters, settings and events help to make this exciting.
● Encourage pairs to make a note of group ideas under headings.

Differentiation
● Encourage groups of less confident children to draw a picture of their favourite event, supporting them as they write a sentence caption for their picture.
● Challenge groups of confident children to write reviews about their first impressions of the story. Suggest that they discuss views and then write their individual reviews.

Review
● Bring the groups together to share ideas and impressions of the story.

2: Satisfying sequences

Introduction
- Recall *Treasure Island* and how a summary helped the children to remember key characters and events.
- Recall how stories follow a sequence of 'beginning, middle, end', with events related to one another.

Whole-class work
- Display photocopiable page 205 'Sequencing events' (or use the interactive version on the CD-ROM). Explain that someone has mixed up the order of events.
- Ask children to read the page and decide which should be the first sentence.
- Highlight this and read it together, encouraging children to read words such as *Hawkins, Admiral, Benbow* using their knowledge of phonemes and graphemes. Discuss alternatives graphemes for the sounds, /ow/ and /aw/. Consider how /ow/ represents a different phoneme in *cow*.
- Find further examples of alternative graphemes, such as 'ai' and 'a–e'.

Paired work
- Provide pairs with photocopiable page 205, photocopiable page '*Treasure Island* summary' from the CD-ROM and access to books.
- Ask them to read sentences aloud, decoding words and blending sounds.
- Invite them to arrange the sentences in order, number them and note the sequence on their whiteboards.

Review
- Gather the class and work through the sentence order together. Number those displayed on the board. Read them in order to see if the sequence makes sense.

Curriculum objectives
- To continue to apply phonic knowledge and skills as the route to decode words until automatic decoding has become embedded and reading is fluent.
- To read accurately by blending the sounds in words that contain the graphemes taught so far, especially recognising alternative sounds for graphemes.
- To discuss the sequence of events in books and how items of information are related.

Resources
Photocopiable page '*Treasure Island* summary' from the CD-ROM; photocopiable page 205 'Sequencing events'; interactive activity 'Sequencing events' on the CD-ROM; simple adaptations of *Treasure Island*; individual whiteboards and pens; scissors

3: Character interviews

Introduction
- Recall previous explorations of *Treasure Island*. Suggest that children focus on key characters and make inferences about why they behaved as they did. Revise the phrase *make inferences* using examples from past lessons.

Whole-class work
- Recall how children made inferences about a character's behaviour during past story explorations – for example, by discussing illustrations and words that demonstrated this behaviour, by considering events that involved this character, and by questioning them in the hot seat.
- Choose a character from Treasure Island and invite children to think of questions to ask that would help them to make inferences about the reasons for this character's behaviour. Write some examples on the board.

Group work
- Invite groups to pick the name of a key character from a hat.
- Ask them to note questions they would like to ask the character about the way they behaved.
- Suggest they take turns to sit in the character hot-seat and answer questions. Encourage discussion of the character's answers and make inferences about behaviour based on these.

Review
- Discuss whether asking and answering questions has helped them to make inferences about why the characters behaved as they did.

Curriculum objectives
- To make inferences on the basis of what is being said and done.
- To answer and ask questions.

Resources
Photocopiable page '*Treasure Island* summary' from the CD-ROM; simple adaptations of *Treasure Island*; individual whiteboards and pens

Curriculum objectives
● To read accurately by blending the sounds in words that contain the graphemes taught so far, especially recognising alternative sounds for graphemes.
● To read accurately words of two or three syllables that contain the graphemes taught so far.

Resources
Photocopiable page 'Treasure Island summary' from the CD-ROM; individual whiteboards and pens

4: Separating syllables

Introduction
● Recall segmenting words into phonemes in previous lessons. Discuss how this helped when reading longer words.
● Ask the child with the longest name to write this on the board.
● Create a rhythmic string by repeating this over and over, for example Henrietta, Henrietta.... Suggest that children beat time by clapping the syllables. Explain that one clap represents a syllable.

Whole-class work
● Display the photocopiable page 'Treasure Island summary' from the CD-ROM. Challenge children to find words with two syllables, for example Benbow. Read these words by identifying the phonemes and blending the word.
● Do the same with words of three syllables, such as citizen.
● Can anyone discover a word with four syllables? (conversation)

Paired work
● Provide pairs with the photocopiable sheet and a whiteboard. Suggest that they write numbers 2 and 3 at the top of the whiteboard. Ask them to underline words of two syllables in green and three syllables in red. Count up the totals and write them under the numbers on their whiteboards.

> **Differentiation**
> ● Challenge confident children to find words of four and five syllables.
> ● Provide less confident children with sentences from photocopiable page 205 'Sequencing events'. Invite them to focus on underlining words with two syllables.

Review
● Bring children together to discuss the effectiveness of the lesson in helping them to read longer words.

Curriculum objectives
● To discuss their favourite words and phrases.
● To make inferences on the basis of what is being said and done.

Resources
Photocopiable page 'Treasure Island summary' from the CD-ROM; photocopiable page 205 'Sequencing events'; interactive activity 'Sequencing events' on the CD-ROM; simple adaptations of Treasure Island; individual whiteboards and pens

5: Favourite event performances

Introduction
● Recall reading the story and summary of Treasure Island, and making inferences about character behaviour (lesson 3).
● Explain that this lesson involves identifying the children's favourite events, words and phrases from the story.

Whole-class work
● Display photocopiable page 205 'Sequencing events' (or use the interactive version on the CD-ROM). Invite individuals to choose which event they most enjoyed reading.
● Read this event from a book adaption, asking children to listen carefully for words and phrases they particularly like. Write some of these on the board.

Group work
● Provide groups with photocopiable page 'Treasure Island summary' from the CD-ROM, photocopiable page 205, and access to book adaptations.
● Suggest a re-enactment of the event, using favourite words and phrases. Encourage children to discuss how they will do this. Suggest they make inferences based on these discussions.

Review
● Invite the groups to re-enact their chosen events to the class. Encourage the 'audience' to make inferences from what they see and hear.

Week 5 lesson plans

This week, children discuss the features of an adventure story prior to planning and writing a narrative about a fictional pirate experience. They play a game involving choosing appropriate pirate adventure words, using information provided and their own knowledge to make choices. They create treasure maps with annotations to link the idea of a 'journey' to the sequencing of story events. Story maps become a natural progression from this, demonstrating how events are related. Children write down their ideas and key words for their stories, and discuss proposed story characters, saying aloud what they plan to write. Finally, individual story plans are written, drawing on information gathered through class and group discussion throughout the week.

Expected outcomes
- All children can plan a story with a beginning, middle and end.
- Most children can write a story.
- Some children can use all expected features of grammar, punctuation and spelling.

Curriculum objectives
- To draw on what they already know or on background information and vocabulary provided by the teacher.
- To write narratives about personal experiences and those of others (real and fictional).

Resources
Six old sheets cut around the edges so that they resemble islands when spread out; items of treasure such as foil-covered cardboard coins, jewellery, shiny metal objects; box made to look like treasure chest; adult pirate costume or accessories; photocopiable page 206 'Treasure chest for planning a pirate adventure' and a set of laminated coins created from this page; small box; individual whiteboards and pens; scissors; laminator; previously explored fiction and non-fiction books about pirates

1: Words to treasure

Introduction
- Recall recent adventure stories children have enjoyed. Talk about what it is they like about them.
- Explain that they will be planning and writing their own adventure story over the next few lessons.

Whole-class work
- Spread the prepared 'island' sheets around the hall and explain to the children that they are now pirates. Divide them into six mixed-ability groups and ask them choose a treasure island each to 'sail' to. Explain that children are going to play a game to find out which pirates know the most about adventure stories.
- Stand with the treasure chest and box of coins (see Resources) on a stage block pretending to be a pirate on a ship, in costume if possible. Hold up a large piece of paper and pretend that it is a list of adventure story words.
- Address a group in suitable pirate language, for example: *Ahoy you scurvy sea dogs! I'm Captain ...., scourge of the sea! Can you shout a word over to me to describe a pirate adventure story?* If you decide that the given word is suitable, pretend it is on the list, shouting *Hoorah! Swim over and choose a piece of treasure from my chest!* Alternatively, *Oooo-arrr! Better luck next time!*
- Continue around the groups twice, using pirate language.
- Display photocopiable page 206 'Treasure chest for planning a pirate adventure'. Suggest that children might use this to help plan their stories.
- Hold up the box of coins. Invite a group to 'swim' over for one and read the word/s on it. They can then suggest suitable word/s for this aspect of planning, for example: *Characters – Roddy Rotten Feet*. Award treasure if applicable. Ask someone to write the successful word/s onto the displayed photocopiable sheet. Leave the coin out of the box.
- Continue around groups until word examples for each aspect have been suggested.
- Count the treasure items each group has gathered. Ask the class to applaud the winning group using loud pirate language. Order the remaining groups to walk an imaginary plank.

Group work
- Back in the classroom, ensure access to pirate books and provide the same groups with the photocopiable sheet.
- Suggest they discuss these headings in turn, choosing an individual to write suggested words for that heading on a whiteboard.

Review
- Gather the class to share word suggestions and make comments on the most suitable for a pirate adventure story.

Curriculum objectives
● To discuss the sequence of events in books and how items are related.
● To plan or say out loud what they are going to write about.

Resources
Photocopiable page 'Pirate's treasure island map' from the CD-ROM; images of treasure maps; individual whiteboards and pens

2: Treasure maps

Introduction

● Recall key features of treasure maps in stories children have read.
● Recall ways of planning a story, including creating a story map showing the event sequence, noting how events are related.

Whole-class work

● Display photocopiable page 'Pirate's treasure island map' from the CD-ROM. Invite children to point out key features.
● Find the 'X' marking the treasure. Talk about how the map links the journey from arriving on the island to finding treasure.
● Explore and compare different images of treasure maps and discuss common features.
● Point out that the displayed map has no words, such as warnings, instructions and signs. Consider how words could provide additional clues to the treasure seeker. Ask for examples.

Paired work

● Provide similar-ability pairs with the photocopiable sheet.
● Suggest that they think of words to add to the map, saying them out loud to one another before noting them on their whiteboards.
● Once they are happy with their suggestions, they can add appropriate annotations to their copies of the treasure map.

Review

● Ask some pairs to read their annotations and say why they think they will be helpful, for example *Warning! Quicksand! Dead man's cave!*

Curriculum objectives
● To discuss the sequence of events in books and how items are related.
● To write down ideas and/ or key words, including new vocabulary.

Resources
We're Going on a Bear Hunt by Michael Rosen; small model pirate; individual whiteboards and pens; large pieces of paper; coloured and black pens

3: Story maps

Introduction

● Read *We're Going on a Bear Hunt*. Talk about the journey the characters take. Suggest that this could be indicated on a story map.
● Discuss previous story maps children have created showing the event journey from beginning to end.

Whole-class work

● Suggest using the *We're Going on a Bear Hunt* structure to plan a pirate story, changing the words to *We're Going on a Treasure Hunt*.
● Recall key aspects of story planning, for example identifying characters, setting and events.
● Draw an island on the board. Ask children to mark where the story starts and ends and draw a path between these points.
● Focus on story events, moving a model pirate along the path following the bear hunt pattern. Keep stopping, shouting *Avast ye!* and asking children to suggest an event to overcome, for example a sleeping crocodile across the path. Mark this on the map.

Group work

● Invite groups to draw a story map, planning out the events as for the class discussion. Provide whiteboards to note key words and ideas.
● Provide resources to draw a large annotated map.
● Modify and extend plans until all children are satisfied.

Review

● Ask groups to present their story maps to the class. Discuss whether the maps give a clear picture of the sequence of events for the planned story.

Curriculum objectives
● To plan or say out loud what they are going to write about.
● To draw on what they already know or on background information and vocabulary provided by the teacher.

Resources
Photocopiable page 201 'Pirate characters'; photocopiable page 'Pirate appearance' from the CD-ROM; fiction and non-fiction pirate books children have read; coloured and black pens

4: Story characters

Introduction
● Recall exploring the pirate characters in stories read and comment on those the children really like/dislike.
● Suggest that children consider some of these when deciding on characters for the pirate adventure stories they are going to write.

Whole-class work
● Hand out photocopiable page 201 'Pirate characters' and show how this can be used to plan the characters in their stories.
● Focus on the names of pirates and decide which ones give effective clues about the appearance of the character, such as *Captain Purplebeard*, and those that give clues about character, such as *Cowardly Slack Jaw*.
● Recall words that children have encountered in stories that describe appearance (*giant, warty*), role (*captain, first-mate*) and character (*wimpish, cruel*).

Group work
● In the same groups as the previous lesson, suggest they make notes about proposed story characters on photocopiable page 201 'Pirate characters', coming to a group decision about names, appearances, roles and character traits.
● Provide each child with photocopiable page 'Pirate appearance' from the CD-ROM so that the children can draw and label pictures of the characters.

Review
● Invite groups to show the pictures of their characters and discuss the roles they play in the proposed story and the most effective character descriptions.

Curriculum objectives
● To plan or say out loud what they are going to write about.
● To write narratives about personal experiences and those of others (real and fictional).

Resources
Photocopiable page 207 'Pirate adventure story plan'; children's completed group versions of photocopiable page 206 'Treasure chest for planning a pirate adventure' (lesson 1); story maps (lesson 3); photocopiable page 'Pirate appearance' from the CD-ROM (lesson 4)

5: Final plans

Introduction
● Recall class and group activities linked to adventure story planning, for example, choosing adventure words, considering setting and events, creating a story map, deciding on characters.

Whole-class work
● Display and read photocopiable page 207 'Pirate adventure story plan'.
● Recall possible titles and characters discussed in previous lessons.
● Talk about where stories might be set, given that they are pirate adventure stories. Perhaps the story will start on land, move onto a ship and visit an island before returning home again, as in the story *Treasure Island*, or perhaps the entire story will be set in one place?
● Consider events mentioned on the story maps children created. Suggest focusing on just two main events for this story.
● Explain that you would like children to use information and ideas gathered in class and group work to develop their own stories.

Paired work
● Provide pairs with access to copies of relevant planning work completed in the last four lessons along with the photocopiable page 207 'Pirate adventure story plan' each. Suggest that they fill these in individually before saying what they plan to write. Make modifications in the light of discussion.

Review
● Ask the class to discuss the effectiveness of previous class and group work in supporting the writing of their plans. Are ready to write their stories?

Curriculum objectives
● To apply spelling rules and guidelines, as listed in Appendix 1.
● To segment words into phonemes and represent these by graphemes, spelling many correctly.
● To learn to spell common exception words.
● To distinguish between homophones and near-homophones.

Resources
Children's completed story plans from week 5; photocopiable pages 200 'Pirate story spellings' and 204 'Matching homophones'; interactive activities 'Pirate story spellings' and 'Matching homophones' on the CD-ROM; individual whiteboards and pens

Week 6 lesson plans

This week children revise work on grammar, spelling and punctuation when writing their story drafts. Focus is on applying spelling rules and guidelines, segmenting words into phonemes and representing them with graphemes, spelling exception words and distinguishing homophones. They explore sentence forms and develop understanding of encapsulation. They re-read writing to check for consistency, and make changes after revising grammatical knowledge through written examples of suffixes, noun phrases, subordination and coordination. They focus on punctuation learned, find examples in books and use new and familiar punctuation correctly in writing.

1: Confident writers

Introduction
● Discuss the need for writing a plan.

Whole-class work
● Suggest that stories are all different even though they follow similar patterns. Adventure stories have the key features children have discussed, but the characters, setting and events are always chosen by the author.
● Discuss how the children's group plans are the strong structure that they can now build their own stories from, adding their favourite ideas for settings, characters and events to create an exciting adventure that is unique.
● Write the following headings on the board: *Spelling, Grammar, Punctuation*. Ask children to recall things they have learned about these aspects of writing over the year. Explain what is meant for grammar, giving examples.
● Suggest examples that fit into each category. For example, display photocopiable page 200 'Pirate story spellings' (or use the interactive version on the CD-ROM) and recall reading and spelling words with alternative graphemes for the same phoneme. Display photocopiable page 204 'Matching homophones' (or use the interactive version on the CD-ROM) and recall identifying homophones and near-homophones. Ask children to recall learning to read common exception words. Write examples under *Spelling*.

Independent work
● Provide children with their completed story plans and ask them to write a first draft.
● Discuss the meaning of 'first draft' and why this is a useful stage in the writing process. Remind children that they will be able to modify this draft in the coming lessons before writing their final version of the story.

Paired work
● Once children have completed their drafts, ask them to find a partner.
● Suggest that partners read their stories to one another and then make comments about their initial impressions of the story.
● Ask children to make a note of comments they think are useful on their whiteboards so that they can consider them again when making any changes to the draft.

> **Differentiation**
> ● Support individuals who struggle without the peer support of their mixed-ability planning group. Suggest that they tell you their story and then help them to write three sentences representing the beginning, middle and end.

Review
● Bring the class together to read their first drafts and discuss initial impressions. Ask children whether they have included things that they have learned over the year.

2: Sentences with sense

Introduction
- Recall pirate books explored. Invite the class to choose a favourite one.

Whole-class work
- Read and write a sentence from the chosen book on the board. Ask children to comment on what the sentence tells us. Consider whether it is a statement, question, exclamation or command.
- Encourage children to understand the concept of encapsulation without actually knowing the word. Recall that sentences are always complete, with a clear beginning and end. Try saying the sentence without the last word. Does it still seem complete? Now miss the first word and ask the same question.

Group work
- Ask groups of four to choose a book and find examples of sentences that are statements, questions, exclamations or commands.
- Suggest they allocate a sentence category to each child so that they can write down the chosen sentence/s.
- Encourage them to discuss whether the sentences are complete and make sense when read aloud.

Independent work
- Ask children to re-read their drafts to ensure they make sense, and that sentences are complete in themselves. Modify if necessary.

Review
- Invite groups to read their chosen sentences to the class. Encourage comments on whether they sound complete and make sense.

Curriculum objectives
- To encapsulate what they want to say, sentence by sentence.
- To use sentences with different forms: statement, question, exclamation, command.
- To re-read to check that their writing makes sense and that verbs to indicate time are used correctly and consistently, including verbs in the continuous form.

Resources
Fiction and non-fiction books about pirates previously explored; children's first drafts of their stories; individual whiteboards and pens

3: Extending sentences

Introduction
- Recall the definition of a sentence and the types of sentences explored in the previous lesson.
- Encourage children to consider the importance of choosing the most effective words to use in sentences within their adventure stories.

Whole-class work
- Write a simple sentence on the board, such as *The pirate was on the island.*
- Ask children to think of ways to extend the sentence to make it more interesting – for example, by creating noun phrases: *The cowardly young pirate, who was frightened of wild animals, hid in a tall leafy tree on the treasure island.*
- Discuss which sentence children prefer and why.
- Demonstrate the use of subordination and coordination by writing two simple sentences on the board and asking children to make them into one sentence using a 'joining word'.
- Remind children about using suffixes to make words longer and change their function – for example, from nouns to adjectives (*sorrow/sorrowful*). Work through some examples using different suffixes.

Paired work
- Ask individuals to read each other's drafts and look for ways of making sentences longer and more interesting.
- Encourage them to talk through suggestions and note ideas.

Review
- Gather the class to talk about their conversations with partners, and to discuss changes they might make before writing the final story.

Curriculum objectives
- To use the grammar for Year 2 in Appendix 2.
- To use some features of written Standard English.
- To add suffixes to spell longer words.
- To expand noun phrases to describe and specify.
- To use subordination (*when, if, that,* or *because*) and coordination (*or, and,* or *but*).

Resources
Individual whiteboards and pens; children's draft stories

Curriculum objectives
● To learn how to use both familiar and new punctuation correctly (see Appendix 2), including full stops, capital letters, exclamation marks, question marks, commas for lists and apostrophes for contracted forms and the possessive (singular).
● To learn the possessive apostrophe (singular).
● To learn to spell more words with contracted forms.
● To use sentences with different forms: statement, question, exclamation, command.

Resources
Pirate books explored previously; children's draft stories; individual whiteboards and pens

4: Perfect punctuation

Introduction
● Recall previous work on sentence forms, and the correct punctuation to use.

Whole-class work
● Ask children to list the range of punctuation they remember on the board, adding your own if necessary.
● Focus on apostrophes and how they shorten words or denote possession.
● Discuss more interesting aspects of text children have discovered – for example, writing words in capital letters, or in different sizes and fonts, so that they stand out from the rest. Consider how this makes the page look more interesting and helps us recognise words the author wants to emphasise.

Group work
● Invite groups to choose a book and identify various examples of punctuation.

Independent work
● Ask individuals to re-read their stories, this time focusing on the overall appearance and punctuation.
● Suggest that they underline punctuation and words they might change, for example adding commas or using capital letters and large lettering.

> **Differentiation**
> ● Support less confident children, asking them to find regular punctuation marks, such as full stops, capital letters and question marks.

Review
● Invite the class to discuss what they have learned about different punctuation and improving the accuracy and appearance of their writing.

Curriculum objectives
● To re-read to check that their writing makes sense and that verbs to indicate time are used correctly and consistently, including verbs in the continuous form.
● To use and understand grammatical terminology in Appendix 2 in discussing their writing.
● To evaluate their writing with the teacher and other children.
● To use present and past tenses correctly and consistently including the progressive form.

Resources
Pirate books explored previously; children's draft stories; individual whiteboards and pens

5: Sharing stories

Introduction
● Recall recent discussions about spelling, grammar and punctuation, asking children for examples of things they have learned.

Whole-class work
● Talk about the need for children to re-read their story drafts one last time so that final changes can be made in the light of the revision lessons this week.
● Remind them about sentences making sense. Write an example on the board of a sentence where verbs are inconsistent, for example: *The pirate jumped for joy as he find the treasure.* Discuss what is wrong with this sentence and make the distinction between past and present tenses.

Independent work
● Provide individuals with their story drafts. Ask them to write the final version of their story.
● Remind them of their notes on proposed changes. Ask them to make sure these changes are included.
● Discuss the importance of choosing the right words, introducing new vocabulary or changing words if they can think of better ones.
● Encourage them to read each sentence, checking they make sense.
● Suggest that individuals present their stories attractively by adding a design around the edge or small illustrations.

Review
● Ask individuals to read their stories to the class.

Curriculum objectives
● To use subordination (using *when*, *if*, *that* or *because*) and coordination (using *or*, *and* or *but*).

Resources
Photocopiable page 'Subordination and coordination' from the CD-ROM; scissors

Grammar and punctuation: Consolidating subordination and coordination

Revise
● Recall previous explorations of subordination and coordination.
● Write down some connectives used for subordination – for example, *when*, *if*, *that*, *because* – and ask children to make up some sentence examples using these 'joining' words.
● Do the same with connectives used for coordination, such as *or*, *and*, *but*.
● Display photocopiable page 'Subordination and coordination' from the CD-ROM. Explain that five sentences have been cut in half and the beginnings and ends put in separate boxes. However, the 'joining words' are missing. Explain that the children's task is to make the sentences whole again by adding the missing connectives.
● Talk about the clues that tell us which is the beginning, middle and end of the sentence (capital letter, connective word and punctuation mark).
● Choose one of the sentence beginnings and ask children to decide which is the ending. Write this on the board and check that it makes sense.

Assess
● Provide children with the photocopiable sheet each and ask them to follow the instructions.
● Ask them to write down their sentences and circle the connecting word in each one.

Further practice
● Join a small group of children requiring support and give them some simple split sentences, for example: *This is my map...and this is my compass.*
● Challenge pairs of confident children to write the start of sentences for their partners to extend using a connective.
● For more support, see page 101.

Curriculum objectives
● To learn to spell common exception words.

Resources
A prepared document entitled *List of common exception words* taken from Year 2 (Appendix 2); photocopiable page 'Common exception words' from the CD-ROM; timer

Spelling: Common exception words

Revise
● Recall how some words do not follow the usual spelling rules.
● Display *List of common exception words* and set the timer. Challenge children to read as many of these as they can in the set time.
● Ask children to move quickly, reading words as you point to them.
● Highlight the words read correctly, and count them at the end.
● Return to words that children did not manage to read. Ask them to try again, with you joining in.
● Repeat this challenge to see if children remember more words the second time around. Always read together so that no one is discouraged.
● Display photocopiable page 'Common exception words' from the CD-ROM.
● Read each sentence together. Provide children with a copy of the *List of exception words* and ask them to suggest a word from this list that might fit the space in the first sentence on the board.

Assess
● Provide individuals with the photocopiable sheet to use with the word list.
● Invite them to fill in the former, choosing words from the list.

Further practice
● Invite confident children to write sentences that include some exception words they have explored with the class.
● Create a simpler version to reflect the reading levels of those who struggle.

Curriculum objectives

● To read accurately by blending the sounds in words that contain the graphemes taught so far, especially recognising alternative sounds for graphemes.
● To read accurately words of two or more syllables that contain the graphemes taught so far.
● To continue to apply phonic knowledge and skills as the route to decode words until automatic decoding has become embedded and reading is fluent.

Resources

Photocopiable pages 'Pirate poems' and 'Ole' Blackeye question sheet' (version (1) or (2) as required for differentiation) from the CD-ROM

Reading: Ole' Blackeye

Revise

● Recall previous reading and discussions about pirate poems. Talk about the things that the children enjoyed as they read aloud – as a class, in groups, pairs or individually – for example, emphasising the rhythm of the words, modifying voices to suit characters and expressing important words by changing the tone and volume of their voices.
● Ask them to recall how much more they have learned to read since the year began. Talk about how learning to read fluently can increase enjoyment of stories and poetry.
● Display the poem 'Ole' Blackeye' from photocopiable page 'Pirate poems (2)' from the CD-ROM, and talk about what children remember about it.
● Read the first verse aloud to the children in a bored monotone and then ask them: *Does you think I gave a good impression of Ole' Blackeye? Do you think that I could have read it differently, perhaps with more expression?*
● Spend time revising their phonic knowledge and skills, for example identifying familiar grapheme/phoneme correspondences in the words of the poem. Ask children to circle words that they read quickly and automatically because they know the phonemes created by the graphemes.
● Invite them to highlight words that they need to think about because they are new to them, such as *'Cause, gotten, Ole'*.
● Find some exception words, such as *eye, were, sold* and contractions, such as *wasn't, couldn't, he'd*. Discuss the role of the apostrophe in *Ole'* and *'Cause*.
● Discuss briefly how sentences are punctuated, pointing out the use of full stops and capital letters, apostrophes and exclamation marks. Emphasise that knowing how punctuation is used when we are reading helps us to understand more about the author's intended meaning of the words.
● Recall how words should be read when there is an exclamation mark. Try reading the three lines that end in these punctuation marks with suitable expression.
● Ask the children read the poem aloud with you, trying to let their reading flow automatically.
● Ask the children to work with a partner and provide them with the poem 'Ole' Blackeye' and photocopiable page 'Ole' Blackeye question sheet' from the CD-ROM. Invite one of each pair to read the poem aloud to their partner and then listen while their partner reads it to them.
● Encourage them to read through the questions, supporting one another in blending and decoding words that they cannot read automatically.

Assess

● Provide individuals with the poem 'Ole' Blackeye' and photocopiable page 'Ole' Blackeye question sheet' from the CD-ROM. (Please note, there are two versions of this question sheet as required for differentiation.)
● Ask them to read each question and then write their answer in the box.
● As this is a focused reading assessment rather than writing assessment, visit children as they work and ask them to read one of their questions and discuss their answer with you. If necessary, ask further questions to support children in showing that they really understand what they have read.
● Observe children as they work, and be ready to support with helpful hints about how to apply their phonic knowledge and skills to decode words they are struggling with. Make note of their successes and difficulties while they are working alone and with partners.

Further practice

● Extend the activity by challenging pairs of confident children to find a new poem, read it and then think of questions to ask their partner about it.
● Support less confident children by providing them with the differentiated sheet and asking them to read the questions and answer them orally. Note any difficulties they have with word decoding and blending.

■SCHOLASTIC

Curriculum objectives
● To encapsulate what they want to say, sentence by sentence.
● To plan or say out loud what they are going to write about.
● To use sentences with different forms: statement, question, exclamation, command.
● To learn how to use both familiar and new punctuation correctly (see Appendix 2), including full stops, capital letters, exclamation marks, question marks, commas for lists and apostrophes for contracted forms and the possessive (singular).

Resources
Photocopiable page 203 'Instructions for making paper look old'; photocopiable page 'Pirate's treasure island map' from the CD-ROM; examples of instructions, for example recipes and instructions about how to make models; individual whiteboards and pens

Writing: Instructions to find the treasure

Revise
● Recall exploring images of pirate treasure maps, and the way that information is presented, for example arrows indicating a certain path, signs showing danger or labels noting features.
● Look at different examples of instructions, such as how to make a model from a box of construction equipment. Talk about how these are presented, for example as numbered sentences with occasional diagrams.
● Recall previous work on sentence structure to extend understanding of encapsulation. Explain how this is really important when writing instructions, as every step must be broken down into separate sentences.
● Explain that children are going to use these forms of instruction to explain to people arriving on a desert island where to find some hidden treasure.
● Recall previous discussions about how instructions follow a sequence, starting with the first thing to do and ending with an achievement, in this case arriving at the island and finding the treasure.
● Notice how the displayed instructions are written as direct commands, for example: *Walk towards the cave*, *Look behind the stone*. Talk about how these commands are in the present tense and discuss how this affects the spelling of words. Consider the importance of continuity, staying in the same tense, whether this is past or present.
● Revise work on using connectives – *and, but, or, when, because, if, that* – to extend sentences.
● Recall sentence writing and remind children about correct punctuation. Consider using exclamation marks to emphasise danger, for example: *Avoid the quicksand!* Talk about contractions and recall the use of apostrophes for possession, for example: *Dead man's cave*.
● Read the instructions on photocopiable page 203 'Instructions for making paper look old', and notice that there are no contractions using apostrophes. Emphasise again that the language of instruction has to be clear and so it does not use shortened words, for example: *Go round the swamp!* rather than *Don't fall in the swamp or you mightn't get out alive!*
● Provide children with photocopiable page 'Pirate's treasure island map' from the CD-ROM, and invite them to annotate this with labels and captions to make the journey from arriving on the island to finding the treasure an interesting one.
● When the map is complete, encourage pairs to tell one another what they plan to write on their instruction sheet.

Assess
● Ask children to refer to their completed maps as they write a list of instructions explaining how to find the treasure.
● Encourage children to invite their partners to read their finished sheets and talk about how easy they would be to follow.
● Randomly choose maps, and their accompanying instructions, to discuss with the class. Give praise for using the correct instructional style. Comment on use of familiar grammar, spelling and punctuation, as well as new features learned in this half term and discussed during revision time. Encourage children to consider how they will improve their writing next time.

Further practice
● Support those who have difficulty by encouraging them to show you their maps and explain orally how to find the treasure, step by step. Help them to write each step down as a sentence using the correct style.
● Challenge confident children to write different sets of instructions, for example how to play a favourite game.

Pirate story spellings

- Pirates, please read each sentence.
- Choose the correct word from the box on the right and write it in the space so that the sentence makes sense.

The cut-throat pirates set _____ to find adventure.	sale, sail
The pirate ship was full of stolen _____ .	lute, loot
The pirates had to _____ on a rope to hoist the flag.	hall, haul
The treasure map will help you to _____ the island.	fined, find
"_____ that ship!" cried Captain Greybeard.	seas, seize
The pirate ship sailed the Spanish _____ .	main, mane
The pirate pulled on the _____ of the tiny boat.	oar, or, awe
The crew sang _____ shanties as they worked.	see, sea
The Black Ghost ship sailed through the _____ .	night, knight

I can read words by blending the sounds and choose the correct ones to put in a sentence.

How did you do?

Pirate characters

- Use the boxes to make notes about the pirate characters in your book.
- Use more than one page if you need to.

Name	Appearance	Role in the story	Character

I can write words that describe the pirate characters in the book I am exploring.

How did you do?

Pirate language

- Cut out the words in the boxes.
- Match pairs of boxes that mean the same thing.

Hello	The Jolly Roger
Close the doors on the ship	Me hearties!
Pull	Ahoy!
The pirate flag	Heave ho!
Friend	Thar she blows!
My pirate crew	Batten down the hatches
There's a whale!	Matey

PHOTOCOPIABLE

SCHOLASTIC
www.scholastic.co.uk

Instructions for making paper look old

What you need

- Sheets of thick paper
- Black tea bags
- Paper towels
- Large bowl
- Heavy books
- A paint drying rack

What to do

1. Tear your paper round the edges to make it look worn.
2. Soak three tea bags in a small bowl of water for about an hour.
3. Take out a tea bag and rub it all over the paper.
4. Carry on until the paper turns dark brown.
5. Throw the tea bag away.
6. Keep doing the same with tea bags until you are happy with the colour of your paper.
7. Dab the paper with a paper towel to dry it.
8. Put a paper towel under the paper and a paper towel on top.
9. Put some heavy books on top.
10. Leave the paper for 12 hours.
11. Take out the paper.

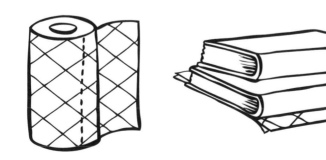

Matching homophones

- Cut out the boxes.
- Match the words that sound the same.
- Use some of the pairs in your pirate poems.

oar	close	peas	sea
sail	dug	awe	nose
see	weak	knot	sell
cell	grown	allowed	sale
week	knows	Doug	peace
clothes	aloud	not	groan

PHOTOCOPIABLE

Sequencing events

- Cut out each sentence and read it.
- Arrange the sentences in the correct sequence to create a story summary.
- Write your own sentence in the empty box to end the story.

✂ -

Jim hid from the others and met Ben Gunn, an ex-pirate.
Jim and his friends set sail on the Hispaniola to find the treasure island.
Ben showed Jim where the treasure was and they escaped.
Jim Hawkins lived with his mother at The Admiral Benbow inn.
Jim heard the crew plotting with Long John Silver to take over the ship.
Blind Pew gave Billy Bones a black spot.
Jim found Billy's treasure map and showed it to his friends.
Jim decided to go to the treasure island with the evil crew.

Treasure chest for planning a pirate adventure

■ Write words and ideas to use in your adventure story inside the gold coins.

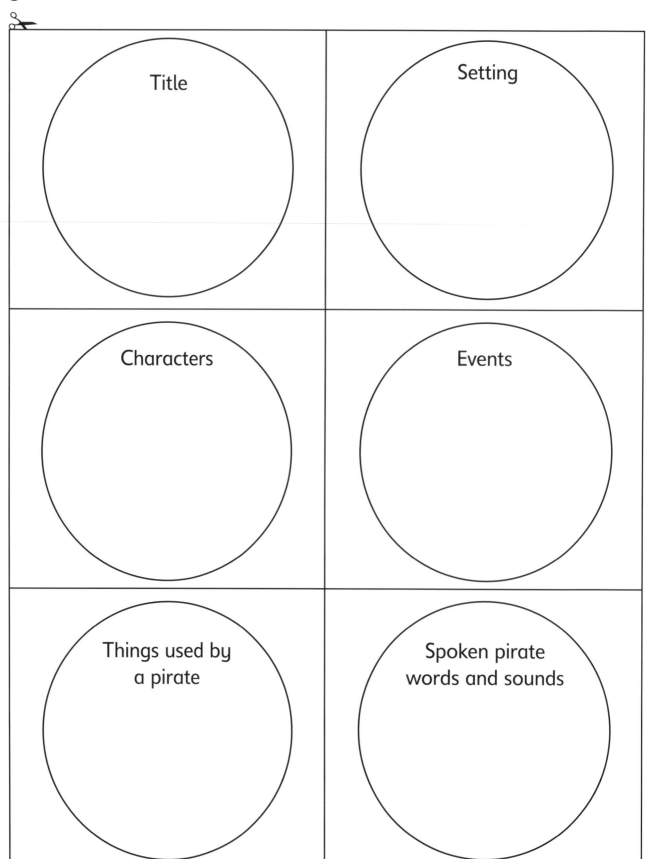

Title

Setting

Characters

Events

Things used by a pirate

Spoken pirate words and sounds

Pirate adventure story plan

■ Use this sheet to plan and write your own pirate adventure story.

Title:

Main characters:

Setting:

Make a note of words you are going to use to begin your story.

Make a note of two main events in the story.

1.

2.

Make a note of words you are going to use to end your story.

I can plan my own pirate adventure story.

How did you do?

SCHOLASTIC

Available in this series:

100 English Lessons

Year 1 – 978-1407-12759-0
Year 2 – 978-1407-12760-6
Year 3 – 978-1407-12761-3
Year 4 – 978-1407-12762-0
Year 5 – 978-1407-12763-7
Year 6 – 978-1407-12764-4

100 Computing Lessons

Years 1–2 – 978-1407-12856-6
Years 3–4 – 978-1407-12857-3
Years 5–6 – 978-1407-12858-0

100 Maths Lessons

Year 1 – 978-1407-12771-2
Year 2 – 978-1407-12772-9
Year 3 – 978-1407-12773-6
Year 4 – 978-1407-12774-3
Year 5 – 978-1407-12775-0
Year 6 – 978-1407-12776-7

100 Geography Lessons

Years 1–2 – 978-1407-12850-4
Years 3–4 – 978-1407-12851-1
Years 5–6 – 978-1407-12852-8

100 Science Lessons

Year 1 – 978-1407-12765-1
Year 2 – 978-1407-12766-8
Year 3 – 978-1407-12767-5
Year 4 – 978-1407-12768-2
Year 5 – 978-1407-12769-9
Year 6 – 978-1407-12770-5

100 History Lessons

Years 1–2 – 978-1407-12853-5
Years 3–4 – 978-1407-12854-2
Years 5–6 – 978-1407-12855-9

---

100 Lessons Planning Guides

100 English Lessons
Planning Guide
978-1407-12839-9

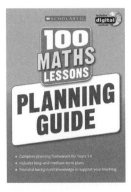

100 Maths Lessons
Planning Guide
978-1407-12840-5

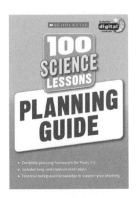

100 Science Lessons
Planning Guide
978-1407-12841-2

To find out more, call: **0845 603 9091** or visit **www.scholastic.co.uk/100lessons**